BODYGUARD

by

Mark V. Lonsdale

ALSO BY MARK LONSDALE
C.Q.B.
RAIDS
S.R.T. DIVER
SNIPER COUNTER SNIPER
ADVANCED WEAPONS TRAINING
SNIPER II
ALPINE OPERATIONS

BODYGUARD

A Guide to
VIP Protection

by

Mark V. Lonsdale

S.T.T.U.

DISCLAIMER

The author, STTU and those that contributed to this book take no responsibility for the use or misuse of the material herein. BODYGUARD is not a publication or training manual of any government agency, nor should the material herein, be taken as the policy or procedure of any such agency.

Bodyguard training and advanced tactical shooting are potentially dangerous activities that could lead to serious injury or death, if not properly organized and supervised. The training methods indicated in this book should only be undertaken by selected personnel, under the supervision of qualified instructors and team leaders. Each and every individual involved in weapons training should act as a Safety Officer, and be constantly alert to any potential safety violations.

No moral or legal conclusions should be drawn from any of the following material—especially relating to the use of force and the possession, transportation and carry of firearms. These laws vary from state to state and country to country so the reader must familiarize himself with the regulations in local jurisdictions. We have tried to present the mechanics of bodyguarding and related training, leaving the legal and policy decisions to the individual or agency concerned.

Several actual incidents and experiences have been included to illustrate points made in the text. The names of the parties involved have been changed to protect the innocent and the guilty, depending on which side of the fence you are on.

Finally, for economy, I have frequently used the generic "he," "him" and "his" throughout this book when referring to both bodyguards and their employers. I realize that there are many female bodyguards, in both government and the private sector, and many women of influence who employ bodyguards. So wherever the reader sees reference to the male of the species, please read in "she" and "her" with equal weight.

BODYGUARD

First Printing May, 1995
Second Printing Dec, 2000
Copyright © 1995 by Mark V. Lonsdale
Los Angeles, California 90049

ISBN 0-939235-06-4

Library of Congress Catalog Card Number 95-68453
PRINTED IN THE UNITED STATES OF AMERICA

DEDICATION

To FWF
for your support when I needed it

and to the memory of
Bob MacKenzie, SCR
Killed in action 24FEB95
—a warrior to the end

ACKNOWLEDGEMENTS

My special thanks to all the operators and instructors that I have worked with in the past two decades, who have taken the time to pass along their invaluable knowledge and experience. Without them, my books would not have been possible.

In addition:

Karen Lewis—Photography and proofreading
Susan Kay Kline—Artwork page viii
Bill Pegler—TEA
Robert & John Forsyth—VSDC
Tim Larkin—Direct Action

. . . and all the companies and individuals who continue to support STTU studies and operations—too numerous to name here. My most sincere appreciation.

AUTHOR'S NOTE

BODYGUARD was written to fill the need for a book directed not at the governmental agencies with unlimited resources, but more to the police officer or private sector bodyguard currently involved in executive, witness or judicial protection.

Over the years I have read numerous books and papers written by self professed security experts but few have given me any indication that the writer spent actual time in the trenches or had a first hand understanding of the day to day problems confronting a bodyguard.

Bodyguarding is neither an academic endeavor nor an exacting science. It is more an art incorporating diplomacy, unlimited patience, a strong presence, a variety of physical and technical skills and the flexibility to adjust to the innumerable small crises that go with the business.

I have spent over a decade running a variety of security operations throughout the United States coupled with extensive experience in Europe, Asia and the Caribbean. At last count, my work has taken me to over thirty countries on all five continents. From black-tie events in Washington, DC and Beverly Hills to the snow-covered slopes of Aspen; from the back streets of Bangkok to the casinos of Monte Carlo; from embassies in Europe to the war zones of the Middle East; from cruising on luxury motor yachts off of Antigua and Martinique to flying corporate jets to Geneva and Rome.

Bodyguarding can be both glamorous and exciting but the true satisfaction comes from planning a complex itinerary, making it move smoothly and safely, while protecting the principal and successfully overcoming the numerous, unexpected challenges created by a wide variety of client needs. Bodyguards know when they have done well because everyone comes home alive and the individual or team is both mentally and physically exhausted at the end of the assignment or overseas trip.

Bodyguarding can also be the most thankless, frustrating and infuriating business on this planet. There are clients who will drive a bodyguard to the point of almost wishing them harm. More than once I have had to use near superhuman restraint when tempted to toss a particularly irritating client overboard or abandon a troublesome bureaucrat on the back streets of some semi-third world country. However tempting, that would simply not be professional.

In addition to the nuts and bolts of day to day protection work, I have also given the reader some personal insights to further illustrate a particular point. These notes are presented in *italics* throughout the text.

Lastly, many young men and women are attracted to bodyguarding for the travel, the money and an opportunity to carry a gun. They will soon find that the travel becomes tedious, the money is not exceptional and the gun is not a significant tool in bodyguarding. The professional must have confidence in his or her training, experience and physical skills, but first and foremost, must be prepared to "Sweat the Details."

—Mark Lonsdale

ABOUT THE AUTHOR

In addition to his current duties as Director of Training & Studies at S.T.T.U., the author has amassed extensive experience training close protection teams and running DVP operations throughout the United States and overseas. In addition, for eight years Lonsdale was retained as a security consultant for an LA based Forbes 400 group where he handled the hiring and training of all security personnel; the design and implementation of sophisticated security systems; the advance work on all foreign travel for the principals; Secret Service and police liaison for official visits; and team leader on numerous operations.

Apart from the hundreds of police, government and military personnel who have benefited from S.T.T.U. programs, Lonsdale has taught instructor level programs for the Federal Law Enforcement Training Center; participated in undercover work for the US Government; run advanced raid programs for the DEA and INS; and given CQB training to US Marines prior to deployment in the Gulf Crisis. Lonsdale is also active in search and rescue, a scuba instructor at UCLA, and a diver and training coordinator for the LA Sheriff's-SEB Marine Company Dive Team.

This is the author's seventh book in a series already well received by the law enforcement and special operations communities.

CONTENTS

II—TRAINING

III—OPERATIONS

INTRODUCTION

"Of all the tasks of government, the most basic is to protect
its citizens from violence." —John Foster Dulles

THE FACTS

Violent crimes such as assault, armed robbery, extortion, murder and
even political assassination have all become common place in our society. One only has to pick up a newspaper or turn on the television to
know that U.S. citizens abroad are being kidnapped; politicians and religious leaders are being attacked for their views; bankers, financiers and
industrialists become targets for disgruntled employees and anti-capital-
ists; celebrities, entertainers and on-air personalities are harassed and
assaulted by deranged fans; our judges and lawmakers are in fear of
their lives from a crazed criminal element; and most public figures are
subjected to bizarre and threatening communications.

Closer to home, society is faced with street gangs, serial killers,
rapists, stalkers, crack dealers, the criminally insane, drug lords, pimps,
perverts, child molesters and extortionists. Now although these various
villains may grow from the "bad side of town," they have come to recognize the affluent neighborhoods as easy pickings, and the rich and
famous as soft targets. Many individuals in the financial, entertainment
and political arenas recognize these threats and have taken steps not to
become "victims."

It is a known fact that conventional law enforcement has neither the
time, budget, personnel nor expertise to handle many of the threats facing prominent members of our society. The police do their best to
respond to the needs of the community, but faced with the current budget cuts, they must now prioritize their responses and cannot be expected to cover any individual twenty-four hours-a-day. Nor are police officers expert in advising the victim or recipient of a threat on the necessary steps to best improve their security.

Out of fear for their personal safety and sheer frustration, many
celebrities have turned to private security as their only alternative.
Unfortunately, most private security firms do not have the resources or
levels of expertise to handle the complex and sophisticated needs of the
rich and famous.

Historically, many private security firms have failed to implement even
minimum standards, their personnel being poorly trained, low paid and
lacking in almost all the skills required for medium to high threat security
assignments. Obvious lack of education, poor physical condition and
unprofessional appearance have also added to their unsuitability for, and
inability to blend into the sophisticated world of high society or international politics.

1

The 6' 4", 350 pound weightlifter type bodyguard of the past has no place in the low-key, high-tech, field of modern security and personal protection. Today, a bodyguard or protective detail should be not only skilled in all aspects of threat management and close protection, but must be able to move discreetly within the personal and professional lives of their protectees.

Faced with this gap in the security industry, several highly motivated security professionals, mostly ex-governmental and military personnel, formed protection, hardware and training companies that could meet all the security needs of any American or foreign VIP. These companies take great pride in supplying the best, most professional experts, protection specialists and training in the security field to date. They have earned the respect of not only the financial and entertainment communities but also political groups and federal law enforcement agencies. They are currently redefining the word "bodyguard" and putting not only respect but prestige back into the security industry. The following is an insiders look at the mechanics of these operations.

STTU and IDS staff working special security during the L.A. riots of 1992

PART I

GETTING STARTED

Herald INTERNATIONAL Tribune

Published With The New York Times and The Washington Post

No. 32,207   PARIS, TUESDAY, SEPTEMBER 9, 1986   ESTABLISHED 1887

Chile Under State of Siege After Attack on Pinochet

United Press International

SANTIAGO — President Augusto Pinochet was slightly injured Sunday in an attack that left five of his bodyguards dead. He declared a state of siege Monday and ordered the arrest of several leftist leaders.

General Pinochet later tore troops into Santiago slums, where opposition forces are known to be strong, and said that no group was too small to track down.

In the attack Sunday, the general was slightly cut on his left hand by shrapnel when his motorcade was hit with bullets and grenades by rebel gunmen who left a trail of death and destruction along a mountain road south of the capital.

President Augusto Pinochet, his hand bandaged, speaks to Chilean television reporters.

Explosion Hits Post Office in Paris City Hall; 1 Dead, 9 Hurt

PARIS — An explosion in a post office at Paris's City Hall on Monday killed one person and wounded nine others, according to first police accounts.

One of the cars from the Pinochet motorcade that was damaged in the attack.

Israel Yields To Turkey on Jews' Funeral

By Henry Kamm
New York Times Service

ISTANBUL — Turkey has told Israel that it would not welcome the presence of a high-ranking Israeli official at the funeral Wednesday of 21 Jews slain in the terrorist attack in Istanbul's largest synagogue last Saturday, a senior Israeli official said Monday.

U.S.-Soviet Ties Take 'Ugly Turn' on Daniloff

By Bernard Gwertzman
New York Times Service

WASHINGTON — U.S. officials and academic experts say Moscow's decision to charge an American correspondent with espionage has strained Soviet-American relations to odds when one called "a very ugly turn."

ON PAGE 3

U.S. Sent Anti-Terror Unit to Karachi But It Failed to Arrive Before Climax

New York Times Service

WASHINGTON — A U.S.

Latin Recession Called Worst Since Depression

By James L. Rowe Jr.
Washington Post Service

Los Angeles Times

THURSDAY, MARCH 24, 1994   DAILY   35¢

Music Executive Slain in Malibu; Woman Held

By Hugo Martin
TIMES STAFF WRITER

Assassin Kills Mexican Ruling Party's Presidential Candidate

■ **Violence:** Gunman in Tijuana reportedly tells police, 'I saved Mexico.' Front-runner's death stuns nation and disrupts election plans.

By Sebastian Rotella and Patrick J. McDonnell
TIMES STAFF WRITER

A man armed with a pistol grabs hold of the man who is suspected of shooting to death Luis Donaldo Colosio, Mexico's ruling party presidential candidate, during a campaign appearance in Tijuana.

5 Palestinians Slain as Hebron Violence Flares

By Mark Fineman
TIMES STAFF WRITER

$3.75-Billion Settlement of Implant Suits Is OKd

Death Will Test the Stability of Political System

Herald INTERNATIONAL Tribune

Published With The New York Times and The Washington Post

No. 32,206   PARIS, MONDAY, SEPTEMBER 8, 1986   ESTABLISHED 1887

Terrorism's Bloody Toll: 41 Killed in Two Attacks

Two men posing as photographers entered a synagogue in Istanbul on Saturday and attacked the congregation with submachine guns and hand grenades. Twenty-three persons died in the attack, which occurred a day after gunmen dressed as security personnel seized a Pan American jumbo jet at Karachi airport. At least 18 persons died in that attack.

Daniloff Charged As a Spy

Newsman to Face Trial; Reagan Appeals Directly

By Felicity Barringer
New York Times Service

MOSCOW — The Soviet authorities Sunday charged Nicholas Daniloff, an American correspondent, with espionage.

23 Jews Slain in Istanbul

By Henry Kamm
New York Times Service

ISTANBUL — Two men on a mission posing as photographers entered a newly refurbished synagogue here Saturday.

A victim of the Pan Am attack is transferred to an ambulance in Frankfurt.

Coffins of the Istanbul victims are removed from the Neve Shalom synagogue.

18 Are Dead in Karachi; 4 Hijackers Being Held

4

1

UNDERSTANDING THE SECURITY BUSINESS

Human nature has shown us that the strong can either prey upon the weak or become their allies. The criminally inclined will become the predators while those with a more developed set of values will become the protectors. Unfortunately, modern man's quest for creature comforts and easy living tends to make him weaker while the tougher lifestyle of the career criminal or terrorist only makes him stronger.

Historically, to offset this imbalance, lords, land owners and merchants found it necessary to retain personal armies or to hire mercenaries to protect their interests. Today, approaching the twenty-first century we find that things have not changed much.

Although many tend to simplify this struggle into the forces of good and evil, it is more accurate to think in terms of the HAVES and the HAVE NOTS. Since cavemen first walked upright, both individuals and groups who did not have have taken from those who had—whether it be material possessions, status or even freedom. Criminals take what they want because they are not willing to work for it, while terrorists take life and deny society freedom so that they may further their cause or achieve a goal.

Since the HAVES have money and influence and want to keep it that way, they have created a need for a buffer between themselves and the threatening HAVE NOTS. With increases in violent crime and attacks on their peers, the HAVES have created a significant demand for security services. Unfortunately, a by-product of any rapid growth industry are the amateurs, the incompetent, "the wanna-bes" and "fly by night" businessmen—all of whom have contributed to the negative image of the security business as a whole. Fortunately, if one takes the time to separate the chaff from the wheat, one will find a small number of dedicated professionals.

Beginning with the rise of international terrorism in the late seventies and early eighties, and compounded by ever increasing domestic violent crime, the security business has become a growth industry with numerous opportunities for the competent individual or enterprising company.

THREE TYPES OF SECURITY

When looking to up-grade security, usually after a scare or a sudden change in wealth or public attention, one is presented with a wide variety of options at an equally wide variety of costs. When first consulting the yellow pages or initiating inquires about security systems and services, one is confronted with numerous choices.

After a few phone calls, one can become inundated with slick brochures and fast talking salesmen, many of whom know little about real security, but all wanting to sell a bill of goods. One will also discover an animal known as a security consultant—some being both knowledgeable and professional, but unfortunately many no more than ex-cops, private investigators and alarm salesmen with no real expertise or training.

If one is perceptive enough to dig through all the hype and BS, one will realize that up-grading security comes down to one of three basic options, or more often a combination of all three. These are physical security measures, electronic security, or some form of guard services. Each with different costs but quite specific applications and limitations.

Physical security is the obvious first step and involves strengthening the doors and locks, building high walls and gates, making the home more secure and generally creating physical barriers around oneself. However, this also causes what is known as "siege mentality". Even with the protection of all these walls, one must still eventually venture out into the world. Even with a bulletproof car, there will still be exposure when inevitably one must leave both the castle and armored limo.

The second alternative is electronic security systems. These serve as an early warning of intrusion and act as some deterrent—but again, they are somewhat passive and often prone to malfunction. They depend on either police response—in twenty to forty minutes in most cities; or preparing to protect oneself—unwise without extensive professional training.

So, if one wants immediate response to an alarm or to have a security escort, there is the third option which is security personnel. Regular security guards may be appropriate at the residence or corporate office, but these minimum wage uniformed security guards are neither trained nor suitable for day to day movement around town or trips overseas. This brings the client to the professional bodyguard and all the problems and recurring costs that go with this type of protection.

ESCALATING LEVELS OF PROTECTION

For the security professional, every contract begins with a threat assessment to gauge just how best to meet the client's needs. Where one bodyguard may be appropriate in limited situations, a full protective team and an integrated system may be called for in others.

There are several aspects to threat assessment and security planning such as protection of property versus protection of people and high versus low threat levels. The assessor will also look to see if there are specific threats or just potential for risk, or if the client's lifestyle is high or low profile.

It is important that the security up-grades be not only effective but that they be tailored to individual clients and minimally disruptive to their lifestyles. Just as new locks must be locked to be effective, poorly designed alarm systems that tend to false a lot, will eventually become a hassle and not used by the client. The same is true for bodyguards. If they cannot blend into the clients' business and personal lives, or they become an embarrassment or inconvenience, then the clients will simply stop utilizing their services.

The first distinction made in the security business is the difference between the protection of **property** and **people.** Property security for estates, houses, industrial sites, corporate offices, financial instruments and valuables, can be classified as manned or unmanned and is normally handled by uniformed security guards or electronic alarm systems. The BG on the other hand protects people, or more specifically one person. In the BG business, everything is oriented toward the protection of people, with property protection being considered low priority and usually relegated to the lowly paid security guard.

The next distinction that must be made in security planning is **high threat** versus **low threat** security risks. High threat generally denotes a known range of threats or prior attempts. For example, a US ambassador in a semi-third world country represents the United States and therefore is a logical target for any individual or group with an axe to grind with American presence. Similarly, an actress who has received very specific threats from a deranged fan would fall into the high risk category, at least until that individual was apprehended.

Low threat is more the day to day movements of a VIP or celebrity with no specific threats identified or suspected—for example, a movie star or wealthy business man moving around a large city or traveling overseas.

Location can also have some influence on the risk level. Most civilized countries being relatively low threat while those associated with the drug trade or wide spread civil unrest being higher risk.

If an individual falls into the high threat category either by status, location or prior history, one BG is not going to be sufficient to improve security. This is now the realm of a protective team operation with all the necessary logistical, vehicular and hardware options.

The next category is the **specific threat** versus the **potential threat.** Most people in their day to day lives are potential targets of crime or violence, but try not to become too paranoid and go about their regular business. This is a kind of "it won't happen to me" mentality and is a common part of life in the big city. However, when there is a specific threat made against an individual, the game changes. People who had no security before, may now get a BG; or if they already had a BG, they may upgrade to a CP team, depending on the nature of the threat. Being targeted for violence or even shot at is infinitely more "specific" than a few crank threatening letters, however, both must be evaluated and taken seriously.

The last category in the assessment is **high profile** versus **low profile** clients. A low profile client, for example a bank president, can be moved quietly, efficiently and safely with the minimum of manpower. However, the movement and protection of the high profile politician or religious leader is quite man-intensive, requiring a professional team, more planning, logistics and coordination. One important protection principle is to utilize unexpected movement and unannounced travel, but both are almost impossible with a protectee who is easily recognized or, like many politicians and celebrities, basks in public attention.

Obviously, the security effort for a high threat, high profile individual who has been specifically targeted by some individual or group will require 24-hour-a-day team coverage and considerable logistical support. This in addition to extensive security modifications to the residence, a state-of-the-art anti-intrusion system, armored vehicles and, after the initial set-up costs, a security budget in excess of half a million dollars a year. More if the client's family must also be covered or the individual frequently travels overseas.

2

ROLE OF THE MODERN BODYGUARD

The word "bodyguard" conjures up a variety of images, with the most generic and often comic being the washed-up boxer or pro wrestler, of considerable size but minimal intellect, working out his "retirement" from the ring as the protector for some underworld figure, loan shark or wealthy benefactor.

In Los Angeles, and particularly Beverly Hills, the bodyguard is often perceived as a large, tanned status symbol for many celebrities. This individual is usually a bodybuilder, private fitness trainer or martial arts instructor trying to make a few bucks on the side and waiting to be discovered by the silver screen.

For the truly rich, famous and powerful, the bodyguard should have no specific image. He or she hopefully has a conservative, professional appearance and the ability to blend in most environments, much like the character played by Kevin Costner in the movie "Bodyguard". When first meeting a prospective client they are greeted with a comment like, "I thought you would have been bigger".

All three of the aforementioned stereo-types are accurate in the private sector, but still only represent a small part of the overall modern bodyguard community. Apart from the private sector, governments, military and law enforcement agencies all have personnel trained as bodyguards for a wide variety of functions.

GOVERNMENT

The US and foreign governments have numerous branches, each with their own need for security, so the following should be viewed as a considerably simplified overview of a rather complex security apparatus.

Governmental close protection personnel work under a variety of names and titles, depending on country of origin and specific purpose. In some countries they are referred to as BG or CP Teams, while others use the terms VIP Protection or DVP, denoting Distinguished Visitor

Protection. In the United States, the preferred title is "Security Detail", which the US government utilizes for a wide variety of domestic and foreign assignments. Best known of these being the not-so-secret US Secret Service (USSS).

Without a doubt, the United States Secret Service is the premier security agency within the US governmental system with both a uniformed branch and the more familiar plain clothed Special Agents. Headquartered out of Washington, DC, the Secret Service has branches throughout the US supported by their own technical division and training facility in Laurel, Maryland.

Best known for the familiar dark-suited Presidential Protection Division, the Secret Service comes under the jurisdiction of the Department of Treasury and, unbeknown to many, also handles several conventional law enforcement functions such as forgery and counterfeiting.

In addition to the presidential bodyguard that one sees on television and during public appearances, there is a legion of unseen support personnel, including the Technical Security Division, Advance Teams, Counter Sniper Teams, Counter Assault Teams, EOD, K-9, drivers, intelligence and communications personnel. Add to this the First Family's security team, the not quite mirror image Vice Presidential Protection Detail and the security teams assigned to America's now long line of ex-presidents, and one begins to appreciate the scope and resources of the Secret Service.

Yet during the presidential election campaigns, every four years, the Secret Service becomes so over extended protecting not only the incumbent President and his family but also all the presidential candidates, that Special Agents are brought in from the law enforcement branches of the service as well as most other federal agencies. A presidential candidate could find himself being protected by a small contingent of Secret Service agents, supported by treasury agents from ATF or Customs and augmented by local and state law enforcement. During fund raising dinners and speeches, there is often an additional contingent of private security to help take the load off of the special agents assigned to close protection.

On a domestic level, the FBI and US Marshals Service also have special security teams trained to handle the protection of federal judges, witnesses or defendants in high profile cases and individuals covered in the witness protection or relocation programs.

Outside of the continental United States the security for diplomats and senior embassy staffers falls under the control of the State Department. The actual security details or bodyguards are members of the Diplomatic Security Service (DSS), a branch of SY. SY being the designator for all State Department security operations which extend well beyond simple close protection responsibilities.

LAW ENFORCEMENT

Both local and state government, can find themselves responsible for the movement and safety of the State Governor and/or other key figures in the legislature who may find themselves at risk or on the wrong side of public opinion. The responsibility for this usually falls to the State Police, Public Safety Department or Department of Justice.

Municipal police and county sheriff's, especially in large metropolitan areas, are frequently tasked with the protection of visiting dignitaries and VIPs. In addition, the Mayor, the DA, the Sheriff and Chief of Police in cities like Los Angeles and New York, will be assigned a police driver/bodyguard for their day to day movements around the city. It is also not unusual for SWAT teams or Special Enforcement Teams to be cross trained in providing close protection for visiting dignitaries, special functions or the transportation of high risk / high profile prisoners.

Many cops also have the opportunity to moonlight as bodyguards for the rich and famous and to augment their incomes by working security at special events. This is especially true in Los Angeles where celebrities grow on trees and the level of street crime is high.

Many celebrities and successful businessmen, many of whom do not really need bodyguards, enjoy the convenience of having off-duty police officers on their payroll, and all the added advantages of that sworn status. They come to expect little favors from the officers like running license plates, fixing tickets, getting their children out of trouble with the law, leaning on troublesome associates, evicting bad tenants and facilitating official paperwork.

The danger to the officers is that they may get drawn too close to the darker side of the client's personal and professional lives. Particularly in the entertainment industry where drug abuse, prostitution and gambling are no strangers, it can get very uncomfortable for the cop who has a strong ethical sense. Anyone watching the OJ Simpson homicide case in July of '94 will have realized the awkward position his off-duty LAPD bodyguards were put in when they were accused of helping evade arrest, and one of them even having supplied OJ with a gun.

THE MILITARY

Most nation's senior command staff and higher ranking generals enjoy the convenience of a personal driver who is often cross trained as a bodyguard. It is also not unusual for members of a general's staff, for instance his orderly or assistant, to receive bodyguard training so as to learn personal protection drills and raise their overall level of awareness. This could range from as little as advanced driver training all the way up to a comprehensive BG course integrating shooting, tactics, foot drills, explosive identification and counter ambush techniques.

The primary responsibility for the security of uniformed personnel, both in the US, overseas and on embassy assignment is that of the Secretary of Defense, better known as SECDEF.

SECDEF security details are usually drawn from US Army CID and are tailored to the task, country and environment. The Secretary of the Navy however, will often draw his own security detail from NIS, even though he is authorized to utilize SECDEF assets.

In a combat environment, special operations command (SOCOM) may take over the security for key Commanders, so it was with no surprise that US Special Forces Delta operators found themselves escorting General Norman Schwarzkopf on his movements in and around the Middle East during the Gulf conflict.

State Department security services would also have had a hand in the overall security effort, especially for the visits of the endless line of Senators and Congressmen who find the need to visit the "front line" (not even close!) and milk whatever political mileage they can out of the "war zone" (read that as photo opportunity).

US embassies abroad also have a use for security personnel and bodyguards. The first line of defense that most visitors to an embassy will see are the Marines of the Marine Security Guard (MSG) Detachments. But behind the men in uniform there lurks the bodyguards of the ambassador and other key staffers.

The bodyguards are often a combination of military, State Department and local police, with some embassies even contracting private firms for security services.

However, when there is an overlap of security services and since the Secret Service is the only group with their own independent communications capability (WHCA—White House Communications Agency), they will take precedent over and coordinate all other security details.

General H. Norman Schwarzkopf with security escort in Riyadh, Saudi Arabia, January 1991

In European countries like France, Germany and Italy, their national counter terrorist teams, such as the GIGN and GSG-9 will often find themselves tasked with bodyguarding their Prime Minister or equivalent Heads of State.

The US national counter terrorist teams like Delta and SEAL Team 6 (now DevGroup) have also been known to sharpen their teeth and hone their skills by doing threat assessments, feasibility studies and security site surveys on US embassies and government facilities around the globe. This gives them first hand experience in thinking like a terrorist; an opportunity to up-date their files on the strengths and weaknesses of certain key structures; and to get a feel for the terrain, should they be called there at some point in the future to effect a rescue.

PRIVATE SECTOR

Private sector bodyguarding comes in many forms depending on the type of client, perceived threat level and geographic local. In countries with a history of instability, kidnapping and violence the bodyguard is not only a familiar sight but essential to every day survival. In the countries bordering on economic collapse or civil war, the wealthy employ whole armies of bodyguards, examples of this being found in Central and South America, Africa, Asia and the Middle East.

In the United States and Western Europe things are not quite so grim, from a social standpoint, or bright from the more adventurous entrepreneur's perspective, but rises in violence and kidnapping activity do tend to stimulate a thriving security industry. For bodyguards, the most common clients fall into one of the following groups.

The Super Wealthy:

Historically the rich have always been the prime target for criminals since they are the "haves" who are most visible to the "have nots". The very wealthy have been the victims of robbery, kidnapping, hate crimes and street violence, so have long taken advantage of personal bodyguards and high tech security systems.

In recent times, the not so wealthy, having less security and being easier targets, have found themselves the target of criminals such as the notorious Rolex Bandits.

Entertainment Industry:

The entertainment industry has a voracious appetite for not only uniformed security guards but also BGs to protect a variety of entertainers, key executives, movie stars, television personalities and rock stars. Even some of the more powerful entertainment agents and attorneys who have attained celebrity status now require personal protection.

Celebrities:

Outside of the entertainment industry there are many individuals who have attained celebrity status, such as sports figures, religious leaders, politicians and controversial authors to name a few. There is also a unique group of retired government and military figures who have had celebrity thrust upon them and become targets for a variety of radical groups or crazed individuals.

Major Corporations:

Large corporations, especially those with overseas interests in unstable semi-third world countries, will often supply bodyguards for valued executives, CEOs, financial advisors or spokespersons. This is particularly true in regions that have shown an underlying anti-American sentiment, where US companies like Coca Cola, Xerox or Bechtel, who have large manufacturing or distribution centers, have been targeted by local terrorist or guerrilla factions. Most now employ ex-Secret Service, FBI or intelligence types to head up their security efforts.

The Underworld:

A darker side of bodyguarding, and one the professional should avoid, is the criminal element. It is obvious from the daily news accounts of drug related homicides and executions that there is no Brotherhood of Thieves or Loyal Order of Drug Dealers. Suppliers, dealers and organized crime types constantly prey upon each other trying to kill key players and rip off other's product for a bigger piece of the action.

The Mafia and mob figures of days gone by were always seen in the company of enforcers and loyal bodyguards, however today it is the king-pins in the drug cartels of Columbia, South America and Asia who have the small army of protectors and gunmen.

It is all too easy for the out of work bodyguard to find himself drawn to the big money, expensive cars and wild women, but he would also be taking a one way ticket to the dark side. Once employed and part of the inner circle, even as just a bodyguard, he would soon find himself "running errands", making deliveries, enforcing collections and, if trusted, asked to make hits on competitors. Once in and a witness to transactions, there is no resigning.

In the inner city, the observant individual will also see this bodyguard relationship with seemingly minor pimps and pushers who are involved in turf wars or feel threatened by the dregs of society that they service. Street level drug dealers find their bodyguards amongst the addicts of gang-bangers who will work for their next fix. But as they hit the "big time" and the money is more significant, they come to realize that they need a more dependable class of protection. This is evident by the fact that one major US city recently arrested several of their own sworn police officers for acting as security to the local drug trade. A trade that routinely takes the lives of other street cops and investigators.

Into this grey area also falls the pawn brokers, loan sharks, bail bondsmen and bookies who move large amounts of cash and can feel the heat. These are businesses that may seem legitimate but taint a career by bringing the BG into a world where human dignity has little value and money buys everything, including people.

3

PROFILE OF A BODYGUARD

From the first two chapters the reader should be developing an overview of the security industry—those aspects that are equipment intensive and those that depend more on the human element. Encompassed within the human elements of the security business are a variety of job descriptions such as industrial security personnel, aged night watchmen, minimum wage uniformed security guards, armed response security services, bank guards, armored car payroll guards, doormen and bouncers at night clubs. These should not be confused with the professional bodyguard or close protection specialist.

This brings us to the question of just how does one become a bodyguard? Does a young man or woman, from an early age, plan a career in bodyguarding? Is it an option that is offered in college? Are there companies out there recruiting potential bodyguards? The answer is "No!" on all of the above. So where do bodyguards come from?

WHO BECOMES A BODYGUARD?

Many individuals, young and old alike, attracted by the stories of high pay, travel, expensive hotels and private jets, are drawn to the supposed glamour of bodyguarding. Some are ex-military or police who are looking for work in the private sector, while others just fall into the role of bodyguard by virtue of their size or through contacts in the entertainment world. Many of the bodyguards for rock musicians and film or television stars are no more than friends of the celebrity who needed a job and showed some aptitude as a minder. Most lacking the training and qualifications to be classified as a professional BG or protection specialist.

From experience as both trainers and employers of bodyguards, we have found that most individuals trying to become BGs generally fall into one of five categories:

- The unemployed
- The bodybuilder
- The off-duty cop
- The martial artist
- The security professional

The first and least desirable is the unemployed individual who has been unsuccessful at finding his niche in life and is willing to try anything. Often with no foundation or necessary skills they simply get caught up in the idea of bodyguarding. Others are products of some State job retraining program as security guards who assume that two days of classroom and a couple of hours with a borrowed revolver are sufficient to qualify them for BG work.

The unemployed are also an easy target for the fly-by-night "Bodyguard Schools" that seem to spring up all over the world. Some last, most don't. They pump the candidates full of hopes and dreams, clean out their savings accounts and give them a worthless certificate, often from an equally worthless instructor. (More on BG schools in Chapter 8).

The truly scary sub-group of the unemployed are the individuals who have no other qualifications other than that they may own a gun or can borrow a gun or just consider themselves "tough enough" for the job. When approached by this individual for a job, just smile and say, "Thanks but no thanks!"

The one group of unemployed that is worthy of serious consideration is the recently discharged military types who have not yet found a place in the civilian work place. A look at their discharge papers (DD-214) and references will give a good indication of their past service and expected performance levels. The prospective employer or trainer should look for the motivated individuals who are fit, disciplined, well groomed, not too rigid, are keen to train and learn a new profession. If they have served in one of the recent military or police actions such as Kuwait, Haiti, Somalia or Bosnia, that much the better.

The second group found to be seeking employment as bodyguards is the bodybuilder, pro wrestler or boxer type looking for a way to support their training and dietary needs. These are the six foot three inch, two hundred and fifty pound mobile barricades, also referred to as "bullet magnets", since when the shit hits the fan, these will be the obvious first targets for the shooter and the slowest to react.

As with any professional athletes, their goals in life lie in sports that often carry with them strict training schedules and frequent travel for competitions, both of which can interfere with work commitments. A prospective employer must also be wary of any potential steroid use and the associated problems, such as violent mood swings or 'roid rage, that go with them.

Understand that this is a broad generalization and not totally fair to all professional athletes working as bodyguards. There are some very intelligent ex-bodybuilders and pugilists who have shown great loyalty to their employers, studied the business and gone on to become excellent personal protectors. However, their value is often limited to positions with celebrities moving in public where high profile muscle is not only appropriate, it can be essential. Although size can be an asset in some situations, it is not a substitute for careful planning, awareness and professionalism. A smaller operator with a "no nonsense" professional demeanor can command all of the respect of his larger counterparts, he just may not be as effective at running interference in a crowd of rowdy rock 'n roll fans.

The third group found in the bodyguard business are the police officers or MPs wanting to supplement their incomes. At least with this group one is dealing with individuals who have some training, an understanding of the law, experience in dealing with people and hopefully a clean background check.

The problems with part-time police officers are: 1/ Their first loyalty will always be to their primary job, not the client. 2/ They are already working one job so are usually tired when working a second. 3/ Basic police training does not necessarily mean they have had any training in security procedures or protection drills.

On the plus side, police officers have well developed powers of observation and the ability to read the signs of felonious intent can be invaluable when protecting a client. In addition, even ex-police officers are still plugged into the police old-boy network which can be very useful when running background investigations or interacting with local authorities. With this group an employer has a fifty-fifty chance of getting either a good bodyguard or someone merely looking for a few extra bucks and an easy retirement.

The fourth group are the martial artists and individuals who have an honest interest in the security business. These are often ex-military types, martial arts instructors, individuals who may have failed the police academy for whatever reason or simply a uniformed security guard wanting to improve his lot in life. In most cases they sincerely believe that they are suited to bodyguarding and have come to realize that they may not advance any further in life's struggle for financial security. From this group we have found and trained some excellent raw material who have gone on to make respectable livings in the business.

The key to finding a good bodyguard in this group is careful interview, a thorough background check and an adequate probationary period so as to better evaluate their motivation and attitude.

The fifth and most desirable is the true professional coming from a Secret Service, military special operations, law enforcement dignitary protection unit, or similar career track.

These individuals blend into teams with minimal re-training, are used to thinking on their feet, have a good basic knowledge of tactics, understand the importance of appearance, are discipline and seldom intimidated by anyone.

In Germany and France, former GSG-9 and GIGN counter terrorist specialists have little trouble landing a job with a wealthy industrialist or large corporation. Out of Israel, the commandos from IDF's specialized units gain experience on foreign embassy security assignments, but eventually end up seeking private employment throughout the world. Former members of the elite British SAS are also in demand both in England and the Middle East, having developed many contacts while serving in the Oman, Saudi Arabia and Africa.

In the US there is quite a cross section of professionals in the security business originating from both military and government service. It is not unusual to find US Navy Seals, Delta operators, Force Recon Marines, and a considerable number of ex-FBI, CIA and Secret Service types rattling around the domestic and international scene. Most have the ability if not the aptitude to become BGs in the private sector.

The more highly trained, college educated and motivated types will seek positions as corporate security directors, security consultants or foreign risk management experts. The operators that have actually served on the sharp end may find little or no satisfaction in domestic "baby sitting" BG jobs but will thrive on the more high risk international assignments.

WHY BECOME A BODYGUARD?

The motivation for becoming a bodyguard is not too complex. As in many occupations, money is a significant factor, closely followed by job satisfaction, benefits, location and the potential for future advancement.

Since few BGs will ever have the opportunity to work the glamorous international assignments, let's first review the more common job opportunities. Granted, some teams have worked throughout Europe, Mexico and the Caribbean, have attended black-tie dinners with the rich and famous and dined in the finest restaurants of London, Paris and Rome, but this is not the norm, nor should it be the prime motivating factor in selecting a career in the protection business.

First and foremost, the fledgling bodyguard must realize that bodyguarding is a service oriented profession—serving the security needs of others. This does not mean that one performs menial tasks or is a servant, but that the bodyguard does work for clients who may often make illogical requests and have whimsical natures. He must possess the ability to cope with constant change and understand that catering to the rich and famous can be frustrating at best and even infuriating at times.

Is there money? A U.S. bodyguard may find himself working for anything from fifteen dollars per hour all the way up to fifty. Two hundred dollars per day is common and a good BG can make upwards of three to six hundred per day on short term contracts. Working full time for one employer or corporation, a BG should expect to make at least forty thousand dollars a year, and up to sixty or seventy with overtime and travel bonuses.

Pay rates very much depend on the individual BG's experience and reputation, the nature of the client and the threat level of the contract. Most BGs who have long term assignments with individuals or corporations can also expect full benefits such as medical, dental, expenses, a car, reimbursement for training expenses and even food and lodging for live-in positions.

The question of job satisfaction is directly related to the individual's suitability to bodyguarding and the relationship with the client. Bodyguarding can be exhausting. Some people just do not have the patience or stamina to be at another's twenty-four hour beckon call. To be willing to travel when they wish to travel; to move when they move, stop when they stop; to go to the bathroom when they go to the bathroom; to dress how they dress; to stay alert while they socialize; and still catch enough sleep to function efficiently.

Pride in one's work is another important factor. One may win the respect of one's peers by demonstrating a sound knowledge of the trade, an ability to handle trouble, good driving skills and proficiency on the range, but the client may be harder to impress.

All too often, bodyguards are viewed in much the same category as drivers, butlers, messengers and other minor functionaries. At the corporate level, the BG may not even have the same status as the junior office executives, since at least those ass-kissing yuppies can show that they are making money for the firm.

Even domestic staff are recognized by the principal as being helpful, adding to his or her comfort factor on a daily basis. On the other hand, the BG just seems to "stand around" and "do very little". The major difference being that if there is a real threat, the BG's value and status will improve dramatically. The client that wouldn't even say "Good morning" the day before will now want to be the BG's closest buddy.

The only time a bodyguard will receive the respect he would like is if he has actually proven himself in a difficult situation, saving the principal from bodily harm or public embarrassment. Over the long haul, a BG that proves himself to be a professional will eventually gain the respect of any employer that understands the value of loyalty and service. The wife or mistress, however, may simply view the BG as a spy, a stooge or a pet gorilla—since she does not share the BG's loyalty.

As to job advancement, if a BG works for one person, who only needs one BG, then advancement is all but non-existent. The most the BG can hope for is periodic increases in pay and improved benefits. If however a BG is part of a large team, or is employed by a corporation, then he could advance to team leader, shift supervisor, job supervisor, operations coordinator, or even security director, all with the appropriate benefits and remunerations.

The alternative, which is the route most FBI and USSS types take, is to do their homework on private sector security and start their own companies, going after industrial, corporate, celebrity, or consular contracts. Those with foreign embassy, CIA or Diplomatic Security Service experience will go after the more lucrative overseas security or training contracts.

DESIRABLE CHARACTERISTICS FOR A BG

Since bodyguarding is considered CLOSE protection, the protectee will greatly appreciate a BG who's presence is tolerable up close and for a prolonged period of time. An individual who is loud, obnoxious, untidy or has a hygiene problem will not be tolerated by the principal or last long in the BG business.

So what gives a bodyguard a professional image? Apart from the essential work related skills, which will be covered in the next chapter, there are some more basic fundamentals that must be considered. Attributes like presence, appearance, personality, education, dedication and loyalty all play a significant part.

The first consideration of image should be during the initial hiring process. A strong resume with extensive training or operational experience may get one's foot in the door, but if one can not sell oneself in the first few minutes of the interview, it will be back on the street reading the classifieds and wearing out shoe leather.

As in most jobs that require people skills, first impressions count and an applicant usually gets only one chance to make a first impression. The prospective BG's appearance, deportment and even handshake should say, "professional—trust in me!".

Author's Note: In 1982, shortly after the kidnapping and subsequent rescue of General Dozier by the Red Brigade in Italy, I was asked to handle security for a high profile visit to Milan. I was contracted based solely on rumors that I had worked that part of the world and on the fact that a representative of the client had seen me on the shooting range engaging multiple targets with center head shots. After a short chat over lunch with the representative and no discussion of actual security procedures I was off to Italy.

Some time later while traveling with the principal himself, he informed me that based on what he had heard prior to meeting me, and even though I came highly recommended, he was sure that he would not like me and was quite prepared to dismiss me upon arrival in Milan. The fact was that his representative had gone back to the corporate headquarters portraying me as a cross between "Rambo and G. Gordon Liddey", who could "put bullets through the same hole".

However, before the client arrived in Italy, I had not only made all the usual preparations involved in advance work, I had taken a crash course in Italian. I had talked to immigration, set-up ground transportation, baggage handlers, selected traffic-free routes to the hotel, confirmed and inspected the hotel suites, visited a few select restaurants, arranged communications and mapped out itineraries.

It was this professionalism, prior planning, attention to detail and knowledge of the area that impressed the principal, not the rumor of my more deadly skills. His trip went smoother than any previous visit, he felt secure, his guests were taken care of and I was assured continued contracts.

Back to first impressions. One of the most important qualities that an employer should seek in a potential bodyguard is a certain type of presence. A sense that this individual is a stand-up character whose mere confidence and presence will calm others and dissuade an aggressor. Someone who can defuse an incident before it escalates into an embarrassment. An indication that he will not be intimidated by anyone when hard decisions must be made. However, this intangible presence cannot be portrayed as belligerence or an overly military bearing, but rather a quiet, professional confidence in himself and his ability. A confidence that the client can feel and from which he can draw a sense of security.

Since a BG will be working very closely with people of power and influence he should be relatively intelligent, articulate and more importantly well read. Well read does not mean a Master's degree in English literature, but more a good general knowledge of world news, geography, politics and the business world. Material that can be gleaned from magazines such as Time or Newsweek, television shows like CNN, a current world atlas and rounded out with a few good novels. It is not necessary for the BG to be a walking encyclopedia but one should at least know where the country is that one is heading for, along with some of the local history, politics and customs.

A BG, like any other staff member, will probably only speak when spoken to by the principal, however it is advisable to at least be able to make an intelligent comment when appropriate. More than one bodyguard has perfected the procedure of "Open Mouth—Insert Foot", by making some observation like " isn't Nietzsche a new flavor of ice cream?" This will only amuse the natives and embarrass the bodyguard.

If the client is involved in the movie industry, the BG should have at least seen some of his or her films, read some reviews, be up to date on current releases and know what sort of numbers they are doing in ticket sales. However, a word of warning. A BG should not try to use a position of trust as a bodyguard as a springboard into an acting career. When a principal hires a BG, he or she is entrusting that person with their safety, and no one is going to put their fate in the hands of an aspiring actor. Many young men have lost the respect of the client and their BG jobs by merely showing an interest in an acting career.

Moving to more superficial considerations, principals will appreciate a BG who is presentable and well groomed. It is advantageous if a bodyguard has some fashion sense and knows what "appropriate dress" means, even though these are things that can be taught and easily changed. Some employers give their bodyguards a clothing allowance, understanding that fine clothes do not come cheap. They also realize that well dressed staff reflects well on them and blends more easily into their elevated social and business circles.

Note: I had one young bodyguard on his first formal assignment with my team, inform me at the last minute that he did not own a tux or have time to rent one. I told him that a dark suit would suffice. That evening he turned up for final briefing in a dark suit, unfortunately it was navy polyester, about ten years out of date and had probably not fit him since high school. To make matters worse, instead of black or even dark brown shoes, he wore casual boots that were a yellowish tan in color. Being somewhat tolerant of the young and inexperienced, I simply took him aside and indicated the way the other team members were appropriately dressed in tuxes and dark suits, and then explained why he was to be stationed on outer perimeter, in a dark back parking lot.

BASIC DEPORTMENT

A budding BG need not be born with a silver spoon in his mouth or be a graduate of finishing school to understand deportment, although in some cases it would definitely not hurt.

Deportment is no more than an appreciation for the basic social graces, personality, manners, appearance, hygiene and appropriate dress. The stuff that hopefully parents and teachers try to instill in every young man and woman from an early age. Arriving for work in full camouflage, heavily armed and unshaven will not endear one to the natives of Beverly Hills. Just as, at the other extreme, wearing a dark business suit when escorting a client on vacation in Tahiti is equally inappropriate.

Social acceptability begins with basic hygiene. BGs have been jerked from contracts when a client complained to a supervisor of a particular individual's bad breath or body odor.

Even though the wealthy do seem to have an overly developed sense of hygiene, in some cases bordering on paranoia, no one enjoys working with an individual who sweats profusely or smells badly. The same applies to greasy hair, visible ear wax, yellow or decayed teeth, dirty finger nails and food stained clothes.

Clothes should be clean, pressed and appropriate for the occasion. In most cases, it is recommended that a BG have a change of clothes, sport coat and a suit handy in the back of his car for those occasions where the clients' plans change suddenly.

When in doubt about appropriate dress for a particular function or trip, ask the client or their personal assistant. If the trip is for vacation, ask if there are to be any business meetings or formal dinners requiring a suit or tux. The actual invitation to most exclusive events will indicate the appropriate attire.

The bodyguard should be quiet by nature, have a pleasant personality, be confident but not brash, and most of all professional in all things. He should be well mannered, polite, discrete, but not subservient. He should treat clients and their guests or associates with the same respect one would treat any employer or elder. The BG must constantly resist the urge to become too friendly or overly familiar with those with whom he comes in contact. All of this is not to imply that BGs are a bunch of choir boys. In fact, many are aggressive, competitive, confident individuals who have quite a wild side that must simply be controlled when on duty. Having had a large number of bodyguards go through psychological testing for suitability we have made some interesting observations. By occupational necessity BGs possess a darker side with a range of deadly skills, a controlled violence, and yet a protective nature. As any psychologist who has worked with police officers or BGs will testify, there is almost a contradiction in personalities. However, the key controlling influences are a foundation in good basic values, integrity and personal self discipline.

One difficulty for many BGs is controlling their egos. On one hand, they train to become proficient in many fighting forms, are motivated, dedicated, conscientious and competitive, and yet must be unobtrusive and content to work in the shadow of a principal. Since the rich and famous tend to lead a softer lifestyle than most, the BG must not make the mistake of judging a client by his or her physical ability or deficiency. If the client indicates that it is too far to walk to the car, the BG should not launch into a story of how he walked forty miles across the hot sands in Desert Storm, but simply have the car brought up. If the client's wife says she is cold, this is not an opportunity to explain the intricacies of arctic survival, the BG should either turn up the heat or give her a jacket. If the principal does not want to carry his own bags, the BG should not tell him it is good exercise, but simply get a porter.

There will be times when a bodyguard may be expected to eat at the same table with a client or guests. This is not the most desirable arrangement, since one can be drawn into polite conversation and distracted, but in some situations it is also unavoidable. For this eventuality the BG should know the correct layout of silverware, the difference between a water glass and a wine glass and basic formal table etiquette—lest he appear to be merely a gorilla in a monkey suit.

All of this emphasis on deportment is for the sole purpose of giving the BG the ability to blend into high society and not embarrass a principal. Studying the clients, their work patterns, social habits, personal tastes and idiosyncrasies will help in avoiding social blunders.

Travel to foreign countries will necessitate some additional research into local culture, customs, politics and religion. For the BG traveling with a corporate executive, this may require minimal study, but if working within the diplomatic community or official delegations, a more in depth knowledge will be called for. (See Chapter 26 for additional notes on foreign travel).

Terrorist Killings Set Problem for the West

NZPA-AP   **London**

Despite frustration and anger, there is little sign that Western countries can take any effective, concerted action to prevent more killings of prominent people in Western Europe.

In the past few weeks, there have been two killings in Paris—an exiled Iranian general and the ambassador of the United Arab Emirates—and in Britain an Indian diplomat was kidnapped and murdered by Kashmiri separatists.

The latest murder victim was the American head of the Sinai peacekeeping force, Mr Leamon Hunt, in Rome.

Responsibility for Mr Hunt's death was claimed by the "Fighting Communists," a faction of the Red Brigades.

A caller to a Milan radio station cited many reasons for the murder, including opposition to the Camp David Middle East accords, Italy's membership in Nato, the Western peacekeepers in Lebanon and American cruise missiles in Europe.

Impotent

Such varied motives frustrate intelligence agencies that try to prevent attacks. And the usual method—abduction or shooting in the street—circumvents the heavy security measures that have turned many embassies and diplomats' homes into fortresses.

The United States Vice-President, Mr Bush, said in Paris last month that the United Nations had been impotent in taking action against international terrorism.

"We are deeply concerned about the increase in terror to effect political change," Mr Bush said after learning of Mr Hunt's death.

"Part of our concern in Lebanon relates to such terror."

A Scotland Yard official, who spoke on condition his name would not be used, said: "There is always a problem with these new groups. We are aware of the main ones, like the PLO, but occasionally you get new ones.

"We have to be as aware of them as we can, but we can only hear of them through other forces and intelligence agencies."

Armed police guard all embassies in the British capital. The main threat in

prove the exchange of information about terrorist activities in the Middle East and Europe.

The *Wall Street Journal*, reporting from Washington, said the CIA was establishing a centre to evaluate the intelligence data. There has been no official confirmation of the report.

Such co-ordination could help to guard against attacks on representatives of the major nations, but might not be so useful in preventing the kind of killings seen in recent weeks.

In France, on February 7, a lone gunman shot dead Iranian former general Gholam Ali Oveissi, aged 65, the brutal military governor of Teheran under the late shah, and his brother Husein. The Islamic Jihad Movement claimed responsibility.

The next day, a lone gunman in Paris killed the ambassador of the United Arab Emirates, Khalifa Ahmed Abdelaziz Al-Mubarak. That killing was claimed by the Arab Revolutionary Brigades.

Arab ambassadors in Paris have asked for more protection.

Kuwait Leader Escapes Bomb Attack; 4 Die

By CHARLES P. WALLACE,
Times Staff Writer

AMMAN, Jordan—The ruler of the small, oil-rich Persian Gulf state of Kuwait narrowly escaped an assassination attempt Saturday when a terrorist drove a bomb-laden car into a motorcade and set off a massive explosion.

The blast killed two security guards at the head of the motorcade and a pedestrian, as well as the terrorist. At least 11 people were injured in the bombing, which took place in front of a gas station near Kuwait's Sief Palace.

The 58-year-old emir of Kuwait, Sheik Jabber al Ahmed al Sabah, suffered facial bruises and minor cuts from flying glass.

'Will Not Dissuade Me'

"The criminal incident this morning will not dissuade me and Kuwait from marching on the road to prosperity," the emir said in a statement after being treated and released from a nearby hospital. Jabber, who has ruled Kuwait since 1977, later appeared on television to reassure his people that he had survived the blast.

In Beirut, an anonymous telephone caller claimed responsibility for the attack in the name of Islamic Jihad (Islamic Holy War), a shadowy terrorist organization.

The caller demanded the release of 17 people being held in Kuwaiti jails in connection with suicide car bomb attacks in December, 1983, against the U.S. and French embassies in Kuwait as well as on several Kuwaiti government installations.

GUNMEN MURDER CAMPUS CHIEF

NZPA-Reuter
Beirut

Three unidentified gunmen murdered the president of the American University in Beirut, Mr Malcolm Kerr, yesterday as he was walking to his office.

Mr Kerr, an American citizen, was shot in the head. He was rushed to the nearby American University Hospital, where he died.

Security sources said the attack occurred as Mr Kerr walked from the lift to his office inside the sprawling campus in Moslem West Beirut.

Beirut Radio said one of the gunmen fired two shots from a pistol equipped with a silencer. One of the bullets hit Mr Kerr in the head.

Bomb Threats

The university is protected by Lebanese Army troops, and guards at the gate do not allow anyone without a special university pass or foreign passport to enter the compound.

The university has received several bomb threats in the past year.

Explosives were found on the campus and defused shortly after the suicide bombing attacks against United States Marines and French troops in Beirut on October 23.

24

4

DUTIES OF THE BODYGUARD

The U.S. Secret Service is an old and well established organization with a long history of experience in the security business. As such, it is a very structured organization with established operational procedures understood by both protectors and protectees. A new agent must simply go through the training and study the SOP manuals to be able to ascertain his or her duties in a variety of situations.

If, after training and study there is still doubt, a senior or supervisory agent is always on hand to answer questions. On larger team operations, such as Presidential travel, newer agents would be initially assigned less demanding tasks, working their way from standing post at some remote location, to outer perimeter, to inner perimeter, and ultimately, to the actual close protection detail.

Even in the corporate security world, large companies have established written guidelines for new security officers to follow. Many also have in-house training programs, or assign a training officer, to better acquaint new personnel with their systems and procedures. Again, if there are questions, an individual can simply read the manual or ask a shift supervisor.

The personal bodyguard, who frequently works alone, does not have the benefit of an SOP manual or the guiding hand of a training officer. The BG must learn from experience, finding his way through the minefield of client preferences, whims and foibles. All the time, trying to educate the client as to what is sound security procedure and what is folly.

DUTIES
The duties of the professional bodyguard can be many and varied but should all focus on one area—to provide the best protection possible within the framework and limitations of the assignment. Limitations such as a client's need to function within his or her business and social world, and the limited coverage that only one bodyguard can supply. These limitations will be covered in more detail in the next chapter.

The duties of a bodyguard, as in most jobs, are generally set by the employer, unless having a BG is a first for the employer, in which case he will need some guidance. The duties begin with who or what the BG is expected to protect and what hours he will work. They may also include doubling as a driver; 24 hour on-call status; taking the kids to school in the morning; locking-up the house in the evening; making travel arrangements; and some record keeping. In addition, there are several less tangible expectations of a BG. Such things as diligence, loyalty, honesty, discretion and a sense of confidentiality may all come under the heading of professionalism but are hard to define in the written conditions of employment.

Although the position of BG is service oriented, there are limitations. On the side of many police cars are the words—To Protect and Serve—but this does not stand true for the professional BG whose motto should ideally be—To Protect but NOT Serve. This is brought about by employers' of bodyguards almost universal misuse of the BG and treating them as "help", available for errands, shopping, feeding the pets, programming the VCR and a myriad of other menial tasks. There is probably no greater cause of discontent between the BG and the client than the misconceptions as to the BG's duties.

This is not to say that a BG never runs errands. In fact, any minder who has never performed some menial helpful tasks probably did not hold jobs for very long. The trick is in knowing when it is acceptable and when it impacts on one's professional status. It will also be directly linked to the actual threat level.

An example of each. It is not acceptable for the BG to allow himself to become loaded down with shopping bags when he needs to keep his hands free to react to trouble. It is also not appropriate to have to fetch the car leaving the protectee waiting alone in a public place. That is the duty of drivers or valets. On the other hand, it could be appropriate to make a quick run to the drugstore for a needed prescription if the principal is safely in for the evening. This would only be the case if no one else is available, delivery is not an option and there is no specific threat at play. Expecting the protectee to make the run to the drugstore is only exposing him or her to added possible danger away from the safety of the castle. (More on this in Chapter 20).

On the subject of non-security related tasks, it is the duty of the BG to use reason and logic to educate the employer on the inherent risks of such distractions and non-essential tasks. It is best for all concerned to head off any confusion as to the BG's duties at the time of hiring, by arriving for the initial interview with a prepared guideline of the acceptable duties for a BG. The personnel manager or client is then offered the opportunity to add or subtract whatever they deem reasonable. At his point the applicant must attempt to educate the client as to the duties of a security professional and the reasons for not being delegated to "non-security related tasks". This can only help one's application and further enhance the BG's standing as a professional in their eyes.

The BG can further protect his position by getting the Conditions of Employment and expected duties typed up and signed by both the client, his administrative assistant, wife and security manager. One should be careful that the employer does not slip in a catch-all clause like, "...and any other duties requested", since this could leave the BG's position open to abuse at a later date.

It is important that the BG not be confrontational on these issues, but it is equally important to stand firm where necessary. Once one starts being viewed as just another helpful staff member, it is very difficult to ever regain professional standing or the respect of the principal.

Since not all situations can be foreseen, educating the client in a polite manner, often by example, becomes a never ending process. It is wise to periodically send memos across his or her desk of changes in security procedures, new technology, changes in the industry along with photocopies of current articles or news clippings related to local crime, his position and potential exposure.

The extent of a bodyguard's duties can also vary with the type of client, size of the client's support staff and level of protection expected. There are bodyguards who are the strong silent types that although very protective and handy in a scrap, could not be trusted with more cerebral administrative duties. Other bodyguards may find themselves handling a variety of semi-security related duties such as travel planning, and this is where we come into the realm of the personal protection specialist.

In recent years, the term bodyguard has been replaced by the title of protection specialist since the duties have expanded beyond just "guarding bodies". To effectively handle a client's protection, the modern BG must involve himself in areas that were traditionally not covered by security. These could include the selection of suitable cars, travel planning, residential security systems, office access control, CCTV monitoring, mailroom set-up and periodic security evaluation.

When it comes to driving, whether a limo is utilized, the BG drives or the client drives his own car, the BG should still take a professional interest in vehicle maintenance. The BG should, at a minimum, ensure that all vehicles are gassed, cleaned, maintained, serviced and inspected for safety features, especially brakes and tires, at regular intervals.

Another possible duty for the BG is travel planning. Even when a client has an in-house travel bureau, the BG should still take an interest in the itinerary especially if he is to be handling the related security. This could be for no other reason than to become familiar with the principal's planned movements, to ensure suitable ground transportation and confirm a hotel room next to the principal.

With time and experience, the bodyguard may also be called upon to make intelligent observations about residential and office security hardware and access control systems. Other duties may be to act as "keeper of the keys", logging visitors in and out of the office or residence and locking-up in the evening.

Although not directly part of the close protection mission, these related duties do improve a client's overall security coverage and are all reasonable expectations of the BG, especially if he or she is part of a team. Tasks that are not part of the bodyguard's duties would include menial chores that could be handled by a valet or errand boy: picking up dry cleaning; making runs for fast food; walking or feeding the pets; cleaning up dog shit; washing the cars; carrying shopping bags; etc.

There are, however, some aspects of BG work, not directly related to the protection of the principal, that a professional BG should be willing to undertake. These are tasks that may require a position of trust or discretion, for example, the transportation of valuable paintings, art works, jewelry, important contracts, confidential communications, cash or negotiable instruments. Having to fly to Rome to transport a rare painting by a seventeenth century Italian master back to the United States could not exactly be viewed as a hardship. In fact, this could be one of the perks of the job.

Additionally, in a corporate environment, once the principal is safely installed in his office for the day, the bodyguard may be entrusted to make bank runs for payroll or cash; hand deliver an important document; deliver the principal's Rolls-Royce for service; or pick-up visiting VIPs from the airport. These are all acceptable duties that call upon the bodyguard's professional skills or position of trust, so should not be viewed as errands.

A word of warning. There are a range of illegal activities, periodically requested by the rich and corrupt, that no matter how much the enticement should be avoided by the BG. These may include: fixing traffic violations; making false statements to officials; lying under oath or committing perjury; the purchase or handling of illicit drugs; delivery of non-specific packages; procurement of prostitutes; debt collecting and strong-arm work; protection and extortion rackets; participation in blackmail schemes; illegal wire-tapping; the general intimidation of business associates; and the disposal of unwanted spouses. Although some of these may sound extreme, they have all occurred, often resulting in arrest and the filing of criminal charges against all concerned.

True Story: Coming highly recommended, a local security consultant/ bodyguard was offered an opportunity to protect a Middle Eastern prince during his pending visit to Los Angeles. At the first meeting the prince's business managers offered the bodyguard a healthy remuneration for his services. They then informed him that he should be aware that the prince liked to have both ladies of the night (prostitutes) and cocaine made available to him during his stay in the city of the angels.

The bodyguard informed the business managers that this should pose no problem, in fact the prince could be assured the safest stay he had ever had in LA. Safe because the bodyguard would happily throw his ass straight in jail. The business managers had not realized that the bodyguard was also a respected Lieutenant with LAPD Metro Division.

Once a bodyguard crosses the line and agrees to help the client with any small illegal act, he has opened himself up for continued abuse. Even though the BG may think he is just being helpful, he will have lost the important elements of trust and respect in the eyes of the principal. Any principal knows that an individual willing to participate in illegal activity simply to protect his job, cannot be trusted as a bodyguard. A bodyguard who can be enticed to illegal activity on behalf of his employer, can also be enticed to turn on his employer.

This is not to say that a bodyguard may not handle certain sensitive matters for a principal. By the very nature of the position, a professional bodyguard has the reputation as one who can be trusted, can get things done, is not easily intimidated, and above all, discrete. Some of these "discrete duties" that the bodyguard may find himself involved with could include: private investigations; the chartering of private jets for discrete but legal business dealings; the pick-up or delivery of a mistress or girlfriend; making discrete hotel reservations for extra-marital liaisons; the cash purchase or pick-up of expensive gifts such as jewelry; and all those other little indiscretions of the rich and famous.

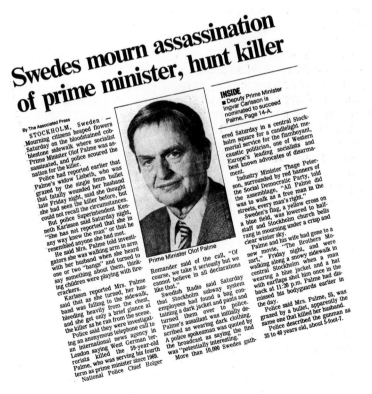

Swedes mourn assassination of prime minister, hunt killer

By The Associated Press

STOCKHOLM, Sweden — Mourning citizens heaped flowers Saturday on the bloodstained cobblestone sidewalk where socialist Prime Minister Olof Palme was assassinated, and police scoured the nation for the killer.

Police had reported earlier that Palme's widow Lisbeth, who was grazed by the single 9mm bullet that fatally wounded her husband late Friday night, said she thought she had seen the killer before, but could not recall the circumstances.

But police Superintendent Kenneth Karlsson said Saturday night, "She has not reported that she in any way knew the man" or that he resembled anyone she had met.

He said Mrs. Palme told investigators she was walking arm in arm with her husband when she heard one or two "bangs" and turned to say something about them, thinking children were playing with firecrackers.

Karlsson reported Mrs. Palme said that as she turned, her husband was falling to the sidewalk, bleeding heavily from the chest, and she got only a brief glance at the killer as he ran from the scene.

Police said they were investigating an anonymous telephone call to an international news agency in London saying West German terrorists killed the 59-year-old Palme, who was serving his fourth term as prime minister since 1969. National Police Chief Holger

Prime Minister Olof Palme

Romander said of the call, "Of course, we take it seriously but we cannot believe in all declarations like that."

Swedish Radio said Saturday that Stockholm subway system employees had found a bag containing a dark jacket and pants and turned them over to police. Palme's assailant was initially described as wearing dark clothing. A police spokesman was quoted by the broadcast as saying the find was "potentially interesting."

More than 10,000 Swedes gath-

INSIDE
■ Deputy Prime Minister Ingvar Carlsson is nominated to succeed Palme, Page 14-A.

ered Saturday in a central Stockholm square for a candlelight memorial service for the flamboyant, caustic politician, one of Western Europe's leading socialists and best known advocates of disarmament.

Industry Minister Thage Peterson, surrounded by red banners of the Social Democratic Party, told the assemblage, "All Palme did was to walk as a free man in the streets, every man's right."

Sweden's flag, a yellow cross on a blue field, was lowered to half-staff and Stockholm church bells rang in mourning under a crisp and clear winter sky.

Palme and his wife had gone to a new movie, "The Brothers Mozart," Friday night, and were walking along a snowy sidewalk in central Stockholm when a man wearing a blue jacket and a hat with earflaps shot him once in the back at 11:20 p.m. Palme had dismissed his bodyguards earlier in the day.

Police said Mrs. Palme, 55, was grazed by a bullet, apparently the same one that killed her husband. Police described the gunman as 35 to 40 years old, about 5-foot-7.

29

5

LIMITATIONS OF THE BODYGUARD

The concept of total security is unknown in the western world, and by this is meant the ability to guarantee a principal's protection from attack. Perhaps during the Gulf War of 1991 Saddam Hussein had almost total security. He stayed in deep bombproof bunkers, protected by his select guard; would only permit his trusted inner circle close to him, mostly relatives or boyhood friends; and never ventured out into public because of the risk of assassination or simply becoming a casualty of the bombing. But who can live like that for any length of time?

Even the US Secret Service, with all their resources, have failed to prevent the attacks on and assassination of several presidents. After the assassination of John F. Kennedy, the only assurance that the head of the Secret Service could give the President was that, "he would not be hit twice with a club." Think about that. They could not even guarantee that the President of the United States would not be struck or shot at least once.

This is not the fault of the large team of highly trained special agents of the Presidential Protection Detail, but more the nature of a Head of State's position. As with any politician, he must come in contact with the people, his voters, and any public exposure brings an element of risk. In addition, if he is to be perceived as being in control, the Commander-in-Chief, he must venture out into the masses "pressing the flesh" to give the image of a loved and respected leader who has nothing to fear from the populace.

In oppressive regimes, supporting a weak puppet or ruled by a hated dictator, the leaders know the folly of getting too close to the people. These tyrants may create fear, but they also live in fear, under almost siege conditions, they exist in a state of constant paranoia of an internal coup attempt.

For entertainers and celebrities, it is their public, their fans, their admirers, but also their obsessive wackos and psychos. Even CEOs and high profile businessmen must still function in the real world of both business and social commitments. So short of total isolation, there are no guarantees. That is the first and most significant limitation of a bodyguard. In the private sector, there are additional obstacles.

Unlike their counterparts in the Secret Service and State Department, the bodyguard working corporate or celebrity contracts has several limitations placed upon him. Where a Secret Service advance team can go into a city, flash official ID and request the cooperation of local law enforcement, a bodyguard can expect little or no cooperation depending on the importance of his client.

WORKING SOLO

A single bodyguard, although not totally useless, is very close to it. He may serve a purpose for celebrities moving in public as a deterrent for unwanted fans or chance encounters, but he will be no obstacle for the premeditated attack of a determined kidnapper or stalker. In fact, under these conditions there is a good probability that a lone BG would be taken out without even seeing it coming.

When working alone, the BG must know his limitations and make these known to his client. Where possible, the BG should request the budget for a partner, especially if there is any significant threat level.

The first and obvious limitation is just how much can be expected from one man. Not even the most highly trained and experience BG has eyes in the back of his head. Nor can he be expected to work long hours with any efficiency or be in two places at the same time. The most fundamental principle of BG work in a crisis is **cover and evacuate.** It is all but impossible for one BG to both react to a threat and evacuate his client to safety simultaneously.

Author's Note: One incident that comes to mind was a time when I was traveling alone with a client and his wife in Hong Kong. Since I was working alone I strongly recommended that we draw as little attention as possible and make our movements around town somewhat low profile. The client saw the logic in this, dressed casually and opted not to use the hotel supplied Rolls Royce on several outings. But I did run into one problem with his wife.

Being blond and quite striking, she already drew considerable attention, but on the day she decided to visit the street markets, she insisted on wearing some very expensive jewelry. All the time knowing that the crowded markets drew a good cross section of thieves, pick-pockets and street gangs.

After explaining to her, at some length, that this was not wise, she simply came to the conclusion that since I was along she would be safe. I asked her husband to reason with her but to no avail.

Finally I confronted both of them with the options: If while in the crowded markets, a thief snatched her two hundred thousand dollar diamond necklace, should I chase the thief with the hope of recovering it. To do this would mean leaving her standing unprotected in a bad part of town. Or should I stay with her and kiss off the necklace.

The point was taken and we went to the markets—one of us a little miffed but less the jewelry.

DRIVING OR ON FOOT

Another problem that a BG will run into is simply moving around town with a client, especially if the BG is required to drive.

Firstly, when driving, both hands are occupied restricting the BG from physically protecting the principal in the case of an attack. Secondly, the driver is often the first one shot in an attempted kidnapping. Lastly, when pulling up to the curb, the principal will often jump out of the car before the BG has had the opportunity to scope out the area.

The obvious solution is to use an assigned driver and leave the BG free to do his job. An alternative is to have the principal do the driving. *(We actually had one client who was a world class race car driver, so it was only logical that he be the one behind the wheel. He agreed).*

Another problem occurs when clients drive their own cars and security follows in a chase car. Apart from the difficulty of just tailing another car in inner-city traffic, if the client runs a STOP sign, the chase car will also have to run it just to keep up. The same problem occurs when the client's car makes a light just before it turns red and the chase car must either stop or run the red.

The solution is to run a lead car and a chase car or to have a BG drive the principal vehicle so as to better coordinate lane changes and intersections with the chase car.

Moving on foot is not quite as big a problem as in a vehicle but there are still limitations. For example, a male BG cannot follow a female client into a bathroom or changing room. In addition, it is difficult for one BG to position himself between the principal and potential danger areas without appearing to bounce all over the place. Two guards can better bracket a client in a more dignified and inconspicuous manner.

When escorting a client's wife or girlfriend shopping, if she does not have a personal assistant with her, the BG will find himself carrying shopping bags and being distracted. This is also one situation where a female BG is more comfortable.

Another limitation of the lone BG is in nightclubs. The client will usually want the BG to escort his wife or girlfriend to the bathroom, just to keep the wolves at bay, but this means leaving the client unattended. If possible, ask one of the other women to go to the bathroom with her and stay with the client. After all, he is the primary target and the one who signs the pay checks.

SCHEDULING

Another problem that a bodyguard will run into is scheduling. An individual can only be alert for so many hours in one day, but a BG's day can begin at six in the morning and not finish until 3 AM, or whenever the clubs close.

We have had contracts where the children are up early playing; the wife hits the gym early; the client may live in LA but is up with the New York stock exchange. From there, it is all go all day. He has meetings and power lunches, she is shopping, the kids have to get to and from school; then they have a benefit that night that goes until the early hours of the morning. It is just not possible for one BG to cover all this, and yet there are employers who try but only succeed in spreading their security too thin.

Some employers may employ a BG for the days only, but then continually keep him late into the night. Even if only one BG is contracted, it is advisable to have several part-timers available on pager to fill in where necessary. This may be up to the BG to do some networking with his peers so that they can relieve each other when the hours become too long and shifts are simply too fatiguing.

GUNS

Firearms can create many problems for the private bodyguard, particularly if he wishes to carry concealed or travels a lot. To begin with, in some cities and states it is very difficult for a bodyguard to obtain a concealed weapons permit, and in some countries, particularly those of the British Commonwealth, it is all but impossible.

In most states, it is not difficult to qualify for an open carry permit as given to uniformed security guards, but there is usually no provision for the executive security type who must carry concealed in plain clothes. This is one of the big frustrations of the bodyguard industry. The standards for uniformed security guards and the minimal training they receive to qualify for a permit to go armed are so low as to be a joke. And yet a bodyguard who is much more highly trained and proficient is often unable to obtain a state concealed weapons permit.

Concealed weapons permits have long been a political favor dispensed by local law enforcement officials, or unreasonably restricted because of the fear of vicarious liability exposure to the city or county.

Bodyguards will also come across clients who do not want them to carry firearms. This may be because of their own fear or prejudice towards guns in general; small children in the house; religious beliefs; or unwillingness to assume the liability exposure of either an accident or an actual shooting.

On some occasions, carrying a firearm may be inappropriate, impractical or unnecessary. Moving celebrities through crowds is a good example. If a path hasn't been cleared and barriers positioned, the BG is better off keeping his hands free to bulldoze through the crowd without the concern of being disarmed. And even if an armed threat is identified, the BG is better off pushing his clients into the masses to shield them from the attack. It would not be appropriate to clear leather and begin blazing away into the largely innocent crowd.

In general, a bodyguard should not consider the gun as a pivotal part of providing security, or that he is significantly handicapped by not carrying one. As stated several times in this book, training, planning, preparation, procedure, awareness and professionalism are far more important than the remote possibility of gun play.

POLICE OFFICERS

In most major cities, police officers can make a few bucks on the side as bodyguards or security consultants. However, even off-duty police officers moonlighting as bodyguards have restrictions placed upon them that are not present when they are working officially.

In the first place, most are required to notify their superiors of their extra curricula activities to ensure that there is not a conflict of interest. It would not, for example, be very appropriate for a police officer to be guarding an individual who is under suspicion or investigation for illegal activity. Secondly, they cannot utilize their law enforcement status in the general execution of their BG duties. More than one police officer or federal agent has been disciplined for misuse of their badge to further the interests of a private client.

If a serious crime occurs in the immediate presence of a police officer, on or off duty, then he may change hats and take an official role. The down side is that at this point he is distracted from his security function, ceases to be an effective bodyguard and may even have to leave his client to deal with the problem at hand.

Reserve police officers have even more limitations placed upon them, some not even being permitted to carry a weapon except in performance of their official duties.

There are some police officers who only make themselves available for static guard duty at night on the estates of the rich and famous. The problem with this is that the officers work all day at their regular jobs and then expect to pull a night shift. The assumption is that once the clients are in for the evening, the BGs can sack out on the couch and catch enough sleep to keep them going for the next day.

If a client is willing to pay for some one to just sleep on property that is fine, but this is not an acceptable arrangement for even low threat level contracts. In actuality, all the client is getting is a tired individual, who will probably sleep through any intrusions, or if awakened, will be reacting in a state of semi-consciousness.

CONCLUSION

The bottom line is that the BG must know his or her own limitations and those imposed by the client, the location and the situation. If the conditions are not conducive to good security procedure, the BG must make this known to the client and request permission to bring in back-up BGs when ever necessary.

Few private sector bodyguards will ever enjoy the resources of the Secret Service. The six agents escorting this limo represent only a small fraction of the hundreds of personnel involved in a presidential motorcade.
(Photo: U.S. Secret Service)

6

THE CLIENT / BODYGUARD RELATIONSHIP

"Uneasy lies the head that wears the crown"
—William Shakespeare, Henry IV

Attempting to understand the inner workings of a celebrity or wealthy principal's mind could easily be a life-long study, filling the journals of a legion of psychologists and behavioral scientists. Since a BG's potential client list includes a wide variety of backgrounds and occupations, it is only with time and experience that the bodyguard will even begin to learn their various preferences, moods, idiosyncrasies, quirks and foibles.

First and foremost, the BG should understand that anyone who can afford a personal bodyguard is of sufficient wealth to be accustomed to doing what they want, when they want, and consider security to be an inconvenience to their established lifestyle. Even a newly elected President of the United States must go through a readjustment period when suddenly finding himself under the protective wing of the Secret Service Presidential Protection Detail. Others in his entourage, particularly the First Lady, often find it even more "inconvenient" and take longer to adjust.

TYPES OF CLIENTS

The types of clients, their occupations and socio-economic status will have a direct affect on the bodyguard and his related duties. A bodyguard in the private sector could find himself working for a number of employers either in the United States or overseas. Countries that are politically unstable or have some level of civil unrest, often created by social injustice and the significant rift between the very rich and the very poor, offer many opportunities for the professional BG, especially if he is a polyglot. In the United States, there is not the civil unrest and uncertainty of a semi-third world country but there still exists a diverse market place for security professionals. Within this land of opportunity there are several different employers of bodyguards, each with their own needs and idiosyncrasies.

The Rich—

Clients of wealth will generally fall into one of two categories; old family money that has been passed on from generation to generation; or the nouveau-rich who may have found success in the entertainment industry, real-estate investment, the stock market, or high technology manufacturing. Whichever group, they represent a significant number of individuals who have amassed a small fortune and wish to keep it. Some may prefer to remain anonymous but unfortunately, those of significant wealth are well known and receive frequent mention in the various social columns and the tabloids. Forbes magazine even goes so far as to publish a who's who list and brief bio of the 400 most prominent.

One advantage of working for the super wealthy, unlike politicians, is their general lack of hidden agendas. BG work is a simple contractual agreement where the employer seeks protection for himself, his family and his home. However, with wealth comes an expectation of superior service, quality in all things and the best that money can buy. If the bodyguard falls short of these expectations he will be quickly replaced.

The Celebrity—

Celebrities retain bodyguards for one of two reasons, social status symbol or a real need for security. The type of crank mail that a celebrity receives and specific threats are a good indicator of the seriousness with which they perceive their own safety. The more serious the threats the more professional the security.

Celebrities by nature have big egos to feed and are used to being catered to. This is not all bad but unfortunately, most also use agents and business mangers to interface with staff and security, and this can create confusion and miscommunication between the BG and the principal. In addition, many celebrities, especially in the music industry, select their bodyguards from their often significant number of friends and groupies, without any consideration for training or suitability. The decision is based more on the fact that they like having a particular individual around so give him a job.

Even when the threat is real and security is more professional, celebrities can be difficult to work for. This is in most part due to the fact that they feed off of contact with their fans and move with large entourages of friends and business associates. This retinue is usually totally dependent on the star for their income and expenses so are always jockeying for favored status. They can also be jealous of the BG's routine closeness to the star, not perceiving it as a necessity of the job.

In amongst all this creativity and court politics, security often suffers. The celebrity may be safe within the group that makes up the inner circle, but new faces are constantly being introduced with no opportunity for the BG to vet them or ascertain their motivations. In the rock and roll industry in particular, the dregs of society, losers, dopers, pimps and whores seem to have little problem obtaining a backstage pass and getting close to an idol.

The Senior Executive—
Corporate moguls, CEOs and key management personnel in multinational companies are some of the easiest clients to bodyguard. They are intelligent businessmen, professionals in their own field, hard working and logical. They may be demanding when it comes to efficiency and performance but there is far less bullshit than dealing with celebrities.

Corporate security is more structured than celebrity bodyguarding but the basic principles are the same. Life revolves around schedules, appointments, meetings and itineraries, and most of the time a business suit or sport coat and tie will be the order of the day. In addition, executive security jobs are usually full time employment that carry full benefits such as insurance, health benefits, expense accounts and corporate cars.

Where one runs into a problem guarding corporate types is in the bottom line—or profit / loss charts. Businessmen view most things in terms of cost factors and return on investment. Everything in their world is expected to show a profit, but security is an overhead, an expense without any visible return.   If the threat level is low, then security seems to be just an added and unnecessary cost center that could be cut when needed. Fortunately the corporate type usually possesses a logical mind. If he himself is not being attacked or threatened, he will still pay heed to newspaper clippings of attacks against individuals in a similar position. All the time, the BG can be reinforcing the fact that the mere appearance of security is a strong deterrent that cannot be quantified.

The Politician—
Very few politicians in the United States, except perhaps the Kennedy family, would be considered high risk security. By nature, the politician seems to avoid strong stands on any significant issue; tries to please everyone; and avoids making enemies. After all, everyone is a potential voter.

However, the rare politician who actually has the "huevos" to take a firm position on a controversial issue, especially one that is politically incorrect, may incur the wrath of not only the voter but also that of an obsessed individual. There is no doubt that the world is full of loose canons and fanatics, all fantasizing about the possibility of attaining the notoriety that comes with assassinating a figure-head.

Security for politicians involves long hours, extensive travel, political breakfasts, business lunches and fund-raising dinners. Although their lives function around carefully scheduled itineraries, and press releases, the BG must be prepared for sudden changes in the program—especially if there is a natural disaster, riot or special event that has political mileage and presents a valuable photo opportunity or a chance to get on the TV evening news.

Another idiosyncrasy of the politician is that image is everything. Therefore, the bodyguard's appearance and behavior must be reflective of the principal's own carefully developed and polished public image. In public, the BG should remain in the background but stay close enough to react to a threat. However, some politicians will not want the BG close at all, since this presents an image that the politician has something to fear from his public.

As with most public figures, the difficulty in protecting career politicians lies in the fact that they must be seen to have not only contact with but also the affection of the people. Through carefully arranged photo opportunities and public events the man at home watching T.V. must get the feeling that every constituent has access to his or her elected official. In the political arena, this contact with the public, shaking hands and kissing babies, is known as "working the crowd" and "pressing the flesh".

The politician's constant close physical contact with large crowds of both well-wishers, and wackos, creates a real problem for the bodyguard or security detail. Unlike the Secret Service, the private or even State or City employed bodyguard cannot cordon off the city block and screen the entire assembly through metal detectors. The BG must instead depend on his own powers of observation and quick reactions to spot and neutralize a threat in the crowd.

THE PRINCIPAL & THE BG

It is important, early in the assignment, to establish a good working relationship with the protectee, especially if the assignment has any longevity. Some contracts are short term for a specific function, as little as a few hours. Some are longer, for several days or weeks, while others could prove to be full time employment. Whichever the case, there needs to be a level of both communication and trust between the BG and the client.

On short term contracts or assignments, there may not be time for a bond to form and the BG must simply do the best he can, maintain a professional attitude and move on. In fact, on some contracts it is good policy to avoid distracting conversations, stay alert and leave when relief arrives. This is true of most police or military protective teams where the personnel are rotated regularly, there is a formal rank structure and the assignment is viewed as just another days work.

However, many BGs in the private sector find full time employment with an individual or family and the situation becomes more complex, especially under the added stress of a specific threat or following a recent attempt. The principals may find considerable comfort in the bodyguard's presence and company, often to the point of inviting him or her into the inner sanctums of their lives.

From experience, male principals with a business background will usually maintain a professional businesslike relationship with their BGs, only forming a personal bond or chatting casually after a considerable time of employment. On the other hand, female clients tend to bond with their BGs much quicker and are often more comfortable with a less formal relationship.

Where the primary principal is a woman of substance in business or politics, and not just the wife of a rich or powerful man, there should be no problem with the same businesslike relationship between the principal and BG. It is women who have not worked in a business environment, or simply married money, who seem to have a problem maintaining a business like relationship with staff. The BG needs to be cautious around women who have attained their status on looks and feminine wiles alone.

Different nationalities also have different attitudes toward employees. Americans are very open and friendly by nature, where as Europeans, the English in particular, are very aloof and conscious of class structure. It has also been observed that individuals who have grown up in very wealthy families are taught from an early age how to interact with staff, while those born less privileged but have attained new wealth are less formal or structured in their households.

Whichever the case, over a period of time, a bond will form between the BG and the principal. At first, the principal will be curious about the BG's life, background, training and past experiences. BG's with past military or police experience who have had violence in their lives are of considerable interest to those who have led a sheltered existence.

Conversely, when no one else is around, especially when traveling, the principal will use the BG as a sympathetic ear to his or her problems, fears, or concerns. Over a period of years, the BG becomes part of the inner circle, having gone through marriages, divorces, mergers, bankruptcies, and other crises with the client. If there has been infidelity, drug or alcohol abuse, or even physical injury, the BG will have gone through all of these, and usually as the one who has helped pick-up the pieces.

At this point, the personal bodyguard is viewed as one who knows the dark little truths and can be trusted. That trust is important in the bond between BG and principal and must never be broken. The BG should not discuss or disclose any personal or confidential information—not while employed and not to the tabloids afterward.

Again, the BG must first and foremost be a professional who establishes some guidelines early on and sticks to them. He should not allow himself to be drawn into the principal's personal life unless it directly relates to a threat. The BG must know when to say No, politely, and when to back off to a discreet distance and just observe.

AT THE RESIDENCE

Working at the principal's estate on a daily basis will require that the BG understand a little about "palace politics". The first question being who is the King?

A male principal may rule at the office, but the BG will quickly find that it is the wife who rules the home, residences or estate. Even with a large domestic staff, majordomo, butler or estate manager, it will still be the

"Queen" who makes the household decisions and sets policy. And here lies the first conflict.

When accompanying the principal, the BG responds directly to the principal's needs, but at the residence, the wife may feel that she has control. This has caused many a problem for the professional BG who is now put in an awkward position. The wife may make requests that the bodyguard knows to be in conflict with sound security procedure, up to and including the wife trying to pay the BG to "off" the husband. But that is extreme. In most cases the BG is merely asked to run errands, help move furniture, walk the dogs or wash the cars. All outside the job description of a trained professional.

These non-security related chores may be fine for Huey the bodybuilder turned bodyguard/gofer, but they are not acceptable for the BG who wishes to maintain his professional integrity. This being one of several good reasons for establishing specific conditions of employment in advance.

Right from the start, the wife may want to establish her authority at the residence and exercise control over the new BG. Any direct refusal or confrontation at this point may cost the BG his job. It is up to the principal to explain to his wife that this is one area in which she should take no active part. However, from experience, it takes a strong principal to risk the wrath of his wife to make this point clear. *(As one client's wife once informed me, "I will make his life miserable until I get my own way". And she did.)* All too often, in the interest of domestic harmony, the principal folds and the wife ends up creating havoc by having the BG cater to her often whimsical and multitudinous demands.

On the brighter side, the confident wife of a truly influential man, who is secure in her position and used to the presence of security teams, will understand the dynamics and limit her input to essential communications that facilitate the smooth running of the estate, without compromising security.

It is good policy that all family members be educated as to the primary purpose and duties of the BG, and how any distractions detract from his ability to function as a protection specialist. However, this too can be a problem with some cultures.

In some countries, particularly in the Middle East, those that hold power see all employees as mere slaves or servants who can be commanded at will, and to be "family" is to have power over all. The BG must carefully and diplomatically skirt this mine field, taking comfort from the fact that the higher the threat level, the greater his perceived value, and the fewer the problems in this regard.

A BG may even find times during his employment where, to be true to his profession, he must risk his job by taking a firm stand as to what constitutes good security procedure and what is unnecessary distraction or interference from family members.

Another problem arises when there is only one bodyguard and several family members to be protected. It is all but impossible for a BG to answer to the needs of, or show loyalty to, two or more people at the same time. Obviously the BG is protective toward all family members, but his first responsibility must be to one primary principal. *(When in doubt, I will usually consider the children my first responsibility since they are the least able to fend for themselves. I have also had clients indicate that in an emergency the children's safety take priority.)*

In a perfect world, the solution to this problem is for the wife to have her own BG—just as the children or other family members would have their own. But we do not live in a perfect world and the cost of several BGs can be prohibitive, so the BG will periodically have to deal with requests that detract from his coverage of the principal.

THE WIFE

To be the BG assigned specifically to the wife can be a unique and challenging experience. As stated earlier, where a male principal will usually take a business like approach to the relationship with his BG, the wife will tend to have a more informal relationship with her staff. This is a danger to the BG who can easily fall into the trap of becoming her friend, co-conspirator, and in some cases, a lover. It takes a dedicated BG to maintain his professional detachment when confronted with the task of protecting a vivacious and often stunning female protectee.

The beautiful, young ex-model "trophy wife" is part of the sociological phenomenon associated with wealthy men, especially if this is his second or third wife. However, all pleasures carry a price, and the price of a beautiful young wife is the basic male insecurity associated with what she is doing when the husband is at work.

The bodyguard may have been hired for no other reason than to keep other men away from the wife, and to send a signal to her that she is always watched. At first she will enjoy the added status of having a driver and bodyguard to help her through her busy days. She will also enjoy having the sympathetic ear of a strong, supportive listener with whom she can discuss her problems, but eventually the yoke of her husband's distrust will begin to chafe.

Author's Note: Every bodyguard that I have known who made the mistake of becoming overly close friends with the wife of a client paid the ultimate price. At first, the BGs would enjoy the special status of having a well placed ear, being able to dress more stylishly or casually, having clothes purchased for them and working easier hours. But that also carries a price.

When the BGs inevitably over stepped their bounds, lost sight of their professionalism or became a symbol of spousal control, and fell from the wife's grace, they fell hard. Having alienated themselves from the other members of the team, and from the principal because of their special friendship with his wife, they were terminated without any possibility of future employment on that team.

Personally, I would go so far as to refuse to work with client's wives or girlfriends so as to avoid any perception of split loyalty. I would instead, in the interest of peace, try to assign female bodyguards or married men to the task. However, often times the wife would request the youngest, most athletic BG since "he blended better in her world". That was a guaranteed recipe for disaster.

As stated earlier in this text, where the primary principal is a professional woman herself, there should be no problem with the same businesslike relationship that there would be between a male principal and his bodyguard. But for the bored wife with too much time on her hands, the BG becomes an all too available target for those manipulative powers that some women find the need to periodically flex.

CHILDREN

Working with the client's children, as with the wife, can also be considered "hazardous duty". Young children, when first exposed to the fact that Dad has a bodyguard, will initially be somewhat timid but quite curious. The BG is a new experience in their little lives and worthy of investigation.

If the BG has multiple duties, as is common when handling security for a family, some of those duties will encompass the children—taking them to school, picking them up, taking them to the park, watching them at play in a swimming pool and general babysitting.

Author's Note: I have had several bodyguards over the years, male and female, who have had an exceptional skill with children. Many had children of their own or were ex-school teachers so had first-hand appreciation of a child's needs. These BGs often volunteered to work with the children knowing that they were less trouble and went to bed earlier than many of the parents. As the BGs showed their affinity for work with the children, and the children became comfortable with them, the parents would actually request those individuals for both domestic and foreign travel.

The pit-fall in working with children is that the BG may find himself in one of several awkward positions, most placing him between the parents and the children. To begin with, many children are cunning, manipulative and politically astute, especially if they have divorced parents and are experienced in playing one parent against the other. To take this a step further, they may add the BG to the equation and request things of the BG that the parents have already denied. For example, eating between meals, candy, skipping homework, having pets in the house, watching horror movies, using the pool, playing in certain rooms, etc. In all cases, it is the parents that must set the ground rules and it is the BG's responsibility to be clear on all of those. If there is doubt, say No! to the child and ask the parents at an appropriate time. Better to temporarily upset the child than usurp the parent's authority.

The more cunning of the little monsters will go so far as to nag their parents into assigning them specific BGs that they like, and then requesting that the BG take them to amusement parks or video arcades. *(One principal, a single parent with shared custody of two daughters that he adored, was so easily manipulated by the "little angel's" begging and tantrums that even his girlfriend was heard to say, "he was pussy whipped by a six year old". Do you think that little girl didn't get her own way with security? Before long, you had a mere child threatening the BG with termination if he did not do exactly what she wanted.)*

The next problem is "quality time". While the parents are at work or traveling abroad, the BG may find him-or herself covering the children, playing with them, and even taking them to movies and amusement parks. The kids only seeing their parents when they can be squeezed into the schedule. This is the fault of the parents for not making more time, but never-the-less, a problem that the BG must deal with.

A time may also come when the kids express a wish to do something with a favored BG rather than with their parents. This can be a direct result of the heavy work loads and social responsibilities that the parents carry, or the difficulty they may have relaxing after work. Some spend so much time dealing with the problems of the world that they do not know how to play at a child's level. Whatever the reason for this situation, the parents must never be led to feel that they are competing with a bodyguard for their own children's attention.

Another problem arises at beaches, amusement parks and places like Disneyland. The BG will often be relegated to swim or go on the more adventurous rides with the children while the parents watch. This gives the children and BG a shared experience that only increases that bond. It is important that the kids like and trust the BG but not at the expense of parental bonding.

Another problem, not unique to children but of particular importance, is the topic of guns around the house. The children will be fascinated by the BG's handgun and will ask to see it, touch it or hold it. All must be firmly discouraged. Weapons should always be concealed, treated with due respect and never left unattended. Over time, the children will come to accept this and forget about the gun. Out of sight—out of mind.

Some BGs, when working around children at home, prefer to lock their sidearms away, only wearing them when in public. This is acceptable if the threat level is low and the estate security and access control are good, but not acceptable where there is any real danger of kidnapping.

All in all, the BG must not get between the parents and their children. This can only be done by constant communication with the parents, knowing their wishes and maintaining a professional relationship, more like a school teacher than a pal to the kids. It is also good policy to request that a nanny or nurse be present at all times so that the BG can concentrate on security. In addition, qualified BGs should be rotated regularly so that no one bodyguard becomes too popular or has too much influence with the wee ones.

TEENAGERS

While small children can be a joy to work with, teens are a whole different nightmare. With the rapid physical changes, peer pressures, fashions and problems associated with adolescence, teens can become quite unpredictable and rebellious. Especially the spoilt rich ones.

The BG tasked with protecting a teen may find himself confronted with all the complications of teenage life. These include but are not limited to: dating, smoking, peer pressure, sex, contraception, drugs, rock 'n' roll, tattoos, cars, and alcohol. All problems that a parent should deal with, but if the parents are too busy with their own lives to attend to their children, it is the bodyguard who must bear the brunt.

The most common problems being the teen sneaking out at night, under-aged drinking, DUI and experimentation with sex and drugs. The BG can also expect to see a contempt for the parent's "capitalist" values, a vocal dislike for the "gestapo" security team, and a demand for more independence, all expressed by radical changes in dress, body piercing and the occasional discreet tattoo.

Again, the best the BG can hope for is that the parents will handle it. Teens raised in a stable home with good solid values will be no problem, but the real hell-raisers from broken homes, who have probably had more money and freedom than is healthy for a teen, will have to be watched carefully. Children of the wealthy will also attract a young, rough, "in" crowd who only value their friendship for access to easy money and nice cars.

PRIVACY

The next aspect of "palace life" that the BG needs to be sensitive to is client privacy. Anyone who has had the need for 24 hour-a-day close protection can testify to the impact that this has on their lifestyle, most significantly, their loss of privacy. For security to be effective, the coverage must be thorough and the bodyguard must be close at hand. This can be so intrusive that clients are often tempted to sneak away from their own security team or bodyguard, just to have a few moments of privacy.

Within the limitations of the assignment, the bodyguard must give the client as much space and privacy as possible. Especially when away from the work environment, at home or in hotels. The client should still be able to call the BG with ease, and the BG must be able to respond quickly.

The client must have the assurance that all business dealings, conversations and affairs, conducted in the presence of the BG, will be held in total confidence.

Note: On my teams we would go so far as to make all new BGs sign a confidentiality agreement, covering not only team business but also the client's business and private life.

A BG should not discuss a client's business with anyone, especially friends, family and staff members. The only exception being the need to brief the team of anything that may impact on security. For example:- pending private or business activities; travel; newly identified threats; expected visitors; or specific client requests.

UNPROFESSIONALISM

There are numerous things that can be construed as unprofessional on the part of a bodyguard—some will create tension between the BG and the client, others will result in termination. Since a healthy working relationship between bodyguard and principal depends heavily on mutual trust, the BG must be careful to do nothing that will impinge on that trust.

Like any job and more so with bodyguarding, it is considered unprofessional to have friends visiting or telephoning one's work place; to use the photocopying machines for personal business; to use the client's car for personal errands; to make long distance calls on business or residence telephones; to eat out of the client's refrigerator; to borrow books or videos from the client's personal library; etc. A BG must organize his life so that he is not taking advantage of the situation and not bringing his personal affairs to work.

Everyone has pet peeves, but few things annoy a principal more, short of sleeping with his wife, than over familiarity with his friends, family or guests. It is accepted that if a BG's duties include working at the house or estate, then a certain relationship will develop with the family, in particular the children. The trick is in knowing the fine line between being friendly and being overly familiar.

When a bodyguard has worked for one client for several months, he becomes a familiar face around the house and office. At this point, friends and business associates of the principal will begin treating him as one of the inner circle, a trusted confident and will occasionally strike up conversations or exchange pleasantries. This friendliness on their part should not be construed by the BG as a sign that they wish to be his friend.

Over stepping these boundaries of professionalism may be manifested by: inviting the principal's friends to play golf or tennis; trying to date their secretaries; or asking professional help of a principal's business associates. The BG may have a legal or financial problem and is tempted to corner one of the principal's lawyers or accountants for some free advice. All bad moves.

The BG should keep his personal and business affairs to himself and not take advantage of the client's associates—unless specifically told to do so by the client, and even then with reservations.

WHAT WILL GET YOU FIRED

Whether working for a client, a corporation, or an agency, there are a few errors that are almost guaranteed to result in termination.

Termination of future employment not one's life, but that may be different in other countries.

Alcohol is always a big one. Drinking on the job, turning up drunk, or even having the smell of alcohol on one's breath, will get a BG his walking papers, not to mention destroying his reputation as someone who could be relied upon. Working as a bodyguard usually entails a twenty-four hour-a-day on call commitment. Like SWAT teams and firefighters, if there is any possibility of a call-out, there should be a minimum of eight to twelve hours between drinking and work.

Another potential problem, more so with novice, gung-ho BGs is unsafe gun handling. This could involve unnecessary gun handling on the property; leaving it laying on a desk or in an unlocked desk draw; failure to maintain proficiency; brandishing a firearm unnecessarily; accidental discharges; or shooting the principal's pesky pooch. These are all signs of immaturity and poor judgement and are totally unacceptable.

Excessive use of force is another problem area. Being overly physical with anyone approaching the principal or his property; assaulting a photographer or member of the press; unnecessary physical searches of members of the household staff; or punching out a waiter who was rude to a female client, will not endear the BG to the client or the victim. The only person that will be smiling is the victim's attorney.

At this point, one would think that all of the above are quite obvious and fall under the category of common sense. Well, in part that is correct but one must also remember that common sense is not that common. So apart from the obvious "terminators" like bad breath, poor personal hygiene, loud polyester suits, racial comments and profane language, there are the following less obvious ones. All true stories.

Indiscretion comes in many forms. An obvious one would be telling the principal's wife about the girlfriend or mistress that he has stashed in the beach house. The less obvious is telling a third party, who believes one to be unassociated to the principal, and then to have it come back through the grapevine, country club or secretarial pool. Remember that gossip is a valuable commodity with high society and a deadly weapon in the political arena.

Not following instructions. A businessman tells BG #1 to wait in his office while he goes to a meeting escorted by BG #2. At 6 PM the principal has still not returned to the office and BG #1 wants to leave. The principal's briefcase is sitting out containing possibly confidential papers so BG #1, in a moment of brilliance, hides the briefcase and leaves.

At 6:30 PM the principal returns to find no BG #1 and no briefcase with the important papers that he needs to read and sign that evening. He assumes BG #1 has taken the briefcase to his residence—but not so. The principal needs the papers so gets on the phone and the search begins. Finally, furious, and after midnight, tracking down BG #1, who had not been wearing his pager, upon arriving back at his apartment.

The moral of the story. If you are asked to wait—wait until hell freezes over or you can contact the principal or a supervisor. Everyone at this level has car phones, hand-held cellulars, pagers, personal assistants, fax/modems or some way to be contacted. At a minimum, BG #1 and BG #2 should have periodically checked in with each other and BG #1 should have been wearing his pager.

Borrowing the client's car. A bodyguard, one of a team of six on a 24 hour-a-day contract, gets off shift and decides to go get a bite to eat. He takes the client's new XJS Jaguar, knowing the client rarely drove it, and goes to a local restaurant for dinner. He starts drinking with a friend, keeps partying, and finally decides to return to the ranch fourteen hours later.

Already two hours late for his shift, driving too fast and still buzzed from drinking, he manages to slide the car off of a freeway off-ramp and gets stuck in the mud. To compound the problem, when the Highway Patrol arrives he cuts and runs knowing that he could not pass a field sobriety test.

Obviously he was fired, not just for taking the car but drinking on duty, being late for work, not checking in and reckless driving. Now this character still took the company to court for wrongful termination. The judge was amused—and he lost.

Now there are times when a client may offer the use of his car or cars, particularly when handling business for him. The BG must use best judgement by not taking the Rolls or Ferrari, not drinking and driving, not swinging by his girlfriend's house to profile, and returning it clean with a full tank of gas.

Abuse of expense money. Working for a corporate entity usually guarantees some form of accountability for funds issued, with expense sheets, authorized expenditures, per diems and receipts expected for everything except tips. However, working directly for an individual or celebrity, one is often given cash with no accountability and in some instances even required to carry the protectee's bankroll. It is not unusual for a BG to be given tens of thousands of dollars to carry for a client when travelling—especially when visiting areas where checks and credit cards are not routinely accepted.

To the story. A protection specialist was brought in to run a potentially hazardous overseas assignment. Within days he realized that three of the principal's staffers were living high on the hog, buying new clothes and pocketing a bundle, all with expense money that required no accounting. In fact they had never had to account for expense money advanced to them and tried to justify this as part of the perks and benefits, but from where the pro stood it was not cool.

Needless to say, this was a habit that they had become all to comfortable with that ultimately cost them their jobs—right after the specialist was hired on as the new security director.

On the same topic of money. It is not uncommon to see a client tipping extravagantly, spending money like water, buying frivolous items or simply spreading the wealth around. The BG should not fall into the trap of thinking that he can spend the principal's money in the same manner.

Where a reasonable tip may be ten or fifteen percent, the principal may choose to tip twenty-five or thirty percent. In some cases he may lay down twenty dollars for a five dollar drink and request no change. That is not acceptable for the BG. He should tip the customary amount unless the principal instructs him to routinely tip more on his behalf.

People of wealth may spend thousands like others spend dollars, but they did not become wealthy by not being money conscious. The first hint of wastefulness or extravagance by the BG at their expense and it is Sayonara.

Punctuality is another important factor in personal protection work. For the Swiss, time is time, but for the rich and powerful, time is money—and they do not like to be kept waiting. It is perfectly acceptable for them to be late, or to keep staff waiting for hours, but the bodyguard had better not only be on time but early and ready to move. Apart from all the minor infractions and tardiness that will ultimately add up to loss of a job, there are more serious instances that will result in immediate termination.

Favored bodyguard, retained more for his personality than skill, we'll call him JD, was told he was to escort the principal and his wife, to Europe and to meet them at their estate for the limo ride to the airport. Well, first JD doesn't show early, then he doesn't show on time. A phone call from the guard on duty at the estate awakens JD asleep at home. In a panic, he races to the estate only to realize that he has no cash so borrows some from the duty guard. Then he can't find his gun so also borrows the duty guard's piece. To make matters worse, JD can't find his passport and even he realized that he could not borrow one of those.

By now it is evident to all that "favored BG" has had a few too many brewskis and the principals are really steamed. To make a long story short, the on duty BG went to Europe and JD was left in LA wondering if he still had a job.

Attempted suicide is also frowned on. Trying to eat the barrel of a gun is another sure way to disturb the harmonious relationship between BG and employer. But Stupid, an ex-cop and shift supervisor with an impeccable record, didn't consider that when he got involved with the female assistant to the principal's wife.

Stupid got so hooked on this young lady that he left his wife and family, made some bad judgement calls and got dumped by the assistant all on the same day. Add to that some self-prescribed anti-depressant medications, ample alcohol and a resulting spiralling depression and Stupid decides to end it all.

His first attempt at this was to OD on sleeping pills and cut his wrists. Unfortunately, even in that state the knife hurt too much so he decides to explore other methods. But just to get even with the perceived cause of his troubles, he phones the assistant at work and tells her to listen while he shoots himself. This is when she freaks and the phone is passed to the security director. Good timing.

Stupid won't listen to reason so the director heads to his location calling the local police and paramedics, and slipping into his heavy body armor enroute. The director finds Stupid passed out on the bed with a small .25 caliber automatic in his bloody hand. The downers had kicked in and he had passed out before pulling the trigger. Police and paramedics arrived within minutes.

Stupid later called to thank the director for his professional handling of the situation and understanding about his decision to fire him. Or did he? Attempted suicide or incompetency? Now here is a trained professional with an arsenal of firearms at his disposal, a SIG and an Uzi in his gym bag, and he picks a .25 caliber pocket pistol. Hell, if a guy can't even kill himself properly, what chance does he have of protecting someone else's life. Just joking. Stupid went into therapy, paid for by the protectee, and got back with his wife. There are several lessons in that story.

Getting involved with other staff members. There are those that say that you can't control human nature. Boys will be boys and the same is true for the fairer sex. It takes an iron will to stay professional when that chemistry kicks in and nature plays its little games to ensure propagation of the species. On top of that, who is to say who can date whom? We are all adults, right?

So, apart from the previous incident, here is the problem faced by another bodyguard. A BG starts dating a secretary at the corporate office. Everyone approves and thinks this budding romance is cute. They are the gossip of the steno pool. But then, for whatever reason, the secretary loses her job under bad circumstances. She files a wrongful termination against the corporation, and all of a sudden the BG finds himself perceived as being in bed with the enemy. The client is uncomfortable so the BG is out of a job.

The wife is another source of danger. On a large contract, two bodyguards were assigned to handle the wife's day-to-day security needs, driving for her, taking her shopping but primarily to discourage the approach of other men. It was easy for these BGs to become attached to the wife, after all, she did buy them new suits and she was kind of fun to be around. So in turn, they swear loyalty to her, feed her the latest palace gossip and promise not to mention her frequent and excessive spending sprees.

The problem. Since marriages do not seem to last forever these days, and hubby has found something younger and more fun, wife #1 eventually finds herself a divorcee. Since "her bodyguards'" have now become friends, and because of their loyalty, she asks to take them with her. The principal and shift supervisor considered both BGs disloyal, so agree to the move. In addition, there is no point in having her spies in his camp during a divorce proceeding.

Ex-wife #1 now learns the actual expense of keeping two full time protectors, the cost now coming out of her spousal support check. That is money that could be better used for something more important like, oh, shopping, and promptly cuts them from the budget.

Two humbler BGs go back to the principal and ask for their jobs back, but by now wife #2 is on the scene and there is no way she will have these disloyal curs on the property. In fact she has already selected her favorite BG from the herd and the cycle of life with the rich and spoilt begins again. End of story.

BGs should be selected for a variety of skills, not the least of which is the ability to handle physical confrontation.

7

SELECTING A BODYGUARD

There are several books, most of questionable value, on the subject of bodyguarding but few address the principal's needs in selecting a professional protector. This chapter is written specifically for the individual who thinks that he or she may need a bodyguard.

The initial thought of hiring a bodyguard is usually brought about by a change in one's wealth or lifestyle, accompanied by some real or perceived threat. Some of the changes that prompt people to consider a BG could be a change in social status, a large inheritance, success in business, a death threat, an ugly divorce, negative press, an attempt on one's life, election to public office or a sudden rise to super-stardom.

The first reality check for a potential employer is understanding the fact that simply having a bodyguard may not save one's life, but that it will most definitely change it.

For whatever reason that an individual may find him or herself in the position of needing or just wanting a bodyguard, some serious thought is called for. The prospective principal should first consider the following questions.

1. Is there a real NEED for a bodyguard or is it just cool to have one?
2. Is there a potential for risk or an actual identified threat?
3. Are you currently being victimized, stalked or threatened or just nervous because it has happened to others?
4. Have the police become involved and do they have the resources to handle the threat?
5. Have you already up-graded the physical security and basic procedures at home and at the office?
6. Have you considered the changes that having a BG requires in your daily routine and life style?
7. Are you willing to accept the fact that you may be giving up a big part of your freedom and privacy?

8. Do you realize that for a bodyguard to be effective the coverage must be complete?
9. Have you considered the potential for litigation if your bodyguard gets physical with someone—even justifiably?
10. Have you run a cost study of the financial commitment of keeping a bodyguard, or even a team of bodyguards if twenty-four hour security is expected? Not just the salary but also medical insurance, liability insurance, additional travel costs, hotel rooms, rental cars, and training.

If after all the above questions have been answered, the principal is still seriously considering a BG then read on. Although bodyguards are a dime a dozen, good ones are not only quite rare, they are quite costly. If, after reading this book, and in particular this chapter, the principal is still determined to get a bodyguard, then he or she should get a good one. Since who, after all, would want a bad one—or even one who is somewhat indifferent.

A potential employer must understand that the value of personal security, unlike a good investment, is not quantifiable. One cannot look at the spread sheets each day to see the results and it is difficult to tell if the presence of a bodyguard is a tangible asset or an unnecessary overhead. Although one may not see the BG fighting back the proverbial hoards of hell on a daily basis, his mere presence may be deterring the unwanted approaches of criminals or crazies. There are very few documented cases where the BG actually saved a client, but there are several where the lack of a competent bodyguard proved fatal.

If all this seems a little intimidating to the prospective employer, a wise first step would be to hire a security professional to work up a personal threat assessment on the principal's position, lifestyle, daily routine, business environment and residence. The individual doing the assessment should not be the one in line for the security contract but rather an impartial third party who can guide the principal through the minefield of up-grading security, purchasing hardware, and if necessary, hiring a bodyguard.

The employer should not go into the hiring process thinking that he can get double value out of a bodyguard by having him perform non-security related functions. There is no greater source of discontent between BG and principal than requiring the BG to work outside of his expected security related duties. This is not just an issue of self esteem for a BG but one of having to compromise security coverage, and when one's life may depend on it, the last thing that is needed is a disgruntled BG.

If one can justify having a BG run errands then the threat level does not justify the cost of a real professional. All that is actually needed is another assistant, chauffeur or man-servant. Conversely, if one needs real security, one should not make the mistake of simply making an existing chauffeur or other trusted employee double as a bodyguard. Not unless they are physically capable, psychologically suitable and the principal is willing to send them out for extensive training.

THE HIRING PROCESS

Before beginning the hiring process, the principal should read a book like this so as to get a grasp of the basic knowledge and skills that a professional BG should have. Many applicants will fall far short of the necessary minimum requirements to be an effective BG, but the principal must at least learn the right questions to ask in order to discover this.

Employers should keep in mind that there are numerous weirdos out there looking for jobs as bodyguards, or any position where they get to carry a gun, so it is advisable to have a professional security consultant oversee the hiring process. He will know where to start the search, how to best word a classified advertisement and then screen the initial deluge of "wanna bes".

Employment and job placement agencies are not the place to look for an experienced professional. Since some States have no regulation over the security industry or basic published guidelines, most employment agencies will be unfamiliar with the differences between low wage security guards and highly trained bodyguards. Those States that do have minimal training requirements before licensing of guards have standards that are so low as to be useless. Add to this the fact that many State and Federal agencies have retraining programs where they run the unemployed or unemployable through cattle like "security guard schools" where the overall standard is scary to say the least.

The employer should also keep in mind that every individual interviewed and turned down for a job, is a potential wacko who may take it personally. To protect the principal, the initial interviews should be done away from both his residence and place of business, either at the security consultant's office or possibly an attorney's office. The applicants should not be told the full extent of the job or the principal's name.

The principal should take no part in the hiring process until the prospective BGs have been narrowed down to a few qualified hopefuls. At this point he should sit in on the interviews to ensure that the applicants meet his expectations in appearance, deportment, intelligence, experience and basic skills. It is also desirable that there be some compatibility or chemistry between a principal and a personal bodyguard, since they will after all, be spending a lot of time together.

Whether one chooses to do the hiring oneself, have the personnel department handle it or have an independent third part take the reins, the process begins with getting the word out or placing an ad in the classifieds. To eliminate the unqualified, the advertisement should emphasize words such as "experienced", "professional", "intelligent", "motivated", "trained", "certified", "with all necessary permits", "clean driving record", "excellent health", "free to travel", "on call 24 hours", etc. However, it is always amazing the number of totally unacceptable types who will answer the ad, but hopefully there will be a few gems in the group.

All initial applications should be in writing with a resume and a photo. After reviewing the resumes it will be easy to eliminate seventy to ninety percent of the applicants. Again, look for actual on-the-job experience, job related experience, employment history, letters of recommendation and certifications.

If one is considering hiring an aspiring rookie, one should look carefully at not only the individual's skills and background but also his motivation for becoming a bodyguard. Is the applicant a true professional just out of work or an ex-cop terminated for excessive force or worse? Is he or she someone on a legitimate career track within the security industry, or a career criminal working himself closer to his potential target? Could this individual be a diamond in the rough or a borderline psychopath who just wants to carry a gun and harbors a real hope of using it?

An employer should also be aware that within the security industry there is, for want of a better term, a significant "bullshit factor". Individuals will claim experience that they have not had and make-up certificates for non-existent training or schools. To detect this BS requires careful study of the applications and a few phone calls to previous employers, schools or instructors, all before they are invited in for an interview. If there is any question about certificates or letters of recommendation, the interviewer should have the applicant bring the originals to the first interview. Where it is just too easy to make changes to documents and run photocopies to conceal them, the originals are more difficult to alter.

THE INTERVIEW

When applicants arrive for an interview, they should be required to complete a standard job application and personal history data form. Prior to meeting with an individual applicant, the employer should take the time to reread both the applicant's initial application and resume and the just completed personal work history data form, looking for discrepancies.

At the interview, the employer should trust first impressions. An individual with the confidence, bearing and presence of a professional will be immediately evident. This does not necessarily mean size or strength but more an intangible presence that says, "professional, confident, competent."

After the initial introductions and pleasantries, the applicant should be given the opportunity to tell a little about himself. At this point the interviewer should be looking for a comfortable confidence without arrogance or nervousness.

The formal questioning should be done with the applicant's resume on the desk, starting with who did they last work for and why did they leave? From there the interviewer should work his way through each line of the resume and each letter of recommendation, questioning the applicant about anything of interest.

Next the applicant should be questioned on all the necessary skills, certifications or licenses required for this position. In addition, the applicant should have a passport, driver license, firearms permit, credit cards and proof of legal residency in the United States, or similar documentation for countries requiring proof of legal immigration.

The interviewer should then probe such areas as financial problems, litigations, pending law suits, health problems, injuries, other part-time jobs, problems in the home or anything that could hinder the applicant's total dedication to the assignment.

If the applicant has made it this far, the employer or representative can discuss the actual assignment, the hours, pay conditions and travel involved. It is important that both parties come to agreement on all conditions and related duties. It may even be that the applicant has more experience in close protection than the interviewer and can make helpful suggestions. If there are specific threats involved, these should be discussed with the applicant and his professional opinion requested. This will give some insight into his range of experience and areas of expertise.

At the end of the interview, if the applicant is still a strong contender, review the written Conditions of Employment and Confidentiality Agreement that all employees would be required to sign. It may also be necessary to have the applicant sign a release for the purposes of doing a background check and contacting previous employers. Also explain that there is a probationary period of three to six months in which he is being evaluated and may be terminated if deemed unsuitable.

Professional BGs take their shooting seriously and practice regularly.

Author's Note: In vetting applicants we found a quick way to eliminate much of the BS. Since most of our work was medium to high risk assignments, we placed substantial value on shooting and driving skills, along with some form of martial arts. For this reason, after carefully reviewing written applications, initial interviews were done at the shooting range to give us the opportunity to evaluate the applicants' gun handling skills and to put them under a little pressure. If they couldn't shoot well and handle a gun safely, the interview was over right there. If they passed the shooting part, the driving test was a simple matter of having them drive us around town to evaluate their precision driving skills, knowledge of the city, smoothness in traffic and application of basic driving tactics.

PROBATIONARY PERIOD

The probationary period is an important tool for the prospective employer. It is during this three to six month period that the new BG is evaluated for compatibility with the family, children, staff and co-workers. The BG should also exhibit total professionalism along with the appropriate deportment, dress, hygiene, courtesy, intelligence and common sense.

His professional skills should also come under scrutiny, particularly safe driving habits, general awareness, attention to procedure, safety with firearms, shooting skills and overall protectiveness toward the principal and his or her family.

LEGAL NOTE: Employers should seek legal advice on the hiring practices and required conditions of employment in their particular area or state. Employee contracts or agreements should also be prepared or reviewed by an attorney.

PART II

TRAINING

**"BETTER 3 HOURS TOO SOON
THAN A MINUTE TOO LATE"**

1

2

3

4

5

Drawing from concealed carry

8

BASIC BG TRAINING

Most individuals entering the business of bodyguarding do so because they already possess some of the necessary skills or aptitudes for the work, with fight training, competitive shooting or advanced driving being the most common. However, regardless of the individual's level of expertise in any or all of these three areas, this does not qualify him or her as a close protection specialist or bodyguard. Prospective BGs must still go through some form of basic schooling or supervised on-the-job training to learn the principles of effective personal protection and the art of working a client.

Professionals, in any field of endeavor, never stop training or learning, and this is especially true for protection specialists. Even for BGs or consultants that are ex-Secret Service with years on the presidential protection team, there are still skills to maintain and new information to review. Just as a police officer continues his studies into criminal behavior and methodology, and a soldier collects intelligence on changes in the enemy's armament and tactics, the BG must stay abreast of the types of criminals and crazies that may be stalking their clients.

To compound the need for continued training, the security business is very much linked to developments in the high technology industries. It comes in the form of computer driven security systems, new forms of radio or cellular communication, surveillance or counter-surveillance hardware, ballistic counter measures, or the cornucopia of other high tech toys offered in a dozen industry catalogs.

When it comes to actual BG training, there are as many different sources as there are subjects that need to be studied or practiced. This is true for both the seasoned professional and the aspiring rookie.

TYPES OF TRAINING

The type of training that a bodyguard requires will depend on his background, prior experience and the nature of the contracts he wishes to pursue. However, there are some commonalities in training and tactics that all BGs will require.

The bodyguard's primary mission is to supply professional close protection for an individual, giving that individual the confidence to go about his or her daily life secure in the knowledge that they have a guardian angel. This requires more than just guns and muscle. The principal needs to be able to draw confidence from the knowledge that the BG is a well trained professional who will steer them clear of danger or react appropriately when confronted.

The first type of training that a prospective BG will need is a course or program that covers all the fundamentals of bodyguarding as covered in Chapters 4, 6, 15 and 19—24. This is not the rough and tough action stuff like shooting and driving, but more the planning, threat recognition and movement drills that make up the foundation of personal protection.

Once the trainee has a firm grasp of the realities of BG work, the next order of business will be to improve personal fitness and enroll in some form of martial arts training (Chapters 9). Then comes a couple of days training in basic protection drills(Chapter 10), followed by a day of first aid and basic emergency medicine(Chapter 11).

Only after all of the above have been completed should the trainee invest time and money in evasive driver training (Chapter 14) and advanced combat weaponscraft (Chapters 12 & 13).

Marine MPs practice CQB and weapons retention.

Notice how shooting comes in last. That is not to diminish the importance of proficiency with arms but to put it in perspective. It would be difficult to find many, if any, instances in the US where a bodyguard successfully shot an assailant in the act of attacking a VIP. Since the BG's first priority is to **cover** and **evacuate,** and that usually takes both hands, it is somewhat difficult for the lone bodyguard to also handle a gun effectively.

Conversely, even though the ability to recognize and avoid an ambush is more important than the ability to drive out of one; and the ability to drive out of an ambush is more important than the need to shoot one's way out of one; if the threat level warrants evasive driving and firepower, then all involved should be proficient in both.

Remember the order in which a BG approaches operations and solves problems:

Know Your Enemy
Plan Movements
Avoid Danger Zones
Identify the Threat
Cover the Principal
Evacuate the Kill Zone (or)
Aggressive Counter Force
Stabilize Injuries
Seek EMS Assistance

This is the same order in which one approaches training. The professional learns to play the game with his brain, not his brawn—but when all else fails, a little brawn (along with a 4000 pound car and a few well placed hollow-points) does have value.

After the bodyguard has absorbed all this training and gained an acceptable level of proficiency, the BG should then expand his training into the areas of anti-intrusion systems, alarm systems, surveillance systems, electronic system design, technical surveillance counter measures (TSCM), and other fields of high technology. This is not with the aim of becoming a systems engineer but simply to be able to recognize, operate and discuss intelligently the hardware with which one is sure to come in contact.

While on the subject of types of training, it is important for the bodyguard to understand the difference between instruction and training; schools and training centers; and instructors and trainers. Many rookies waste time and money when they confuse knowledge with skill, or time in the classroom with training experience.

BG schools and instructors are sources of information, techniques, tactics, methodology, and general higher learning on the subject of personal protection. Training centers and trainers, on the other hand, take that new knowledge and turn it into practical application. The primary differences between the two groups being time and sweat.

Some schools structure their programs around classroom lectures, and admittedly, a skillful teacher with field experience and good audio-visuals can make time in the classroom a worthwhile learning experience. But no matter how much one concentrates and takes notes, there is only so much that the brain can absorb in one sitting.

The better schools are training centers where the instructors use lectures as primers for hands-on training and field training exercises (FTX). Without the opportunity to immediately put theory into practice, new knowledge is soon forgotten. Without the opportunity positively reinforce newly acquired skills through many successful repetitions, those new skills will never become habit or reflex.

In a business where attacks come fast and hesitation could mean the difference between life and death, reactions must be reflexive. To hone skills to a reflexive level there is no substitute for repetition and positive reinforcement under the watchful eye of an experienced instructor/trainer. This requires time, dedication and hard work—three things that are seldom mentioned in BG school brochures.

Police officers practice cover and evacuation during an STTU
VIP protection course.

SAMPLE TRAINING PROGRAMS
The following is a list of topics in which the bodyguard will need to receive training. The general order of progression starts with essential initial training in Individual Skills, moving on to more advanced Team Skills, and finally into the more specialized areas of study.

Initial Training
Basic BG Procedures
The Role of the BG
Responsibilities of the BG
Types of Clients
Basic Threat Assessment
Working the Residence
Corporate Security
First Aid & CPR
Terrorism Overview
Basic Explosive Identification
Defensive Tactics for Close Protection
Close Protection Foot Drills
Vehicle Selection & Modification
Precision and Performance Protective Driving
Basic Combat Weapons Training
Close Quarter Protective Shooting

Advanced Training
Advanced Weapons Training
Ambush Identification & Avoidance
Evasive & Offensive Driving
Close Protection Team Drills
Risk Management & Reduction
Counter Surveillance
Advanced Unarmed Combat & CQB
Emergency Trauma Medicine
Terrorist Method and Motivation
International Travel
Corporate Aircraft Security
Running the Advance Team
Special Event Management

Specialized Training
Electronic Counter Measures
Security System Design
Bomb Search Procedure
Maritime Security
Alpine Ski Security
Threatening Mail Interpretation
Criminal Psychology

SOURCES OF TRAINING

When reading both foreign and domestic gun or adventurer magazines, one could be lead to believe that bodyguard schools abounded and that bodyguarding was the fastest growing industry in the United States, if not the world. If the truth be known, there is not that much work out there for individuals with no more experience than a diploma from a BG school, and many of the schools that one sees advertising last no more than a year in business (except the government run programs).

Bodyguard training is available under a number of titles such as Executive Protection, CP or BG Training, Counter Terrorism, VIP Protection, etc, but it all comes from one of two sources, the government or private sector.

Government training is primarily for federal agents, military and sworn law enforcement, while private sector schools cater to the civilian bodyguards. There are times however when police and military make use of private sector schools, and select civilians are permitted to participate in government training.

GOVERNMENT

Many police departments, federal agencies, and military units have some use for close protection training. This can come in both formal programs and informal on-the-job exercises.

The best known of the federal protective teams is the US Secret Service. Like many special agents of the Department of Treasury, Secret Service personnel receive their basic training at the Federal Law Enforcement Training Center (FLETC) and then move onto their own training facility, the James J. Rowley Training Center, in Laurel, Maryland. The Rowley Center is utilized by both the Secret Service uniformed branch who guard the white house, and the more familiar special agents who move with the President, VP and first family. It is here that agents perfect driving skills, learn advanced weapons and tactics, close protection drills, CQB and water safety.

Both the Secret Service in DC and FLETC in Glencoe, Georgia, offer a number of VIP security programs for various law enforcement agencies with a need for that type of training.

This would include major metropolitan police departments that have officers assigned to dignitary or diplomatic security units within their cities. In some cases these are full time dedicated teams and in others they are drawn when needed from Special Enforcement or Metro SWAT divisions. All at some time in their careers will work or train with the Secret Service.

Outside of the more formal programs offered by the Secret Service, it is not unusual for the officers from specialized police units, along with ex-Secret Service agents to offer training programs for fellow officers or other qualified individuals.

In the US military, the Military Police and counter terrorist teams of all branches of the services, run BG and CP schools for their own personnel who may be tasked with the protection of general staff officers. The same is true of foreign units like the SAS, GIGN and GSG-9 who host much sort after BG training programs for both police and military personnel.

PRIVATE SECTOR

Without prior police, government or military training in VIP protection, an individual can find it difficult to break into bodyguarding. However, there are many who learn their trade on the job, at some point given the opportunity to act as bodyguard for a celebrity and then figured the rest out as they went along. Bodybuilders and martial artists, working as bouncers in nightclubs or security for event management companies, will periodically be offered a chance to cover a model, actress, rock n'roller or similar celebrity. From there, befriending the celebrity and landing a permanent position as their bodyguard. But these types will have trouble graduating to a career in professional protection without more substantial formal training.

In the private sector there are numerous sources of security related training. Some schools thinking that they can train a bodyguard from start to finish while others concentrating on only one particular skill like driving or shooting.

For the individual wishing to avoid the big single expense of a multi-week BG school, there are several related specialty programs that will help a budding BG into the business. These courses will also help bring the rookie up to speed on individual skills, better preparing them for more advanced BG training.

Local community colleges and shooting ranges often offer a variety of security related classes at a reasonable cost. If security guards are state regulated in that state, then one can start by going through the state required guard training and firearms training. In California these programs are run at most indoor shooting ranges and provide the trainee with a state Guard Card and a Gun Card with minimal *(and I do mean minimal)* training in civilian powers of arrest, search, seizure and the defensive use of deadly force. For the more academically inclined, many colleges offer administration of justice programs, police science degrees and even formal security industry courses.

Classes in emergency medicine, certification in basic life support, First Aid and CPR are available through the Red Cross, American Heart Association or most community colleges.

If not already active in martial arts, the hopeful BG should enroll in a reputable dojo or gym that offers not just traditional karate, aikido or judo but applied self defense programs that are more street oriented.

For two of the more fun parts of VIP protection, driving and shooting, there are dozens of schools available offering either or both of these skills, but only a few are worth the money.

For driver training, Tony Scotti, Bob Bondurant, Direct Action and BSR all offer excellent programs in high performance and evasive driving. Some programs are generic performance driving while others are tailored more to corporate bodyguards and chauffeurs (See Chapter 14).

For basic and advanced tactical firearms training, such schools as Gunsite Training Center in Paulden, Arizona and Thunder Ranch in Kerrville, Texas offer a variety of excellent programs. Other good schools are ISI, MISS, LFI and the Chapman Academy, all being well known and well respected (See Chapter 13).

However, even with proficiency in first aid, martial arts, shooting and evasive driving, the novice bodyguard still lacks the mission specific drills, defensive tactics and protocols of a close protection specialist. Since these subjects are only superficially covered in driving and shooting schools, the BG must learned more either on the job or at a reputable executive protection school.

Professional schools like Richard Kobetz's Executive Protection Institute, in Berryville, Virginia are probably the best place for a private bodyguard to begin his training. Their program titled Providing Protective Services, takes the student through all the intricacies of planning, movement, procedures, etiquette, protocol, liability and the legal issues of BG work, to ultimately become a school certified Personal Protection Specialist (PPS).

Selecting a school is very much a case of "let the buyer beware". There are many less reputable schools that promise the world and produce very little. The total novice may be impressed by their slick brochure and bells and whistles programs, but with time and experience will realize that most are just smoke and mirrors.

In selecting a school, the BG should look first at the credentials of the instructional staff, since it is not necessarily the name of the school that will look good on a resume but rather the credibility and reputation of its instructors within the industry. These schools are not cheap and when adding travel and accommodation expenses, they can be all of a young man or woman's savings.

For those not wanting to spend the time or money on the longer one or two week programs, groups like the Executive Protection Institute run a series of two day seminars around the U.S. covering such subjects as: VIP Protection, System Design, Corporate Aircraft or Yacht Security, and Contemporary Terrorism. Tony Scotti's school also has traveling programs on Executive Security, primarily in the areas of Protective Driving, Bomb Recognition, Attack Recognition, Route Surveys and Vehicle Communications.

PERSONAL ENDEAVOR

Unlike government agents who are constantly in training, or at least have numerous schools available to them, the private bodyguard, as in most civilian professions, must constantly seek out sources of training and knowledge to help further his career. In fact, for many bodyguards, the advanced training becomes the most interesting part of an otherwise often boring job.

The first and most available source of information is books, magazines, periodicals, case studies and academic papers. There are literally hundreds of publications on the market covering every aspect of executive protection and its many related subjects. Apart from just bodyguarding, the serious student should read up on past assassinations, attacks on executives abroad, terrorism, international politics, sub-national conflict, explosive devices, developments in security technology, etc.

To stay abreast of recent incidents, the professional can read the newspaper, watch CNN and subscribe to Time or Newsweek magazines. Another source of valuable information and training are security industry and tactical law enforcement associations. Most of these publish newsletters, have conferences and host a number of excellent trade shows and training seminars each year.

Shooting skills can be maintained by frequent trips to the range while driving skills can be honed by simply becoming a more alert, smoother, safer driver. Personal fitness will benefit from a controlled diet and frequent trips to the gym or dojo. Add to all this an increased situational awareness and the individual is well on the way to becoming a more effective protector.

"The road to excellence is never ending—
so the search must be unrelenting."

1

2

3

4

Drawing from a shoulder holster

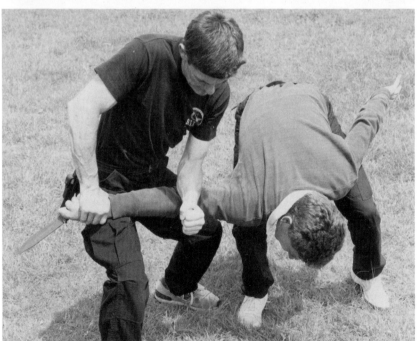

Defensive tactics for BGs must be simple and effective.

9

FITNESS & DEFENSIVE TACTICS

An understanding of defensive tactics (DT), self defense and physical fitness are all important assets to an aspiring bodyguard. Clients will be impressed by any individual who has had formal martial arts training, works out on a regular basis, stays in shape and can possibly give self defense lessons to his family members. A bodyguard, working for one client full-time, may find himself becoming not only a protector, but also to some extent, a convenient companion and work-out partner. This is especially true with clients in the entertainment industry who feel the creep of time and suddenly decide it is time to lose forty pounds and get back in shape.

BG's traveling abroad with clients may also find themselves being coaxed into the hotel gym or swimming laps and playing tennis. For these reasons, and others, it would behoove the aspiring BG to be not only comfortable in a modern gym but also well read on nutrition and general fitness.

From a more practical view, one foundation of the bodyguard's trade is the expectation that, when necessary, the BG has the ability to physically intervene in a developing situation. This is an important skill matched only by planning ability and early threat recognition. Handling physical confrontation requires physical conditioning, mental preparation, a working knowledge of the principles of self defense and a few specific DT techniques suited to BG work.

THE BASICS

Exercise for the sake of exercise can be tedious. This would include weight training, running, aerobics and swimming, and although all excellent sports in their own right, they lack practical application to everyday life. Self defense and martial arts training, on the other hand, can be a challenging form of personal fitness with the added benefit of protecting life or at least dignity in the face of danger.

Since not everyone can afford a team of bodyguards, and the police cannot be in all places at all times, it is up to the individual to accept reality and make the decision that, "I will not be a victim!" Then make the commitment to prepare for the worst.

This is not paranoia, but common sense born out of living in violent times. Just as one up-grades the locks, latches and exterior lights on a house, one must also prepare mentally and physically for confrontation. In security terminology this is known as "hardening the target", or making oneself a less desirable potential target to an attacker.

People who are strong, confident, alert or purposeful in their manner are seldom the victims of street violence. It is the same with BGs. It is the meek, the weak and the unaware that are easily ambushed or intimidated. Understanding this, it is our first goal to change our appearance so as to not fall into the profile of "victim" or easy target.

A large percentage of physical security is appearance and deterrence. We seldom hear of martial arts Black Belts or professional fighters being attacked in the street. It is not that the potential attacker knew that this person was a Black Belt, it is that he sensed a quiet confidence and awareness that worked as a warning signal that screamed, "This one will fight back!"

It does not take years of formal martial arts training to become a good BG, although it would be considered a plus to have a black belt in some legitimate fighting form. In fact, many of the martial arts, in their traditional forms, have little street value and some techniques would prove suicidal if attempted under less than ideal conditions. A BG must take only the most effective techniques from karate, aikido, judo and other fight styles and integrate them into an effective form of self defense. As with the STTU CQB program, the techniques must be simple to grasp, easy to learn and effective in application.

A BG must first study how and where attacks occur; how to avoid these situations or locations; and then develop the necessary defensive reactions. This will include "soft options" like breaking grips, control techniques, wrist and joint locks, choke holds and pressure points; and the "hard options" of striking, kicking, blocking, throwing and strangling. Remember, there are no rules in the jungle and only the fittest survive.

Fighting fitness requires four things:
1. A fundamental knowledge of defensive techniques
2. The physical ability to apply them effectively
3. The presence of mind to handle a stressful situation
4. A fierce determination to win

In BG work, planning is more important than fighting. Avoiding an ugly situation is always preferable to having to deal with one. The following are just a few tips on life style modification and defensive mind set that apply equally to any individual as they do to a BG moving with a protectee.

- Avoid high crime areas and neighborhoods known for drugs, prostitution or gang activity.
- Stay away from bars and clubs that have a reputation for trouble or a rough clientele.
- At night, stay in well lighted, public areas avoiding dark streets, parks, beaches, back-alleys and parking lots.
- Young ladies should be wary of guys that just "want to party"— since this may be the prelude to rape.
- Be alert to who and what is happening around you. Do not allow strangers to get too close.
- Be extra alert when using public restrooms or ATM machines which are both common locations for assaults.
- Keep car doors locked and windows rolled up when driving through bad areas. If you must stop, do it in a well lighted gas station or shopping center.
- Do not wear excessive or expensive jewelry in public.
- Do not wave a thick wallet or a lot of cash around.
- Dress according to your environment and avoid drawing attention to yourself. Much as we love it, ladies should be especially careful where and when they wear tight, revealing clothing.
- Avoid clothing and shoes that may hinder your ability to flee or fight.
- Do not enter your house or condo if there are signs of a forced entry. The intruder may still be inside.
- Maintain a quiet, confident manner.
- STAY ALERT—STAY ALERT—STAY ALERT !!!!!

PHYSICAL CONDITIONING FOR SELF DEFENSE

Modern living makes law abiding citizens soft and dulls their less civilized primal skills that were once necessary for survival and self defense. This is not true of the career criminal who lives rough on the streets and refines his trade in the State run Grey Bars Hotel. One only has to see the muscle bound monsters who frequent the iron pits in the prison system to realize that these animals are not getting softer. Quite the opposite in fact. The tax payer is paying for their post graduate studies in intimidation, violence and mayhem.

On the other hand, we drive or limo everywhere, avoid stairs, take elevators, seldom carry our own bags, eat processed foods, use remote garage door openers, power windows, and with multi-media channel changers don't even leave the couch to change TV channels, program VCRs or adjust sound systems. If this wasn't bad enough, we now have the information super highway and telecommuting to beat freeway traffic, so it seems technology is taking us to a point where we won't have to move at all.

The advocates of push button technology say that this will only give us more time to pursue our sports and interests. Unfortunately, all too many people are just lazy by nature and will push-button themselves into total inactivity and an early grave.

For the security industry, this may actually be good for business. The weaker the rich become, the more they will feel the need for a BG. Just as in early times, it was only when the barbarian hordes were beating at the city gates did the warrior class become valued and respected members of society.

People develop a false sense of security based on the belief that "it couldn't happen to them", or that the police will be there when needed. Others place their faith in changing the locks on their houses, installing alarm systems or carrying aerosol cans of CS, CN or the newer OC. Although each of these precautions may contribute slightly to personal safety, they fall far short of the mark when one is confronted with the terrifying reality of an attack. Random street violence and attacks by stalkers can occur without warning, take only seconds, but leave physical and emotional scares that last for years.

Eventually one must admit that on occasions, calling "911" just doesn't cut it. One has to be prepared to physically defend oneself or hire a BG who can. For the BG it means improving both general fitness and basic combative skills.

A healthy life-style, general cardio-vascular fitness, good nutrition and simple awareness are pluses when preparing for martial arts training. But self defense, like any sport, has certain physical requirements and task-specific muscle conditioning to consider. Fighting, and that is basically what self defense is, requires some degree of **strength, stamina, flexibility** and **speed.** This in addition to technical know-how, repetitive training, presence of mind, determination and a strong will to win.

Physical **strength** in self defense is divided into two areas and does not include the ability to lift heavy objects. Firstly, one needs sufficient strength in specific muscle groups to break an assailants grip and/or deliver strikes with sufficient force to incapacitate or cripple the would-be attacker. Secondly, one needs the strength to redirect an attack or utilize the attacker's size, weight and momentum to your advantage. To quantify the amount of strength required varies from individual to individual and from situation to situation, but it is small by power lifting standards. This is not to say that there is such a thing as too much strength. All things being equal, strength could be the deciding factor in a fight.

Upper-body strength plays a big part in the fight game, as seen with boxers and martial artists who have well developed shoulders, arms (especially triceps), backs (lats), and to a lesser degree chests. Well conditioned abdominal muscles are also a valuable tool in fighting in that they allow the fighter to absorb more punishment to the body while adding tremendous power to strikes and throws that require upper-body rotation.

For female BGs, who genetically have less upper-body strength than men, they can make valuable use of their strongest muscle group—the legs. Fight-specific leg conditioning will increase kicking effectiveness along with adding power to upper-body moves. Most of the power generated by the legs in martial arts, is drawn from the upper leg and hips so squats, leg extensions and lunges will prove to be the most valuable exercises.

Strength, although an asset, is not the main ingredient in a successful counter attack. The speed and accuracy of the attack, against a known weak point is far more important.

Stamina is also essential so that one can either show discretion and run from a confrontation, usually not an option for a BG, or continue a counter-attack to the point where the assailant is beaten. The one punch knock-out is strictly the domain of John Wayne and the silver screen. In the real world an attacker is going to be neither deterred nor subdued by a single counter strike, unless that strike is delivered by a very powerful and skilled individual, or is delivered with sufficient force to a vital area of the human anatomy.

The pain and injuries incurred in the heat of combat may not be sufficient deterrent to a determined attacker, but **extreme pain** can be quite effective. Target soft body parts with a response that is violent, forceful, accurate and sustained.

Stamina training required for self defense centers around both cardiovascular conditioning (running, cycling, swimming, jumping rope, aerobics, etc.), and muscle stamina achieved from doing high reps with specific weights and in a specific range of motions designed to replicate fighting. Dumb-bell front throws, flies, bench-press, triceps cable pulldowns and incline-bench sit-ups/crunches are all examples of conventional exercises that will enhance defensive tactics training.

Flexibility training, an aspect that many of us neglect, is one area where women usually have the advantage over men. Although high kicks are not recommended for street application, flexibility in the legs will add ease of movement and speed to any technique. Overall body flexibility, agility and suppleness are beneficial in all aspects of martial arts training and greatly reduces the chance of injury.

Flexibility can be gained from personal stretching routines, stretch-aerobics or even yoga classes.

Speed is the fourth ingredient in a physical conditioning program. A determined counter attack is wasted if it is not delivered with speed and surprise. It is difficult to surprise an assailant with a slow move, so speed becomes an important ingredient. Speed is also an integral part of power. A punch or kick delivered with both speed and strength will be more effective/destructive than one that lacks either contributing factor.

Once again, speed and power can prove ineffective if delivered without accuracy and an understanding of the human anatomical weaknesses.

The single best method to develop speed in fighting is with a willing training partner, coach or instructor. Benefit can be derived from working with the various types of punch bags seen in most fight gyms, but eventually a live opponent must be used so as to gauge one's own speed, sharpen the reflexes, develop coordination and timing, and get a feel for human movement. Unlike strength, stamina and flexibility, speed and timing are hard to develop outside of the formal martial arts class or without a private self defense trainer.

In conclusion, general physical fitness brings with it a feeling of well being, confidence and high self-esteem that increases alertness and often serves to deter an assault. Unfortunately appearance alone does not stop an attack with certainty. Self defense fitness requires muscle specific conditioning that must include training for strength, stamina, flexibility and speed. The strength to escape a grip and/or subdue/cripple an attacker; the stamina to run from an attack or continue the counter-attack until the assailant is neutralized; the flexibility to move easily and avoid injury in training; and the speed to surprise the attacker by delivering a devastating counter-attack.

MENTAL CONDITIONING FOR SELF DEFENSE

There are several steps involved in the mental conditioning of an individual if he or she is to be able to handle a violent confrontation effectively. The first step, and foundation of all others, is acceptance that "it could happen to you or your client" and recognizing that city life can be hazardous to one's health.

Once one accepts the realities of violent crime, one must also accept the right to fight back with whatever force is necessary to stop the assault or protect a client. No-one has the right to touch, hurt or violate another individual, his children or loved ones—and the very thought of such an action should trigger a fierce protective instinct within the BG. Unfortunately these primal instincts to fight are often buried by many layers of "civilized conditioning" to the point that many cannot find the right trigger mechanism, or are afraid to use it. The survival instinct must be re-learned, cultivated, flexed and exercised. This can only be done through realistic and effective defensive tactics programs, where the student is confronted with a wide variety of simulated assaults. Attacks that will trigger all the human responses, including shock, anger, indignation, fear and finally aggression and self preservation.

Fear is a healthy defense mechanism built into the human psyche which saves people from injury, especially when confronted with activities or incidents beyond their abilities. A classic example would be the fear of approaching the edge of a cliff and therefore avoiding the possibility of falling.

From a self defense viewpoint this could be equated to staying away from rough neighborhoods and low-life bars, there-by avoiding a nasty confrontation. Unfortunately fear can have both a positive and a negative effect on human performance. Fear can help in avoiding danger or supply the added strength /adrenal rush to fight for our lives. On the negative side, fear has the ability to totally paralyze an individual causing panic and confusion in the face of eminent danger. The increased pulse-rate, the nervous tension, the tightening chest, the hot flush, and the acute awareness are all indicators that the increased adrenaline output is taking effect and the body is going into the "fight or flight" mode. Under these conditions the human body is capable of great feats of speed and strength—as long as one does not freeze in fear.

To overcome, or at least control fear, avoid panic and react effectively, one must understand more about how assaults occur and how best to defend oneself. The whole self defense process is not just learning some fancy moves but the study of actual assaults, the counter-attacks and then being subjected to realistic simulations. When the student begins to recognize some of the common points in the attacks and then realizes that he or she has the power and ability to disable the attacker(s), a new confidence and strength is born from within.

Anger is another emotion that can have either a positive or negative effect on one's performance. It can cause blind illogical behavior or, on the up side, it can add power and determination to a counter-attack. A BG has every right to experience fear and anger when his client is assaulted, but these two strong emotions must be harnessed into right-eous indignation and fierce determination and then coupled to a crippling counter-attack.

Individuals not used to dealing with violence can be frozen into inactivity by the surprise of the initial assault. This must be immediately countered by some positive, assertive action that will trigger the more physical defense mechanisms. In the popular anti-rape programs taught throughout the United States, the students are conditioned to shout "NO!" in a very strong, authoritative voice as the prelude for defensive/offensive moves. Once the decision to fight back has been made the victim must become the aggressor. The counter-attack must be swift, violent and effective. For the BG, verbalizing the perceived threat to the fellow team members or the principal should initiate the necessary contact drills.

This controlled aggression or violent counter-attack does not come easy for many people, especially women who have been conditioned by society to be caring, loving and gentle by nature. It is not unusual to have a female defensive tactics student that believes she is incapable of the aggressive techniques required of her, for example; eye gouging, groin kicking and head stamping. The student may even go so far as to show concern for the attacker's safety and well being. This is where it is up to the instructional staff to graphically explain to the student what could happen if she does not fight back; to document the results of similar brutal attacks; and then expose her to several realistic simulations, with class and staff encouragement.

The instructors who role-play as "attackers" in DT programs must be schooled to imitate, verbally and physically, actual attackers as much as possible within the training structure. These "attackers", when fitted with protective gear like the RedMan suit, must be taught to react realistically to the counter-attacks launched by the students. In this manner the student is exposed to violent behavior that will accompany the assault and not find the experience so shocking should he or she be confronted by the real thing. In addition the trainee will experience the confidence building that goes with not only surviving but winning.

Once the trainee BGs have mastered the basics of self defense and defensive tactics, they should move on to third party attacks. These are simulated BG situations where the role player(s) is attacking a third part, the principal, and the BG must cover and evacuate. This should be done with one, two, three and four man BG teams working together.

Role playing and simulated assaults will also teach the BGs to evaluate the attacker and seek out the most advantageous time to launch the counter-attack. The main purpose of the role playing process is to take the mystery, and with it some of the fear, out of street violence and the nature of attacks or attempted kidnappings. After all, it is the unknown that we fear most.

Along with DT training the students must be taught mental rehearsal of theoretical attacks and counter-attacks. These are called the "What ifs...?". Experienced law enforcement officers use the same technique as they patrol the streets, approach a disturbance or enter a suspect location. They will run a series of "what ifs..?" through their conscious thought process. This could consist of: "What if someone is waiting around this next corner..?"; "What if he goes for a weapon as I approach him...?"; "What if I am walking into a set-up...?"; "What if I hear gun shots..?"—These are mentally answered by plans to go for cover; draw a weapon; return fire; retreat; call for assistance; etc.

The BG can do the same thing as he jogs in the park; passes a group of rough punks on the street; finds himself in the sub-way with a suspicious individual; enters a parking garage; or hears a noise in the house at night. By consciously rehearsing contingency plans to avoid, escape or fight the BG is conditioning the sub-conscious to react correctly under stress. When and if the assault comes, he will be already one step ahead of the attacker. This is not a sense of paranoia but what some call "Condition Yellow", relaxed but alert and a more common sense approach to urban survival.

With the decision to fight one must also accept a degree of pain and the possibility of injury. This is especially true when knives, broken bottles and sharp instruments are involved. The probability of getting cut is very real. Even Black Belts do not intentionally take on berserk, knife wielding assailants if there are other options, but when unavoidable, they still expect to get cut.

Even in a confrontation where no weapons are involved there will still be bruises scrapes and falls. Shock, anger, fear and adrenaline will mask much of the discomfort but when one experiences pain one must try to block it and continue the counter-attack with vigor and determination. A little pain while fighting off the assault is preferable to the permanent physical or psychological injuries, or even death, that accompanies failure.

With the acceptance of reality and some effective training comes a new confidence and awareness. The student is more capable of identifying and avoiding potential trouble spots. Recognizing some of the pre-indicators of an ambush or attack may give the BG time to escape or better prepare for the confrontation. If the assault comes as a total surprise, the BG will have well ingrained conditioned responses that should kick-in automatically without the need for the slower conscious thought processes. During the fight the potential victim or BG will become the aggressor with a small but effective repertoire of crippling counter-attacks, blocks, strikes, kicks and throws.

Training with Redman protective equipment

PRINCIPLES OF SELF DEFENSE

The mean streets, home of criminals and crazies, is an arena where the only rule is that there are no rules. With this in mind, and before moving on to actual techniques, the following eight basic principles of self defense should be learned and memorized.

1. FIGHT DIRTY—There is nothing "sporting" about self defense. Attack the eyes, throat or groin; use a weapon if one is available; show your attacker you are at home with street fighting and gutter techniques.

2. ATTACK VITAL AREAS—When confronted with a determined attacker, do not waste time trying to "punch above the belt". There are no rules so go for the most vulnerable and sensitive areas of the body. Attack the eyes, throat, groin or any other weak point that presents itself.

3. ATTACK THE ATTACKER—Nothing surprises a bully or mugger more than finding himself on the receiving end of a crippling attack. An aggressive counter attack is a winning strategy.

4. SIMPLICITY OF TECHNIQUE—Do not confuse attacks that "look good" with those that work. Keep counter attacks simple, direct and effective.

5. MOMENTUM OF ATTACK—Seldom will a single blow fell a determined attacker. The initial counter attack must be followed up with a series of effective techniques, delivered with controlled aggression, until the attacker is totally subdued. With multiple attackers, one must move quickly from one to the other without giving them time to regroup.

6. EXPECT TO GET HURT—No matter what style of fighting you have been taught, be prepared to absorb some punishment in a street confrontation. Better a few bumps and scraps than ending up dead or brutally raped.

7. DO NOT GO TO THE GROUND WITH AN ASSAILANT—Stay on your feet and maintain mobility and flexibility in your defenses. If your assailant goes down you may be able to use stamping kicks to finish him or simply run to safety.

8. MENTAL REVIEW & AWARENESS—Stay alert and constantly run little "what if?" scenarios through your head. Where can I run to; what would I do if; who is close to us; is this area safe?

EFFECTIVE STRIKING

The average red-blooded male believes he has the God-given ability to throw the perfect John Wayne punch and drop any assailant with a single blow. Many learn through hard experience and often some pain that this is not so.

Firstly, no one is born with the ability to punch well. Secondly, any one can be taught to strike effectively immaterial of size, weight or sex. The "average male" will usually break his hand or simply fail to have any effect when he lashes out at a determined attacker, and women with no prior fight training will also find their punches having little or no effect. When the decision to strike back has been made, the counter attack must be launched with crippling effectiveness. Lashing out ineffectively may only serve to enrage the attacker and result in additional injury to the victim.

There is far more to striking than simply knowing how to make a fist. In fact, in many strikes we do not use a fist at all, preferring to opt for an open-hand technique. For a strike to be effective it must have speed, power, accuracy and surprise. This is in addition to being technically correct in terms of molding the hand into a striking implement.

The preferred strikes for BGs are the palm-heel strike, the hammer fist, the horizontal punch, the vertical punch and the quarter punch, with some variations on each. Each striking technique is designed to meet a specific need in reaction to different attacks and available targets.

The palm-heel strike is an open-hand technique that is usually targeted at the upper lip and just underneath the nose of an assailant. It is a very effective up-ward driving blow that can be used to cripple or simply to break contact with the attacker. After driving the head back because of severe pain to the nose, the assailants throat is left wide open for follow-up attacks, as is the groin and solar-plexus.

For the BG, the palm-heel strike can be used to disable an attacker from the side or behind, targeting the temple or base of the skull with equal effectiveness.

The hammer punch is a closed fist technique which is usually employed as a horizontal blow to the sternum or a down-ward blow to the head or neck. The hammer punch is a powerful technique that can also be used to break grips or strike any unprotected part of the attacker's body.

The horizontal and vertical punches are directly related and most resemble the conventional punches that most are familiar with. The selected vital area and the distance to that area will dictate which punch is utilized. Horizontal punches when one requires full reach and vertical punches for closer in-fighting. It is essential that the self defense student carefully study the correct formation of the fist before attempting punches on the training bags. An incorrect punch can result in painful injuries to the knuckles and wrist.

It is not uncommon for street brawlers and untrained fighters to sustain broken fingers and knuckles as a direct result of poor technique and incorrect fist formation. It is important that the fist be in-line with the wrist and that only the first two knuckles be employed as the primary striking surface. During training the students first master fist formation followed by light strikes against a pad or focus mitt. Once the instructor is satisfied with form, students can move on to developing more power against the heavier punch bags.

There is less chance of knuckle breakage with the palm-heel strike and hammer punch so those are usually taught first, especially to women and small men who do not have substantial bone development in the hands.

Another open-hand technique that is easy to learn and extremely effective is the cupped hand directed against the ear. This cupped slapping technique causes a pocket of air to be compressed into the ear, resulting in a burst ear-drum, severe pain, disorientation and loss of balance. In some cases the pain is sufficient to cause unconsciousness.

The quarter punch is a half fist (where the first two knuckles are rolled in but not the entire fist) that also requires considerable training to master but is very effective against soft targets such as the throat and groin. However, none of the strikes are effective unless accompanied by the four elements of speed, power, accuracy and surprise.

SPEED—An attacker will block or stop a counter punch if he sees it coming and has time to react. A half hearted technique, a faint or one that lacks determination will only serve to warn an attacker of intended resistance. The counter attack must be fast, effective and continuous until the attacker is beaten or flees for fear of his own life. A heart warming sight.

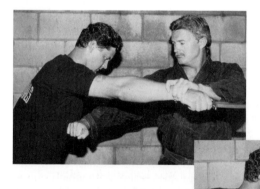

**Two applications
of the hammer punch**

POWER—It is not necessary to have the arms of the Hulk or the training of Mike Tyson to be able to put power into a punch or strike. Arm strength is only a small part of the power behind a good punch. The bulk of the power will be drawn from the shoulders, back, legs and body rotation. As with any counter attack, one must close distance with an assailant—attacking the attacker! The very motion of lunging forward will add both body weight and leg power to a strike. The shorter, closer strikes will draw more power from the arms and shoulders, developed by shoulder and triceps exercises in the gym.

ACCURACY—The human body has a tremendous capability to absorb punishment, but there are areas that cannot withstand even a moderately powered blow. To rain blows on an assailant's back, chest, shoulders, upper arms and thighs may only serve to tire you and enrage him. Pick your target and attack with conviction. The eyes, throat and groin are all excellent soft targets to begin with. Fight dirty! In addition, attacks to the ears, nose, temples, solar-plexus and heart can prove very effective.

SURPRISE—The element of surprise has won battles since the dawn of time. The attacker who is used to intimidating his victims may be a cowardly bully at heart who gets his rocks off by targeting the weak. When you pick your target and explode into action with potentially crippling counter attacks, he may well be surprised into fleeing if not dropped by your initial strikes. Once you initiate your defense give no quarter, show a fierce determination to win and attack with a calculating, controlled aggression.

Only on the rarest occasions will one punch or strike end a confrontation. A trained Black Belt or professional boxer may be able to place his best shot with sufficient power to incapacitate an assailant but the average person will need to follow-up the initial counter-attack with two or three other strikes. The general rule is to continue the attack until the assailant is no longer a danger.

If the assailant does break and run, it is not recommended that one run after him, even if there is a belief that the attacker needs more of his own medicine. He may be leading his victim further from assistance; into a trap with more of his degenerate friends; or out of public view. As far as the law is concerned, one may only defend oneself "when in FEAR of life or safety" and may only use sufficient force to "stop the attack." It is not the place of the BG or trained victim to mete out justice to every miscreant that crosses his path. It can even be unwise to try to hold an assailant until help arrives. He may fight even harder if he believes he is cornered and about to be arrested. The victim or BG's sole obligation is to survive with as little harm as possible to oneself and the principal.

The danger of high kicking in the "real world"

Axe kick

Rising front kick

EFFECTIVE KICKING

There is nothing sporting about street crimes such as rape, robbery and assault. To survive, one must draw on every ounce of strength and every defensive tactic available. There is no such thing as "a fair fight" or "sporting behavior" when one is confronted by the realities of city life. Kicking the stuffing out of some mugger, rapist or stalker is not only acceptable behavior, it will be applauded by most law abiding citizens (even the police).

Kicking techniques are a big part of close quarter fighting since the leg muscles are considerably stronger than the arms and therefore capable of inflicting more damage. Add to that the fact that the BG will need to keep his hands free to control the principal or draw a weapon.

The first step towards developing kicks as an effective defensive tool is to realize that the high-flying spinning round-house kicks seen in various kung-fu movies have no place in a down and dirty street fight. A martial arts expert or PKA kick-boxer with years of training may be able to make one of these flashy high kicks work but most would opt for a lower, faster more devastating technique.

When trying to high kick to the head, the foot has considerably more distance to travel than if it was directed to the knee or groin. This gives your opponent more time to see it coming and more time to react. You also expose your groin, sacrifice your balance and risk having your leg caught in mid air. A nasty situation to be caught in.

Kicks are divided into two categories: kicks with the foot which can be used at medium to close range; and kicks with the knee for closer in-fighting. The knee to the groin is probably the one that people are most familiar with and is still a valid technique. It is also the counter-attack that is most expected and therefore defended against.

After a blow to the stomach or groin an injured attacker will tend to double forward at the waist. This is a good time to grasp his hair or head and deliver follow-up knee strikes to the face, head or chest. The most common mistake made during training is for a timid individual to attempt a knee to the groin or upper thigh prematurely or without conviction. Thus warning the attacker.

From a BG perspective, a knee driven into the side of the thigh (known as a Charlie Horse) can serve as an excellent crippling techniques against an unwanted adversary confronting a client.

The primary foot kicks utilized are the stamping kick, the front kick (two variations) and the side kick—each with its own advantages and applications.

The stamping kick is utilized in two situations. The first, stamping down onto the attacker's foot to create pain and aid in escaping their grip. If done with a hard-soled shoe it will have considerable effect and make difficult an attacker's further pursuit. The other occasion this technique can be utilized is when the attacker is already down and the victim has the opportunity to stamp down onto the villain's head or any other available body part.

The front kick is practiced in two forms; a straight kick where the foot is picked up and then delivered directly to the knee or groin; and a rising kick which is slapped up directly between the attacker's legs. Again, the groin kick is an expected self defense move so must be delivered with speed and surprise. Kicks to the knee cap are less expected, harder to stop and equally effective. An attacker with a broken or dislocated knee will have considerable trouble continuing the attack and will be easier for the police to locate.

The side kick is usually delivered to the side or back of the knee or to the head or throat of an already downed attacker. The side kick utilizes the outer edge of the foot and is also considerably more effective when combined with a hard soled shoe.

When training for any of these kicks the student must first warm-up, stretch-out and then concentrate on maintaining balance while kicking. The danger with kicks is that one is sacrificing some balance for the speed and power of the technique. Once the student has mastered the move the instructor should have the student kick at various striking bags with increasing force. After delivering the kick the student must immediately return to full balance and decide whether to flee the scene or follow-up with additional counter attacks.

The next step in a realistic training program is to attempt these kicks in regular street clothes. Most classes are done wearing sweats that give more freedom of movement than modern fashions. Tight skirts and pants can hinder movement and make it more difficult to raise the leg high enough to kick. High-heeled or leather soled shoes, although effective weapons, give less stability and mobility than a flat, rubber soled variety. It is not necessary to invest in baggy pants and combat boots, but the BG should consider what he or she wears when working.

The student must not be squeamish about "putting the boot in" and kicking once the attacker is down. Sporting behavior such as allowing the attacker to get back up is absolutely suicidal. The counter attack must continue until the attacker is no longer a threat. This will usually mean kicking until the attacker is unconscious or incapacitated.

Do not be fooled by the cowardly attacker that fakes injury or begs for mercy so that you will stop your attack and give him the opportunity to recover and get the upper hand. You only get one chance to surprise an attacker. Once he realizes you have had some training he will be more cautious on his next approach, and being a cunning animal of the streets, may not be deterred by your small amount of training—just more cautious.

In conclusion, it takes special training to be able to kick effectively, but more importantly, it takes experience to know exactly when to kick or strike back. This experience can only be gained through professional training where emphasis is placed on realistic scenarios that replicate actual real confrontations.

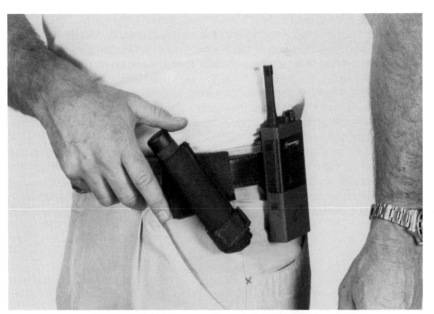

*Retracted ASP baton in Eagle Industries belt carrier
(check local and state requirements before use)*

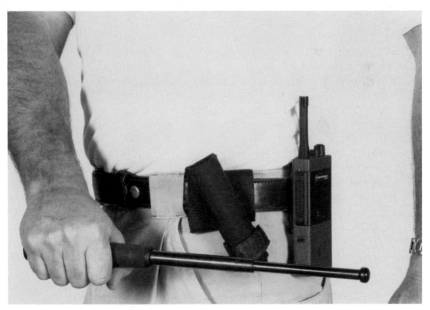

*Extended ASP baton—an effective and concealable impact weapon
for close protection*

COVER & EVACUATE

The concept of first covering and then immediately evacuating a client from a dangerous situation is the foundation of all bodyguarding. Where the danger comes from a single assailant, there are basic drills and techniques utilized by bodyguards to block and then extract their client from the situation. Many of the initial blocking and covering techniques have similarities to basic fight principles and martial arts, varying only in that the attack is being deflected from a third part and therefore not technically SELF defense.

In some cases, where gun play is not an option, strikes and kicks can be utilized to neutralize an attacker, if only long enough to move the client to safety. In other cases, joint locks and pressure point techniques may be required to control or subdue an assailant until back-up arrives. These are covered in more detail in Chapter 10 and STTU's CQB manual.

Federal agents practice close quarter shooting drills.

10

CLOSE PROTECTION DRILLS

The basic team drills used when covering a client on the move are the foundation of close protection (CP). It is not difficult to restrict access to a client when they are safe at home, in the office, on an airplane or in a hotel room. These are all areas that present natural physical barriers to an assailant. However, when the client is moving on foot or in the car, the potential exposure is greatly increased.

The best example of this exposure would be a politician or dignitary moving through crowds, "pressing the flesh", and making public appearances. Celebrities and entertainers making public appearances face the same threats so it is at this time that basic protection drills become most important.

When moving in public, awareness and basic procedure are far more important than armament or shooting ability. It has been proven time and again that the BG seldom has time to recognize the threat, draw a weapon and return fire. In most cases, considering the few seconds it takes to complete an attack and the confusion and panic it creates, the best solution is simply to COVER & EVACUATE.

The purpose of the foot drills is to constantly place the bodyguards between the principal and any potential threat. This will either discourage the attacker, restrict a clear shot at the principal or at least slow the attacker. The drills should in theory also place the BG in a better position to intercept any approach or preempt an assault.

Whether it is a full team or a single BG, there are basic drills for most public occasions. Which drill, or the type of drill, will be dictated by the location, number of security team members, proximity of other people, available cover, and potential threat level. This part of BG work is also known as "working the principal", and calls for the BG to be constantly, and discretely, readjusting his position to best cover the principal.

To best understand the drills, we need to prioritize the BG's tasks—with or without an identifiable threat. The first part of any movement is the planning phase, which involves planning the best time and route to safely get the principal from "A" to "B". After planning, the BG's responsibilities fall under the Four Ds—Deter, Deny, Detect, Delay. To deter an assault, deny access, detect an approach, and finally delay the attacker long enough for the principal to be evacuated from the scene.

In many cases the BG's positioning of himself in a visible but professional manner will deter unwanted strangers or fans approaching a client. This may be something as simple as escorting a beautiful female client when she goes shopping and deterring any unwanted "come-ons" from would be Lotharios.

To deny access, the BG must actually place himself between a client and the crowd or any likely direction of attack. In this way, a potential nuisance or attacker must physically pass the guard to get to the principal.

To detect a threat, the BG must be ever vigilant, constantly scanning the crowd, profiling individuals or simply looking for physical hazards. The danger is not always an attacker, it could just as easily come from unseen stairs, a cable across the ground, traffic, or even a waiter with a scalding hot coffee pot.

In most cases, when one detects a potential threat, it must be verbalized to the team or directly to the client if the BG is operating alone. In an exigent circumstance, the BG will find it necessary to physically grab the principal to move him or her out of the line of impending danger.

Once a threat or potential threat has been identified, the BG must delay the approach or attack long enough for the principal to realize that there is a threat and seek refuge. Or in the case of a security team, for those assigned to cover and evacuate the principal to go into action.

Since most attacks come at close range, it is in this phase that we go by the rule of "arms reach". If a threat is within arms reach, it is faster to simply jump on the attacker than to try and draw a weapon (as seen in Hinckley's attack on President Reagan). If the client is within arm's reach, but not the threat, it is best to turn, cover and evacuate—unless there is a real risk of getting shot in the back.

There will be times when a BG's sole assignment will be to evacuate the client. This could occur when the attack is directed against some other personage at a function and it is simply best to move your client to a safer location. The same would be true in the event of fires, quakes, plane crashes or natural disasters. Amidst all the panic and confusion, the BG would be expected to maintain his head, know the nearest exits and location of emergency equipment like fire extinguishers, and extract his client from danger.

When all of this is put into practical application it becomes the protection drills. Alone or part of a team, there will always be some place in relation to the principal that it is best for the BG to position himself. The same is true whether on foot or in vehicles. These drills have sufficient flexibility to conform to just about any situation.

As part of a four or five man team, a BG's position in relation to the principal is somewhat fixed. When working alone or with one partner, the bodyguard's position is more flexible covering an entire arc around one side of the principal.

TEAM DRILLS

Before discussing actual team drills, the BG must come to consider the team as a coordinated single entity that literally functions like one beast with one brain. The team leader is the brain, the BGs the limbs and the radio becomes the nerve link between the brain and the limbs.

One potential problem with team operations is that as the team becomes larger and the operation more complex, there is an increased potential for confusion and miscommunication. To offset this problem, many teams, including the Secret Service, use portable radios with ear pieces and remote mics. Some years ago these were Motorola MT 500s with flesh toned wiring running to a hard-wired ear piece and sleeve microphone. These have now been replaced by Motorola Sabers with a clear plastic ear piece and coiled tubing. The mic can be incorporated into the ear-piece, worn on the lapel or clipped to the cuff. Some exceptionally low profile units even use a wireless ear piece that receives a signal directly from the radio worn on the belt or in a shoulder rig.

Although the radio systems designed for dignitary protection are low profile and somewhat concealable, the ear piece still clearly marks the protection team. However, having radios and being identified is preferable to not having communications and risking confusion.

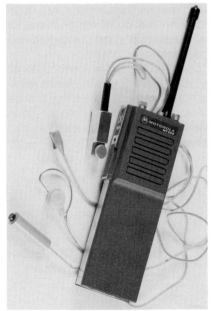 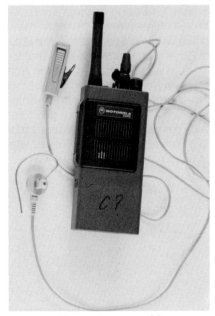

MT500 with 3-wire
COMMS system

Motorola expo with
2-wire system

The radios, although a big help, are not essential. Just as an individual can coordinate movement of his limbs without conscious thought, each team member, from practice, should know his position and responsibilities in relation to the principal. This practice being a critical part of successful team movements.

The fundamental principle behind team movement is that each member of the team has an assigned arc of responsibility, not unlike a military patrol moving through hostile territory.

For ease of understanding and briefing purposes, the individual arcs can be referred to by use of the clock-ray method. That is to say that if moving in a diamond pattern, the principal is the center of the clock's dial, the point becomes 12 o,clock and tail 6 o'clock. Therefore the BG to the principal's right would cover 12 through 4, the BG to the left would cover 8 through 12, point would cover 10 through 2, and the tail man would cover 4 through 8 with some overlap.

The second important principle of team drills is that the BG should not allow activity in other areas to distract from his or her arc of responsibility. The BG must trust in the drills and the other BGs' skill to handle any activity in their arcs.

The ideal, when moving on foot as a team, is for four or more agents to form a diamond or box pattern around the client. This gives cover from all sides and is then adjusted for various scenarios such as working a crowd, passing through doors, entering and exiting vehicles, etc. If an attack comes from the right then those on the right respond to it or cover, while those on the left evacuate. The point and tail of the diamond close in where most needed and look for secondary threats.

If the attack comes from the front, then the BGs in back evacuate as those in front and on the sides block or engage the attacker. When working motorcades or around vehicles, specific team members will be assigned to specific tasks such as opening doors, riding shotgun, riding with the principal or in lead or chase vehicles. The vehicles can be used in a similar manner as BGs are used when moving on foot.

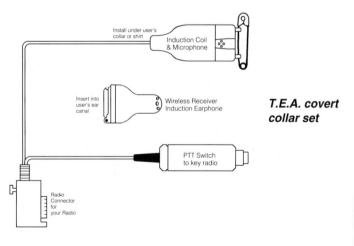

Install under user's collar or shirt

Induction Coil & Microphone

Insert into user's ear canal

Wireless Receiver Induction Earphone

PTT Switch to key radio

Radio Connector for your Radio

T.E.A. covert collar set

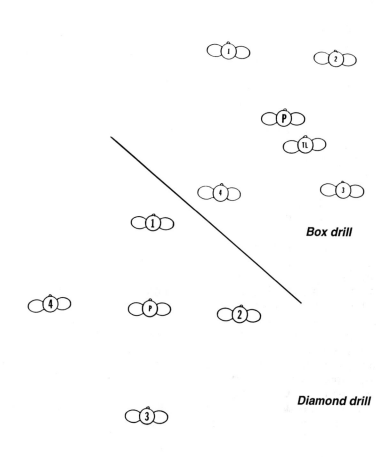

Box drill

Diamond drill

Responding to threat

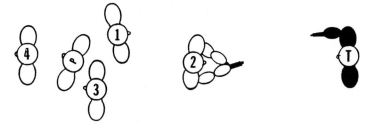

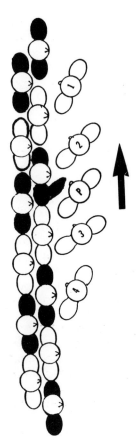

Politicians and celebrities working the crowd. #3 carefully watches the individual that the principal is shaking hands with.

Responding to the threat: #2 and #3 close in and evacuate the principal as #1 and #4 cover the movement.

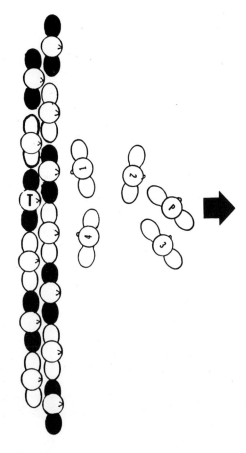

SOLO BG DRILLS

The lone BG will seldom enjoy the luxury of a full protective detail, so the best he can do is position himself in the most advantageous way. The first consideration is for the BG to position himself between the client and any possible threat or potential line of attack. If this is not possible, he should position himself so that he at least has a clear view of the areas of greatest potential threat.

When working a principal, it is important that the BG concentrate on the people and areas around the principal and not the actual principal. It is very easy to get distracted and drawn in to watching the principal as he or she moves about the room, greets important guests, or makes public addresses. The BG must learn to watch the crowd around the principal since that is the primary source of danger.

In some cases, where the BG is standing or moving very close to the principal, the BG will actually turn his back on the principal and look outward. Unfortunately, this really only allows him to scan one direction or arc. When working alone, it is usually better for the BG to stand or walk a little behind the principal, keeping him or her within his peripheral vision, and looking past the principal for potential threats.

A right handed BG, walking with the principal, should walk to the right rear of the principal. This keeps his right hand free to draw a weapon as he grabs, moves or covers the principal with his left.

When moving through crowds the BG can take a lesson from the Secret Service. Since he should be busy scanning the hands and faces of the surrounding people, it is difficult to also keep visual contact with the principal. To solve this problem, Secret Service agents have learned to lightly latch on to the principal's coat-tail with their left hand, allowing them to feel the principal's movements without having to look away from the crowd.

When working a slow moving motorcade or vehicle, the BG can use the same technique. By placing one hand on the car's fender the BG can watch the crowd and still maintain pace and detect changes in speed or direction.

Even though the BG will routinely move at the right or left rear of the principal, he should move to the front when approaching doors, elevators and vehicles. The BG should be standing between the principal and any door or elevator before it opens. When riding elevators, the BG should stand between the principal and the elevator doors, so that as the doors open the BG gets first look into the lobby.

When leaving a building, the BG should exit onto the street first so that if there is a potential threat, he can block the principal from exiting or push him back into the protection of the structure.

When approaching a car or limo for a curb-side pick-up, the BG will want to first verify the correct identity of the driver, before allowing the principal to get in. With limo dropped-offs, the BG should exit the front passenger door first and immediately block the principal's door with his knee, until he is satisfied that it is safe to de-bus.

Lastly, on all foot drills, the BG must stay close enough to the client to be able to physically move him or her out of the line of any attack. People not trained to react to an attack will tend to freeze and must be physically moved or evacuated. While the principal is still in shock or looking to see what the commotion is, the BG should be already in action placing himself between the principal and the attacker or physically pulling the principal out of the danger zone.

Note: Back when I was a martial artist training in France and long before I ever became involved in professional protection, I was asked to bodyguard Miss France at an indoor volley ball championship in Paris. During the game I stood in the front left corner of her VIP booth and within about two meters of where she was seated. I tried not to pay her any attention or watch the game, concentrating more on the people passing or approaching her location.

At some time during the event I caught a blurred movement out of the right corner of my eye, and reacting solely on reflex, shot my hand in front of Miss France's flawless face. My hand connected with the volley ball with a resounding crack sending it flying off into the crowd.

It turned out that one of the players had accidentally spiked the ball in our direction. If I hadn't been on my feet and alert, that ball would have hit Miss France full in the face. It wasn't terrorists or stalkers but she was very appreciative of the fact that I had saved her both injury and embarrassment. Her companions sat motionless, still frozen in shock.

NOTE: The accompanying photos and diagrams in this chapter will better illustrate the foundation of all close protection drills. (TL = Team Leader; T = Threat).

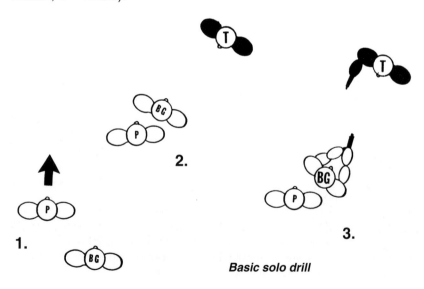

Basic solo drill

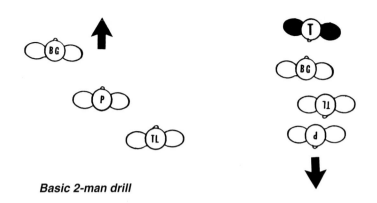

Basic 2-man drill

Police practice witness protection drills.

Two cover while two evacuate.

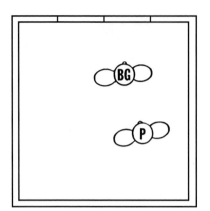

Working doors or elevators

BG exits first

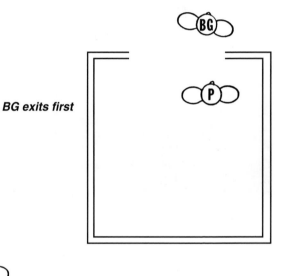

When BG gives the "all clear" the principal exits and the BG drops into the right rear position.

11

FIRST AID & MEDICAL EMERGENCIES

As stated several times in this text, bodyguarding is more than just two hundred and twenty pounds of "have gun will travel" mentality. It encompasses any and all aspects of ensuring the client's health and safety—one of those being basic accident management and emergency medicine. Whether it be a sucking chest wound from a gunshot or a small cut from broken glass, a professional BG should be able to provide assistance.

Life support is one of many areas where private sector bodyguards can take a lesson from the Secret Service. Special Agents assigned to protective details are taught and practice a skill known as Five Minute Medicine. This is the essential life support skills necessary to keep a protectee or team member alive for the five minutes that it takes to transport to a hospital, or until professional emergency medical assistance arrives.

At a minimum, all BGs should be certified in First Aid and CPR, and able to handle the following basic Red Cross life support guideline:

1. RESCUE the victim and yourself.
2. Restore or maintain BREATHING and HEARTBEAT
3. Control heavy BLEEDING
4. Treat for POISONING.
5. Prevent SHOCK.
6. EXAMINE the victim carefully.
7. Seek MEDICAL HELP.
8. KEEP CHECKING the victim until medical help is obtained.

In the protection business, the BG should always be aware of the nearest source of medical assistance, whether it is a hospital, emergency room or paramedic service. These will have been identified and logged in the advance survey work and/or threat assessment. So the only decision that the BG will need to make in the event of a critical injury is transport immediately or stabilize and wait—after activating the local EMS system.

The following is the basic life support outline used during all STTU tactical programs. It is given only as a guide to the minimum knowledge required, so should not be taken as a substitute for professional training and certification.

Consider:
    a. Location of nearest hospital / trauma room
    b. Route to the hospital with or without police escort
    c. Having paramedics on hand or on stand-by
    d. Having EMT/Paramedic trained personnel on the team
    e. All team members having First Aid & CPR certification

A. BASIC LIFE SUPPORT
- Stop / Think / assess / prioritize / get help
- Position / immobilize
- A.B.C. (Airway—Breathing—Circulation)
- Stop obvious hemorrhage
- Treat for shock
- Maintain thermal balance
- Other injuries / fractures / near drowning / burns
- Rest and reassure
- Transport / monitor

B. ABC / CPR
Establish and manage airway. Two full breaths and check pulse. Administer 12 breaths per minute (child 15/min, infant 20/min). If no pulse go to CPR.
CPR requires 15 compressions / 2 breaths when working alone and 5 compressions / 1 breath for two person CPR.

C. AIRWAY OBSTRUCTIONS
6–10 abdominal thrusts, then check airway for foreign body.
Continue with ABC when obstruction is dislodged.

D. SHOCK
- Depresses bodily functions, takes priority; weak and rapid pulse, cool and clammy skin, altered consciousness.
- Comfort, soothe, maintain comfortable temperature, elevate feet, oxygen, fluids by IV only, supportive measures as above.

E. HEMORRHAGE
First and foremost, apply direct pressure to the wound.
- Direct pressure
- Elevation
- Pressure Points
- Tourniquet

F. SUCKING CHEST WOUND
- Direct pressure
- Injured side down to keep good lung high and dry
- Use a plastic backed bandage

G. FRACTURES
- Splint
- Immobilize
- Be especially careful with spinal injuries

H. DEHYDRATION
Cramps, fatigue, headaches, dry mouth, concentrated urine.
(urine should be clear, copious and odorless)
Prevention is best—lots of cool, clean water.

I. HYPERTHERMIA
Dehydration, nausea, vomiting, dizziness, fainting, sweating.
Heat exhaustion = pale, clammy, sweating.
Heat stroke = flushed, dry, no sweating, rapid pulse; a life threatening emergency.

J. HYPOTHERMIA
- Weakness, drowsiness, impaired coordination. Shivering in early stages only.
- Passive rewarming only, dry blankets.
- "Mammalian diving reflex"—cold-water near drowning, depressed vital signs to the appearance of death.
- Victim should not be declared dead until rewarmed and dead.

K. OTHER INJURIES
Burns—flush or bandage minor; thick dry sterile dressing on major; dry, insulated cold packs may be used.
Eyes—flush minor; dry bandage major—do not remove object.
Poisons—may cause respiratory failure.

L. DISPOSITION
Monitor and transport.

Although training is the priority, a fully stocked first aid kit is also highly recommended. Not some rinky-dink little five dollar band-aid kit from the local drug store, but a carefully designed custom trauma kit suited to protective work. In fact, we suggest two kits. One with the major essentials sealed for emergencies only, and a second smaller one with handy items such as band-aids, Aspirin, Advil and antiseptics, etc. for the common minor cuts and scratches. Those that are trained to administer it should also have a medical oxygen system on hand.

The trauma kit should be in a strong case with individual compartments for the specialized contents. For local use we favor the search & rescue soft type case or backpack that can be stowed in the trunk of the car. For air or overseas travel the rigid aluminum Haliburton type cases are better suited to hold up to the airline luggage handlers' abuse.

If a client or a member of his family or entourage has a pre-existing medical condition or unusual blood type, it is strongly suggested that a medical professional be added to the support team, or placed on call. If traveling to a foreign country (see Chapter 26), the concerned individual's doctor should notify a local hospital or physician of the condition and make whatever arrangements necessary.

It is also good policy for the BG to carry a brief medical history form with blood type, allergies, prescribed medications, etc. for all of his charges. This is essential when dealing with clients who may be allergic to bee-stings or Penicillin, on special heart medications, are asthmatic or hemophiliacs. Being able to supply this information to doctors or EMS personnel can greatly expedite assistance and possibly mean the difference between life and death in an emergency.

If the client frequents remote parts of the country or participates in such sports as hiking, snow skiing or scuba diving, then the BG should be even more concerned about emergency medical training and the ability to cope with injury. When accompanying clients snow skiing in particular, the BG should model his belt-pack trauma kit after those carried by the local ski patrol, after all, they are the experts in alpine injuries. For scuba diving, the BG should be Water Safety and Rescue Diver certified, have access to the Divers' Alert Network (DAN) and ensure that oxygen is available at the dive site.

Author's Note—As a team leader, I have always tried to include at least one RN or paramedic, or at a minimum a certified EMT or corpsman, on any large assignment—especially where children are included in the party. Nothing gives a parent a greater sense of security than knowing that their children have been considered and that the BGs have humanitarian skills to offset their more deadly purpose.

Professional BG teams should have trauma kits and oxygen on hand.

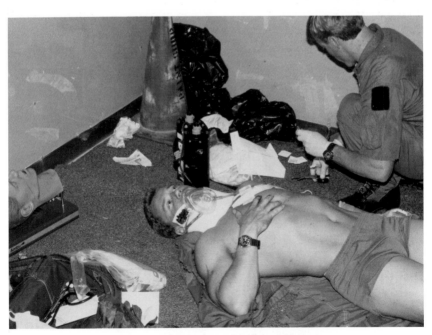

*More important than the First Aid Kit is
advanced training in trauma medicine.*

Wilson custom combat .45 Government Model

Novak/HRT model Hi-Power

12

FIREARMS SELECTION

As any security professional will attest, the probability of ever having to use a gun on a BG job is slim to none. But as with sworn law enforcement, firearms and firearms training constitute a significant part of a bodyguard's training.

Whether a BG carries a gun or chooses to work unarmed, may be dictated by the nature of the contract and the anticipated threat level. Some bodyguards, for example those working rock 'n roll stars at crowded concerts, chose not to carry a gun at all, and those working the usual range of domestic executive protection contracts often have no real expectation of ever needing one. The BG may also come across clients who request that no firearms be carried on the job or even brought on to their property. In these cases it will become a judgement call for the individual BG as whether he is willing to work under those conditions.

Teams or individuals involved in high risk assignments or overseas contracts will almost always go armed. Working delegations traveling in semi-third world hot-spots, or protecting members of the judiciary in Columbia, would require the BG team to gear up for a higher probability of action.

However, whether it be a corporate CEO in Houston, a celebrity in Los Angeles or a judge in Bogota, most employers will expect their bodyguards to not only be armed but to have a reasonable proficiency with firearms.

Author's Note: When working with International Diplomatic Security almost all of my team were ex-military special operations, police instructors or federal agents with exceptional shooting skills. The team was very competitive on the range, several of us being good enough to compete in combat shooting at a national level. This level of expertise was known to our principals who drew both pride and confidence from the knowledge that their security personnel were some of the finest combat shooters in the country.

An individual does not need to be a nationally ranked combat shooter to be a good bodyguard but he should have an acceptable level of proficiency and a solid working knowledge of the types of weapons suitable for BG work, methods of carry, safety, training, transportation and storage.

The legality of specific weapons systems or the laws relating to concealed carry are beyond the scope of this book since they vary from state to state and country to country. It is the responsibility of the individual to research and conform to local regulations so as to avoid problems with local law enforcement and embarrassment for the client.

On that note, do not make the mistake that one bodyguard made when he went to Washington, DC to escort Senator Kennedy on a junket to South America. He was arrested by the Capitol Hill Police when trying to check his firearms at the front desk of the Russell Senate Office Building. The police were not amused by the fact that he was in possession of not only a handgun and ammunition but also two submachine guns—all in a district with some of the most restrictive gun laws in the country.

This highly respected bodyguard had worked for Kennedy for several years, was a former California police officer, licensed to carry in California and authorized by State Department to use the guns in foreign countries. But he was still charged with three counts of DC gun law violations.

To further illustrate the stupidity of some of these gun laws, after having the guns seized, he was released on his own recognizance and was able to join Kennedy mid-trip. He was then to be provided firearms by the US embassy in each of the countries Kennedy was visiting.

The very nature of BG work places some limitations on the suitability of various weapons. Since most operations are in plain clothes and require the carrying of the weapon concealed, this precludes the use of any firearm except the handgun. But not all handguns are suitable. An eight inch barreled .44 magnum revolver, reminiscent of Dirty Harry, is not only heavy and difficult to conceal, it is slow to draw and difficult to shoot. On the other end of the scale, a small .25 caliber pocket pistol is equally unsuitable.

On the subject of Dirty Harry, there seem to be a number of aspiring bodyguards seeking employment that have a Rambo-like approach to life in general. Keeping in mind that select personnel, good training, common sense, careful planning and constant vigilance are more important than firepower, employers and BG team leaders should be highly suspect of "closet commandos" who carry multiple weapons or turn up on the range with enough hardware to equip a small revolution. Look more for the quiet man who carries one gun in a discreet manner and is very competent with it.

HANDGUNS

Although the military considers the handgun a secondary weapon, only to be used if the submachine gun or assault rifle malfunctions, it is in fact an extremely effective primary weapon for close quarter confrontations, provided that the shooter is adequately trained. The handgun is a weapon that can be carried unobtrusively at all times while performing the day to day tasks of a working bodyguard. Even teams that have access to shotguns and submachine guns will find limitations in their applications for close protection, so must concentrate on handgun proficiency.

Concealability however, is not the prime consideration in selecting a handgun. A common mistake made by bodyguards is carrying too small a gun simply because it is lighter and easier to conceal. Apart from the fact small semi-auto handguns are notoriously unreliable and finicky about ammunition, they are also difficult to draw and shoot well. This is partly due to the small grips and partly because of the poor point characteristics of a very short sight radius.

If one is justified in carrying a gun, then one should carry the gun that will do the job well. No one in their right mind would chose to be in a tight spot with a puny .380 back-up when they could have been carrying a full-sized combat handgun. If concealing a gun, for example a Government Model or SIG 228, means wearing a jacket on a hot day, so be it. This is far more professional and efficient than carrying nothing more than a diminutive five shot .38 in a pants pocket.

In selecting a handgun, the shooter should consider several things other than advertising hype or low cost. A combat handgun must be first and foremost a reliable weapon with a proven record of good service under prolonged use. In addition, it should have the following:

• Simple, rugged design with good ergonomics
• Sufficient power and penetration to reliably stop an assailant
• Reasonable accuracy, but not so tight that it is unreliable
• Good clear, rugged sights for rapid alignment
• A clean, crisp single action or smooth double action
• Adequate capacity for serious "social work"
• A corrosive resistant, no glare finish

Finally, the caliber must be large enough to do the job but not so powerful as to slow recovery time or second and third shot follow-up on a determined attacker. A weapon must also be controllable enough as to allow rapid shot placement on multiple targets with minimal recovery time between shots.

As with a large percentage of police departments in the nineties, most BGs are carrying high capacity nine millimeters, such as the Beretta 92F, SIG 226 & 228, H&K P7M13, Glock, S&W, and Browning Hi-Power, with many of the hard-core shooters sticking to their .45 ACP Government Models. The newest caliber on the block is the 40 S&W, falling between the 9mm and the .45 ACP in terms of performance and available in most of the above weapons.

Which manufacturer or model handgun one chooses is largely dependent on personal preference and prior experience. LAPD officers carry 92Fs, as do LA Sheriff's deputies who also have the option of carrying

H&K P7M13s—the same gun issued to the German GSG-9 counter ter-rorist team. The Secret Service, along with most other federal agencies currently carry SIG 228s. LAPD SWAT, Delta Team and many other elite groups carry reworked forty-fives. In fact, both US Special Operations Command (SOCOM) and the FBI hostage rescue team (HRT) have issued contracts for custom forty-five caliber combat pistols. Ex-British SAS and Israeli military types have long favored the Browning Hi-Power but current members are issued SIGs.

The revolver has been all but discarded for SWAT, HRT and even duty carry owing to its meager capacity of six and difficulty to reload quickly, under stress. This is a reasonable position for police work since officers may find themselves out gunned by drug dealers, gang-bangers and survivalists. However, in BG work, where one is not out on the street looking for trouble, if the problem can't be solved with six rounds, the solution probably won't be found with fourteen.

There are many professional bodyguards, especially old school retired Secret Service agents, who still favor the revolver for its simplicity and reliability. Even BGs who carry a high capacity semi-auto as a primary weapon, favor the smaller revolvers like the .38 Special Model 60 as a back-up gun.

Another reason to keep current with a revolver is that in some coun-tries, a working BG will not get a permit for any firearm except a .38 Special revolver. This is partly due to antiquated laws but more to the prohibition on any firearm of a military caliber like 9mm Parabellum.

Arguments abound centering around which caliber is the "best" man-stopper—usually from self professed "experts" whose lives have never depended on the gun in their hand. So, as John Wayne would say, "Now listen and listen good, pilgrim". Any of the current combat calibers, such as 9mm, .45ACP, .357 magnum, 10mm, 40 S&W, in the hands of a good shooter, will do the job. Although bullet design, velocity, diameter and construction play some part in the performance of a bullet on human tissue, shot placement is the single most significant contributing factor in stopping an assailant. As long as the round has sufficient power and weight to penetrate the intervening body tissue, to reach a vital organ, everything else is secondary.

Conversely, there is a difference between killing and stopping a threat-ening individual. Under ideal conditions, any small caliber will kill if the round enters the "brain housing group", or may mortally wound, resulting in death some time after the shooting. This is not what the professional is looking for. The BG needs dependable stopping capability under the less than ideal conditions of a close, quick confrontation.

In general, the larger the caliber, the larger the wound cavity; and the heavier the bullet, the more consistent the performance. This allows for a rushed, reactive shot that is not so well placed to do sufficient damage to stop all threatening action by the assailant. It is not necessary to kill the attacker to stop him, one must merely inflict enough physical dam-age so that the body cannot continue or the spirit looses the will to fight.

Note: My initial military training was with the 9mm Browning Hi-Power, but that was only considered a back-up to a battle rifle or submachine gun. When I began combat shooting in earnest in the late seventies and early eighties, I quickly realized that the Government Model was a superior weapon system and that .45 ACP was a more reliable man stopper. At about the same time, many top shooters who were also professional gun toters and instructors, came to the same conclusion. Since we represented the cutting edge in combat pistolcraft, it was with no surprise that the top US hostage rescue teams and SWAT teams adopted customized forty-fives as their weapon of choice, and that foreign manufacturers immediately tooled up for this caliber.

Now, although I feel quite confident carrying a 9mm SIG, H&K or Beretta, one of my favorite guns being a Novak/HRT Browning Hi-Power, I always feel more secure with the familiar weight of a .45 ACP on my belt or in my hand. However, I also maintain proficiency with a number of other weapons including a Model 60 .38 and a small 9mm back-up gun, but these would not be my first choice as primary weapons.

If working as part of a team it is advantageous if all members carry the same type and caliber of weapon, but this is not as important as it would be for a SWAT or HRT team member. It is more important that the individual BG be competent with his weapon of choice and that the weapon function reliably.

New weapons should be thoroughly tested before going into the field or carried on duty. It is recommended that a new weapon, along with ALL its magazines, be used in training for at least 500 to 1000 rounds without malfunction before it can be considered reliable. Then the weapon should be inspected before and after each training session for cracks, wear or loose screws.

The only acceptable modifications to a combat weapon are those that enhance performance and reliability, and do not include non-functional gadgets that could loosen and become a liability. Appropriate modifications could include: changing the grips to better suit the shooter; adding high visibility sights; smoothing the double action trigger and cleaning up a single action one; polishing the feed ramp; opening the ejection port; adding night-sight inserts; or anything proven to enhance reliability with a particular weapon.

Most of the currently available combat handguns (Beretta, SIG, HK, S&W, Glock, Colt) require little or no custom work, and can be considered "combat ready" after checking for zero and firing a few hundred rounds for reliability.

Most feeding problems and malfunctions with semi-autos can be traced to bad magazines and inferior or incompatible ammunition. The recommended way to identify these problems is to shoot the weapon with proven reliable magazines and high grade ball ammo. Magazines should be marked and numbered to facilitate the identification of one that consistently causes malfunctions. If magazines have been dropped on a hard surface, the lips may have become bent, changing the angle of attack of the round trying to transition to the chamber. Some can be repaired, others will have to be discarded.

With revolvers, the most common reliability problem is light hammer strikes that result in a failure to fire. This can be caused by worn mainsprings or amateur gunsmiths lightening the springs to help smooth the trigger. Let your gunsmith know that if he is doing any action work, not to lighten the springs. The reliability of a trigger that is a little on the heavy side is far more important than a silky smooth action job and a gun that won't go bang 100% of the time.

D&L .45 government model with Safariland holster,
Wilson magazines and Davis pouches

SIG 228, 9mm, current issue to several federal agencies

Eagle attache case with built-in holster (shown on outside).

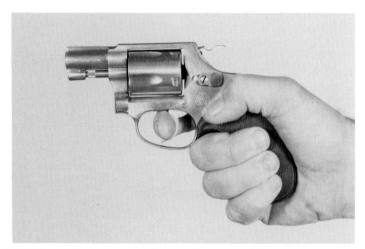

S&W Model 60, 38 Special, favored by many BGs as a back-up gun

SHOTGUNS

For many BGs, the next step up from a handgun would be a 12 gauge shotgun. The shotgun has application on larger fixed locations like ranch or estate security details or contracts in higher risk areas. Shotguns were a common sight during the LA Riots of 1992 when BGs and security guards were contracted to cover industrial properties, businesses, and to make pick-ups from check-cashing centers in the heart of South Central.

Shotguns are excellent multi-purpose weapons in many situations. They are readily available, require no special permit to procure, and are relatively inexpensive. But the role of the shotgun in BG work is restricted.

There is no denying the knock-down power of a full load of buckshot at close range, but the shotgun's limited magazine capacity (4—8 rounds) and marginal accuracy make it unsuitable as a general duty weapon. In addition, the shotgun's length makes it all but impossible to conceal and the heavy recoil only serves to slow second shot follow-up.

Another negative of the shotgun is that any weapon intended for close quarter shooting must be able to make guaranteed close proximity hostage/head shots. The increasing spread of the shot pattern (approximately 1" per meter) could endanger the client being held hostage, fellow DVP team members or innocent by-standers.

The advantages of the shotgun include a high visibility deterrence and, with the addition of a fore-end light mount, an excellent weapon for night patrolling on ranches and larger properties.

For simplicity and rugged reliability, the Remington 870 police shotgun is hard to beat. If budget allows, one of the optimum shotguns for this type of work is the Benelli Super 90, marketed by H&K in the United States. It is an 8 shot weapon with excellent handling characteristics and accuracy with either buckshot or solid slugs.

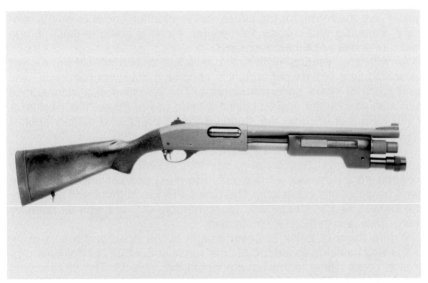

Professional model Remington 870 with tactical light mount. Scattergun Technologies.

SUBMACHINE GUNS

SMGs would usually only be considered for the high-risk contracts—probably in countries other than the US. In addition, although a compact and effective weapon system, few civilian BGs would ever have the opportunity to get enough time behind the weapon to become truly proficient.

Even though the US Secret Service has Uzis in briefcases, and other government teams carry MP5Ks and Colts in nondescript soft cases, these are still slow to bring to bear in an emergency. A BG with a handgun will clear leather long before a sub-gun can clear its case.

The primary advantages of the submachine gun are greater ammunition capacity, increased fire power and compact size. But more importantly, it is the number of accessories that can be attached to enhance performance.

In selecting an SMG, keep in mind that it must have not only the capability of rapid fire at close range, but also extremely accurate select fire. In close proximity crowd situations, it will be important to engage the armed suspect with precise, confident, surgical shooting, without endangering the principal or by-standers. A "hose job" is not an acceptable form of shooting when dealing with close protection or rescues.

Another advantage is the psychological effect that SMGs may have on an adversary. A terrorist may be less inclined to try anything when it is noted that the security team is armed with automatic weapons. That said, do not count on the mere presence of superior fire power to prevent an attack. There are always political or religious fanatics who will gladly give their lives for the cause, not to mention society's ample supply of criminals and crazies. Remember, if one is going to flaunt it, one had damn well be prepared to use it.

As with any weapon system, the selection criteria should be: rugged reliability; time proven performance; accuracy; quality construction; and availability of spare parts and service. The selection of a submachine gun may well be the easiest choice a team has to make. The Heckler & Koch MP5 has become the standard for all police and military special operations, and the one by which all others are judged.

The MP5 has become the trade mark of the world's elite—both abroad and domestically. This is not to say that the MP5 is the only suitable weapon on the market—it is simply the most popular and has proven itself on countless occasions. The Colt CAR-15s in 9mm and .223Rem, the Beretta M-12S (9mm) and the venerable UZI are also all used by teams tasked with dignitary protection.

Where there is a risk of being caught in the open and a little more range and power is called for, as in a vehicular ambush or maritime protection detail, some teams have adopted the H&K-53. The 53 is almost identical to an MP5 in appearance and function but has more punch and a longer effective range since it is chambered for the more powerful 5.56mm(.223) assault rifle cartridge.

The MP5 and the HK53 make for a good partnership since both function the same and require no operator retraining. For the team that is already familiar with and using the M-16, then the CAR-15s in 9mm and 5.56mm may be a more convenient or cost effective alternative. Retraining requires time, money and considerable effort.

The submachine gun's most significant advantage over the handgun is the number of accessories that can be integrated into the weapon system. These include but are not limited to:

• Integral or detachable fore-end light mounts
• Conventional scope sights for long range precision shooting
• Red-dot type laser projectors for enhanced shot placement
• IR laser aiming devices to be used in conjunction with night vision goggles
• Suppressors for those times when noise could compromise an approach
• Blank firing attachments (BFA) for training purposes
• Fixed or folding stocks

The most important accessory being the light mount. It is difficult, at the best of times, to juggle both a flashlight and a weapon, let alone open doors and search buildings. With the light attached to the weapon, the BG can conveniently bring the weapon to bear, where ever the light is pointed. Light mounts are not intended as aiming devices, but definitely hasten and simplify the aiming process.

H&K MP-5 with light and laser mounts

Shooting position with MP5K

Beretta M12S

AMMUNITION

Ammunition is probably one of the single biggest expenditure incurred in training. It is not unusual to shoot 500 to 1000 rounds per week, per man or 200 to 400 rounds per day, per man when involved in firearms training.

After initial weapons skills have been mastered, a BG should still allow himself 100 rounds per week as part of his personal maintenance training program.

The basic criteria for duty ammunition is:
• The ammunition should come from a large, reputable manufacturer
• It should be of a consistently high standard
• It must function reliably in all personal weapons
• It should have sufficient penetration to reach a vital area
• It should be combat accurate

The BG should avoid the expensive trick ammunition, "super hot" loads and "killer" bullets that are constantly being advertised as the solution to all problems. They tend to be too expensive to train with, have erratic feeding and function, and are seldom very accurate. It is better to go for consistency, reliability, accuracy, quality and economy.

GUNS FOR THE CLIENT

Many celebrities own guns for personal protection. Some just keep them in the home or office, others consider it necessary to carry them at all times. Not always without incident.

Many well known actors, sports celebrities and musicians have been arrested for carrying a concealed weapon without a permit. This often happens as a direct result of a late night traffic stop or a suspected DUI. Some have even been stupid enough to try carrying a gun through an airport, being picked up by security metal detectors and x-ray. This all creates some unique problems for the bodyguard.

It is not unusual for a client to ask the bodyguard to procure a firearm for them so that they will have a weapon when the BG is not present. Others may already have a weapon and insist on keeping it at hand.

The problem is one of competency and training. Few civilians, including many bodyguards, take the time and energy to become truly proficient with a firearm. At best they take a couple of trips to the local range, shoot probably a hundred rounds with mixed results, and then never practice again. This creates a false sense of security on their part and a hazard to all around them.

Unless someone lives with a handgun, shoots on a regular basis and has been schooled on all the dynamics of gunfighting, they are no more than an accident looking for a place to happen. Even if an individual is "a good shot", this does not prepare him or her for the shock, fear and confusion of deadly conflict, and the split second decision making needed to resolve it.

If the client insists on having a firearm, the bodyguard has a moral obligation to insist that he or she receive professional tuition and train on a regular basis.

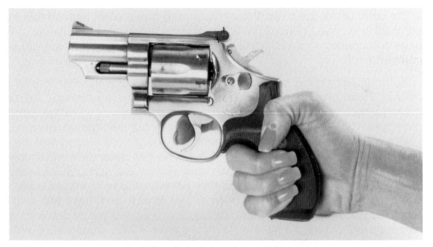

S&W Model 66 stainless .357 mag

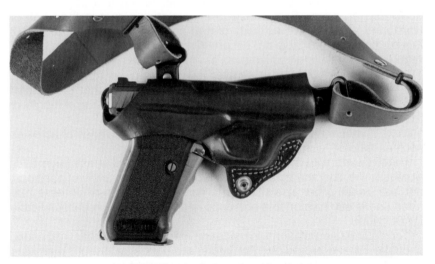

H&K P7-M13 in Galco shoulder holster

HOLSTERS

A good holster is like a good pair of shoes—and those who spend twelve hours a day or more on their feet know and appreciate the importance of quality footwear.

Unlike patrol officers and uniformed security guards, the BG must carry his weapon concealed, and to conceal a weapon, it must conform to the contours of the body. If the holster and gun are not comfortable to carry for prolonged periods, walking, sitting, or driving, the amateur will have a tendency to want to put in a desk draw or leave it in the glove compartment.

Author's Note: One hot night I was working outer perimeter in a dry river bed with two other BGs with whom I had not worked before. About midnight we found ourselves in a confrontation with six armed gang members. When we lit them up, they fired at us but then turned and ran.

When the smoke cleared, I realized that it was probably good that they had chosen not to stay and shoot it out. The two other BGs were now hugging the dirt and I was the only one with a weapon drawn. I was steamed at the lack of back-up and they were feeling very embarrassed.

It turned out that since it had been so hot all day, and these two amateurs did not want to wear their jackets, they had elected to leave their weapons in the cars. I now take the time to check who I am working with a little more thoroughly.

Successfully concealing a full-sized handgun, in such a manner that it can still be drawn quickly, is an art in itself. An art that begins with a good holster. Some BGs chose to simply stick a gun in their belt or waistband—and we are all guilty of it at some time in our careers—but this is neither comfortable nor secure. One will be constantly checking or readjusting the weapon as it moves around.

In selecting a holster, the shooter looks for several features. Firstly, the holster should fit the gun correctly. This means that the holster should be made specifically for the model, caliber and barrel length of the gun to be carried.

Next, it should hold the gun securely through a wide range of activities such as running, climbing, sitting and driving.

Thirdly, even with a secure holster, the shooter must still have easy access to the gun and be able to draw quickly from a variety of positions, not just standing but also sitting in a car. If a holster has all these features and is still comfortable and concealable then it is probably suitable for BG work.

The four basic positions for sidearm carry are right/rear, appendix, shoulder rig and crossdraw. For years, the right side or right rear were the two most popular methods of carrying a combat handgun, and to this day, are still the best positions for prolonged carry when one is moving about.

In recent years, as a direct result of the holsters developed for combat pistol competition, many professionals have gone to carrying a pistol inside the pants on the strongside/ front. This has become known as appendix draw. There is no doubt, that this position is one of the fastest and most convenient positions to carry a gun, even though it is a little unnerving having a loaded semi-auto pointed directly at one's genitalia. (That's sexual organs for the non-latin speaking readers). The other downside of appendix carry is that it is not comfortable when one is sitting or driving for prolonged periods.

The two most comfortable carry positions for drivers or those required to work a desk, are conventional crossdraw or in a shoulder holster. The two problems with shoulder holsters are that they make for a slow draw, and can become uncomfortable and irritating in hot weather.

Finding a holster that fits the body and is still concealable is a process of trial and error. It is not unusual to go through several holsters until one finds one that suits his or her build, clothing and duties. See the accompanying photos for more details.

Over the years, we have seen both BGs and police officers experience a variety of embarrassing situations with their holsters. The following are in addition to the literally hundreds of police officers who drop their handguns each year because of poor holster design or carelessness.

Case #1—A detective running down the stairs in the Los Angeles Courthouse suddenly sees his revolver fall from his inverted-draw shoulder holster and go skidding across the marble floor. It had become unsnapped and the spring had lost tension. Even without the snap, a holster should hold a gun by tension alone.

Case #2—A BG running to meet a private jet at Aspen Airport has a small automatic fall from his ankle holster. He scoops up the gun before anyone notices, but not until that evening realizes that the loaded magazine was missing from the grip. No doubt still on the tarmac in Aspen. Poor holster design, bad positioning and a lack of awareness.

Case #3—Several off-duty police officers, enjoying an evening at an amusement park, decide to try their skills on the small Malibu Grand prix race cars. Upon leaving the cars in the pits, an attendant reaches into the cockpit of one of the cars, and in front of the awaiting crowd, holds up a PPK Walther and asks if this belongs to someone. An embarrassed officer needed to flash his badge to get the gun back.

Case #4—A bodyguard working an American client visiting a Monte Carlo casino has his gun in the back of his pants. Unfortunately he did not realize that his jacket had ridden up and was caught behind the grips, totally exposing the weapon. Luckily a young lady discreetly warned him and saved him considerable embarrassment.

Case #5—A BG working in Nice, France without a gun permit had chosen to carry his .357 magnum in his briefcase rather than on his person. Unfortunately, while preparing to board a private jet to fly to Paris, he allowed the pilot to carry the briefcase. Before he could stop it, the pilot had put the briefcase on the conveyor belt through the X-ray machine. He then had some serious explaining to do to local authorities.

Case #6—Secret Service agents working in the Caribbean had elected not to wear jackets because of the heat, and chose to carry their handguns in the small men's handbags favored by Europeans. Unfortunately, they were not used to carrying something in their hands and were consistently misplacing their loaded purses. A little embarrassing to say the least.

Case #7—A trainee BG turns up to training with "the new hot setup holster". After exiting a vehicle, running to a barricade and going for his gun, realizes that it was not there. It was simply a design problem with holster and the car seat had pushed the gun forward and out of the holster.

Case #8—Another case of a BG with a new holster. This was a good holster but the gun could not be drawn because of a defective pull-at-the-dot thumb snap. Once snapped, the snap required a pair of pliers and no small amount of effort to be undone.

Case #9—A BG turns up on the range with a new Beretta 92F but a shoulder rig from an older gun. Upon drawing his weapon he realized that he had drawn the receiver but the slide and barrel were still in the rig. It turned out that a protrusion in the holster pushed on the disassembly button on the side of the Beretta and successfully stripped the gun when drawing. It does pay to test your equipment in training, before carrying it on duty.

Case #10—An experienced police officer has a holster cut away in the area of the trigger guard, allowing him to get on the trigger before the gun cleared the holster. He thought it would be faster. It was. He had the fastest time from the whistle to the first shot on the range—right into the side of his leg. The lesson is obvious.

Beretta 92F / Eagle inside-the-pants holster

Colt/Galco

Colt/Galco

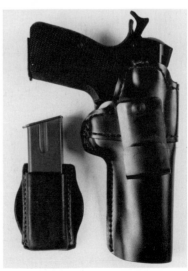

SIG 226/Safariland

Browning/Safariland

SIG 226 with Davis leather

Novak Hi-Power with Davis leather

Nova six pack with Davis leather

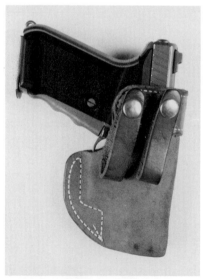

*P7M13 with Robar NP3 finish and
Davis leather*

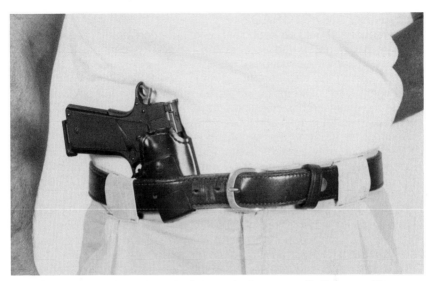

Safariland inside-the-pants holster in the appendix draw position

Galco shoulder rig. See page 69 for the technique of drawing from a shoulder holster.

CLEANING AND STORAGE

All weapons should be kept clean and in a good state of repair. Before training, weapons should be checked for cracks, unusual wear, loose screws and barrel obstructions.

After training the weapon should be immediately cleaned and moving parts lightly oiled. The inside of the barrel should be left clean and dry. During the disassembly, cleaning and reassembly the weapon should be checked again for cracks and loose screws.

Security for firearms and ammunition is important. A weapon should be kept in one of two places: either in the holster or under lock and key. A loaded weapon should never be out of the direct control of its owner, and when not being carried, firearms should be locked away in a safe out of the reach of curious fingers, particularly those of children.

Firearms safety and security becomes paramount for BGs working estate security where they may be living or staying on property. The same is true with weapons in hotel rooms and around the office. Any carelessness with firearms is grounds for immediate dismissal.

True Story: A bodyguard staying in the bunk house of the ranch where he is working decides to clean his revolver. After cleaning the gun he does some dry-fire practice aiming at a tree that he could see through the window.

Upon finishing his practice he reloads his revolver and leaves it on the table. About this time the phone rings and he is distracted by the call. Upon hanging up the phone he picks up the gun to dry-fire at the tree one more time—forgetting he had reloaded. BANG! Luckily it was just a window and a tree and not the gardener or a horse.

Lesson: Firstly, he should not have been cleaning his weapon on a job sight. Secondly, he should not have had the weapon unholstered or been dry-firing while working. Lastly, he was just stupid and careless—and unemployed soon after.

CONCLUSION

What ever the weapons selected, the BG must take the time and expense to master them. There is no substitute for many hours of disciplined training and time behind the weapon.

Where training time is limited, the BG must perfect individual shooting skills on his own time, and save those all too precious training days for working on team skills, walking drills and counter ambush procedures. Team members who are not willing to spend some of their own time and money on individual training are not an asset to the team and should be replaced by more motivated individuals.

13

FIREARMS TRAINING

Many bodyguards, particularly those in the entertainment industry, have no use for firearms training, knowing that in their world a gun would be more of a hinder than a help. In a situation where the greatest threat comes from the crush of adoring fans, a bodyguard depends more on low animal cunning and brawn than the need for firepower.

Conversely, there are all too many individuals seeking employment as bodyguards whose sole motivation is to find a job where they can carry a gun. These are the types who cannot meet the minimum standards to become a federal agent or have already been turned down by the local police academies. Not surprisingly, these same "wanna bes" are probably not suited to BG work either since they have no perception of just how minor a role guns play in close protection. Responding to a threat with deadly force will always be secondary to the fundamental principles of Cover & Evacuate.

However, in today's violent society, both bodyguards and those who employ bodyguards know that there are high threat situations and locations where only an armed professional, or better still a team of armed professionals, can bring peace of mind. But, keeping everything in perspective, both groups should know that it would be a rare occasion when the bodyguard would actually have either the time or opportunity to clear leather.

Accepting the reality that shooting would be a last resort, if one intends to carry a gun, one must make the commitment to become competent in its use and educated in its applications. Carrying a gun professionally carries an awesome responsibility, as would any activity that requires decisions involving life and death. In shooting, as with medical training, an error in judgement could result in death or serious injury, so the time and energy spent in training will always be disproportionate to the expected real world application.

That brings us to the subject of training and the specific needs of the modern bodyguard. As with any skill, there must be some specificity in training related to the arena in which it is to be used. The shooting techniques taught to patrol officers, on the standard 25 yard police shooting range, are not effective for the close confrontations that occur while escorting a high profile VIP or protected witness. Similarly, an individual with proven rifle ability will not necessarily have equal proficiency with a handgun. So where range time and budget are limited, the training must be specifically adapted to suit the imposed demands of the close protection specialist.

Before covering the actual mechanics of modern combat pistolcraft, a training program must first address the all important topics of shooting policy and weapons safety.

FIREARMS POLICY

Whether a contract security company, a corporation that employs bodyguards or an independent BG, all must have some form of policy or guideline regarding firearms—their use, applications, storage, cleaning and transportation.

In developing policy for private sector security personnel and BGs, one must keep in mind that a private sector bodyguard has no more law enforcement power than the average citizen in the street. In fact, even sworn police officers working as private bodyguards may not enjoy the full protection of their sworn status, especially if working outside of their jurisdiction.

Without the intent of contradicting any existing policies that an agency may have, the following could be used as a general guide to formulating a policy.

Firearms:

Only agency approved firearms should be carried and they must be kept clean and in safe working order. In addition, the policy on handguns should address:

- Authorized type(s)
- Authorized ammunition type and caliber
- Details on use where, when and how
- Serviceability, maintenance and working order
- Frequency of shooter qualification or check-out

Policies must also cover the use of Special Weapons:

- Authorized rifles, shotguns, SMGs, stun munitions, tear gas
- Employ when, where and how, in clear and concise statements
- By qualified personnel only—to avoid legal problems, public criticism, embarrassment, or disciplinary action

Additionally, the policy needs to cover:

- The use of batons, mace, OC spray or heavy flashlights
- Company policy, legal ramifications, etc

Training:
All armed personnel must attend range practice on a regular basis and maintain proficiency. Personnel failing to meet minimum standards will not be permitted to carry a firearm and risk suspension or termination.

Carry of Firearms:
1. Only those employees who have met the State standards, have a valid permit and adhere to all legal requirements may carry a firearm.
2. Agents will carry their approved weapon(s) on their person, holstered, with an adequate supply of ammunition. Deviation must be with prior approval.

Use of Deadly Force:
1. Agents are not to shoot any person except in self defense, when they reasonably believe they or another person are in danger of death or grievous bodily harm.
2. Firing warning shots is expressly prohibited. Agents will not fire at fleeing suspects except when the circumstances of self defense exist, ie, fear of death or grievous bodily harm exists.
3. Shooting at a moving vehicle, tires, etc., with the intent of rendering it incapable of being operated poses a significant danger to innocent parties and is prohibited except in extreme circumstances. However, this does not preclude firing at persons inside the vehicle when justified; but the hazards of an uncontrollable moving vehicle must be taken into consideration.
4. Firearms will not be used to intimidate or coerce suspects who are not threatening an agent or another person. Agents will not brandish or unnecessarily display a firearm in public areas. This does not preclude drawing a firearm in a situation which is threatening or potentially threatening. Agents will always use sound judgment in displaying firearms.

There should be complete and total understanding on this subject since policy and safety violations could result in tragedy. The foundation for all policy on deadly force is that it is to be used in "Defensive of Life Only". Either one's own, the principal's, that of a fellow BG or an innocent third party. Unfortunately, not all confrontations are simply black and white. There are several that fall into a "gray area" that will require some difficult judgment calls on the part of the BG involved.

One example of a tough call is the situation where an attacker appears to have surrendered by putting his hands up, but still has a gun in his hand. You order him to drop it but he does not comply immediately. Now, knowing that action is faster than reaction, if he makes the decision to shoot you, and carries it out with speed and conviction, he will probably win. Some agencies are recommending that if the suspect does not drop the weapon immediately, the agent involved should probably shoot. It is just too dangerous to try and play "the catch up" game after he initiates a threatening act.

A similar situation occurs when an individual is bending to pick up a weapon. Although the gun is not in his hand, the potential for danger is significant. From the time he gets his hand on the gun and makes the decision to take you out, to the time he fires is only fractions of a second. You may have to shoot even though he technically does not have a gun in his hand.

Another aspect of shooting policy that must be addressed is that of the actions of the BG immediately following a shooting. This is a subject that requires more legal guidance than can be presented here, but some considerations would be:

- Ensure the client's safety
- Call the police and emergency medical services
- Identify potential witnesses if possible
- Immediately contact a supervisor and/or lawyer
- Make no public statements
- Keep statements to the police simple and honest, emphasizing an "in fear of life" situation
- Be honest and objective in written reports
- Reports should be the facts leading up to and including the shooting
- Team members may compare recollections, but should avoid carefully tailored reports
- The best way to protect oneself is to know the firearms policy ahead of time, and only discharge a firearm in compliance with the policies and procedures laid down by the State and the agency.

The punch and draw used for very close quarter confrontations

RANGE SAFETY

The next item on the agenda, prior to actual range training is a working knowledge of the basic rules and procedures for safe firearms handling. The following is a sample guideline used for advanced tactical firearms training.

Range Rules:

Tactical firearms training is considerably more demanding than basic target shooting, requiring an increased level of alertness for potential safety violations. Training will involve fast movement with loaded weapons; simple and complex team drills; increased levels of stress; and a departure from traditional range procedure.

The instructor and range staff demand the full attention of all participants. If a trainee does not understand an exercise or range command—ASK!

Firearms Handling:
1. Treat all weapons as loaded
2. Do not point a weapon at anything you do not wish to destroy
3. Keep all weapons holstered until instructed to shoot
4. Keep the muzzle down range at all times
5. Keep your finger off the trigger unless preparing to shoot
6. Know your target and what is down range beyond it
7. Reholster before turning around after shooting
8. Long guns will be carried muzzle up, safety on
9. Listen to all range commands carefully
10. Use ear and eye protection when on or near the line
11. Never leave a weapon unattended—loaded or unloaded
12. Do not engage steel targets closer than 10 yards

Personal Conduct:
1. The instructor or rangemaster has total control of the firing line
2. Everyone is a safety officer—use common sense
3. Do not attempt any exercise that you believe is beyond your personal ability
4. Anyone can call a "cease fire" or "stop" if they see a potential safety hazard
5. To maintain the training momentum it is necessary that the instructors have your full attention at all times
6. Reload magazines whenever there is a pause in training
7. Change or patch targets immediately when the line is safe and declared "clear"
8. Obey all range commands immediately—especially "STOP" or "CEASE FIRE"

BE ALERT—BE SAFE

CLOSE QUARTER SHOOTING

Close quarter shooting (CQS), usually taught as part of a more complete BG program, was developed to meet the needs of the individual operator, under close combat conditions. CQS has little in common with target shooting under ideal range conditions, and is designed more to replicate reality.

The conditions found in attacks or attempted kidnappings include:
• Some form of diversion or distraction
• Fast, unexpected confrontations
• Relatively short ranges; 3 feet to 45 feet.
• Often at night
• Limited room to maneuver
• Multiple assailants
• Bystanders in close proximity to armed assailants
• Noise, confusion and panic

For the trainee BG there is no value in enrolling in an advanced CQS program until one has mastered the basics—the ability to hit a single target, with reasonable speed, at seven to ten yards. Only once one has demonstrated this minimal skill level, should one advance to more demanding mission specific BG weapons training.

There is no substitute for professional tuition, diligent practice and a lot of shooting under the watchful eye of a competent instructor. There are several good sources of basic and advanced combat pistol training listed in Appendix C, but for a shooter to improve, he must first recognize the existing deficiencies in his own ability. This requires more than just a lot of shooting.

All shooters, even the world champions, have some deficiencies in their technique, so correcting those flaws or overcoming previously learned bad habits is an essential starting point. At first, training under any respected shooting instructor will benefit the novice BG, but with progress, he or she must seek out instructors who have a more intimate knowledge and experience in close protection.

If a new shooter is willing to abandon the common misconceptions about shooting, likes to train and shoot, enjoys excelling, and is willing to push personal limits, he or she will achieve levels of speed and accuracy that were previously unattainable. This however, does require time, dedication, ammunition and quality instruction.

PRINCIPLES OF CLOSE QUARTER SHOOTING

To be a good combat shooter requires more than just a good eye and a steady hand. In addition to those, it requires familiarity with basic tactics, physical agility, a competitive nature and above average shooting skills.

When confronted with a potential kidnapping or assault, the BG can find himself in very close proximity to armed attackers, with very little time to evaluate the situation. If the BG does not react quickly and shoot reflexively, he may well end up as a statistic along with the principal.

The principles of combat shooting are well known: Tactics—Accuracy—Power—Speed (T.A.P.S.). This means that it does not matter how good a shooter may be, any tactical errors could prove fatal. Accuracy is important but only relative to the task at hand, hitting the kill zone on a man sized target. Not a difficult feat under ideal conditions, but then the speed and confusion of combat is far from ideal. The power is inherent in the weapon system, type of ammunition and the number of shots fired—generally two or three to the chest and/or one or two to the head, if the assailant fails to respond to the chest shots. Speed is essential but dictated by proximity, size of the target, danger and personal ability.

To be able to shoot fast, without sacrificing accuracy, requires modification to the accepted fundamentals of basic target shooting—stance, grip, sights, breathing and trigger release.

The key features of the STANCE are still comfort and balance but for combat there must also be the **flexibility** to move quickly. There is a natural tendency to bend the knees slightly when shooting, but this must not be over exaggerated by squatting or bend forward at the waist as in the old classic FBI crouch.

In BG work, the DRAW becomes an important part of basic training. Firstly, the holster must be designed and positioned so that the shooter can access the weapon quickly, with the first grip on the stocks being the same as the shooting grip, without having to readjust on the way to the target. Once the gun clears leather, it should be pushed along the most direct line from the holster to the target. This is one brisk, positive motion where **smooth** is more important than **fast.**

The GRIP on the weapon should be firm but not a white knuckle death grip. Excessive pressure on the weapon will adversely affect accuracy. The extent to which the arms and weapon are extended toward the target will be governed by the distance to the target.

SIGHT ALIGNMENT, in the conventional sense, is often impossible because of low light, the need for speed and stress induced target fixation. When confronted by an armed assailant, it is almost impossible to draw ones attention away from the imminent danger, his gun, and back to the sights. In addition, the distances involved are often close enough to be able to depend on muscle memory and natural WEAPON ALIGNMENT.

Any hope of controlling BREATHING in a high stress situation is pointless. At best, the shooter can consciously force himself to relax and breath naturally. Breathing will increase dramatically as part of the "fight or flight response" of the human body. Only when the shooting stops, will the shooter again make a conscious effort to calm his racing heart and ragged breathing.

TRIGGER CONTROL must also be modified. There is no longer the time to slowly increase pressure on the trigger in search of the perfect surprise break. In combat, the weapon must fire at the instant the shooter has a clear shot, and before the gunman can shoot first. With the correct training, the trigger finger will become programmed to respond to visual input and squeeze the trigger with minimal conscious effort. This is not a sudden jerk that may cause a miss but more a fast compressed-time squeeze.

When engaging MULTIPLE TARGETS the shooter will come to depend on rapid weapon alignment and almost subconscious trigger release. Longer shots and smaller targets however, will often require the use of a more precise, conscious sight picture and more deliberate trigger control.

The SPEED with which one shoots will be dictated by three factors. The DISTANCE to the target; the SIZE of the target; and the shooter's personal ABILITY. One should never shoot faster than one can guarantee hits since misses are an unacceptable part of training and a serious hazard in the field. For those longer shots, the shooter should take the extra quarter or half second that it takes to align the sights and to guarantee a hit, giving the gun the opportunity to settle into the kill zone.

FOLLOW THROUGH is another basic fundamental that has little to do with close quarter shooting. With time, experience and practice, the shooter will develop the confidence to shoot fast and move on without having to pause to verify the hits on hostile targets. The shooter will know when the shots feel right and move his attention immediately to other possible threats. Operationally, one should shoot until the threat is neutralized or falls, but with static, non-reactionary targets, one must develop the confidence to shoot and move when speed is of the essence.

Range programs should be designed to reflect reality as much as practicable. It is also essential that trainee BGs make every effort to handle their weapons in a manner consistent with good "street procedure". This requires attention to not only safety but also press checks, drawing, post shooting cover of the target, reduction of stress induced tunnel vision, reloads and malfunction drills.

Press Check—Many of the more progressive training groups and instructors run a "hot range" when training experienced personnel, as a BG school should be. Therefore, it is essential that the shooters get into the habit of verifying that there is a round in the chamber before starting or entering a new exercise. This is known as the press check. A simple matter of pulling the slide back a quarter of an inch or so, to verify that one can see brass in the chamber.

Draw—Many shooters become very complacent (sloppy) about their draw when they are starting exercises with the gun already in the hand. To reinforce good habits, the draw should always be a positive, efficient, crisp movement, with the finger off of the trigger.

Target Cover—Shooters should not be permitted to reholster immediately after shooting. There must be a brief pause where they are conditioned to evaluate the effects of their shots on a dangerous assailant. After engaging a target, or simply drawing on a "no shoot" target, the shooter should continue to watch the suspect, depressing the muzzle of his weapon to about groin level on the target. As he becomes satisfied that the suspect target is not a threat, the weapon can be pulled back to the close-cover position at about belt level. The final step is the reholster. This technique is also known as "fading"—a systematic downgrading of the threat level.

Tunnel Vision—We know from experience that a life threatening situation has several physiological effects on a shooter. One is stress induced tunnel vision. To condition trainees to break out of this, we encourage them to scan the area, or at least look at the targets on either side of theirs, immediately after shooting. This will make them more aware of the surrounding situation and other impending threats.

Reloading—In combat firearms training, the instructor should not need to tell the shooters when to reload. They should be reloading as necessary and topping up magazines between drills. During an exercise, they may use the tactical reload or combat reload, as the situation dictates. A combat reload is a fast reload done when one makes the error of running dry in the face of danger. The empty magazine is dropped directly from the weapon and a fresh one inserted, simultaneously chambering a round. The tactical reload is more of a deliberate action performed during a tactical pause or when behind cover. The partially expended magazine is slipped out and replaced by a fresh one. The partial magazine can then be pocketed for possible future use.

Malfunctions—In tactical training, range drills do not stop for weapons malfunctions (jams) and trainees must be conditioned to clear malfunctions in an expeditious manner. The two most common drills that must be almost reflexive are the failure to fire drill of "Tap, Rack, Bang" and the stove-pipe drills of either "sweep" or "invert and slingshot".

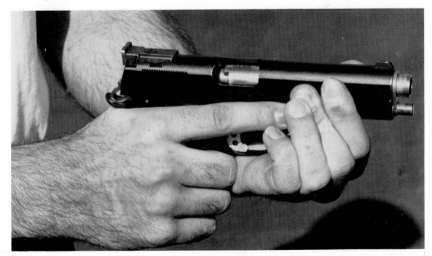

Press check to ensure a round is chambered

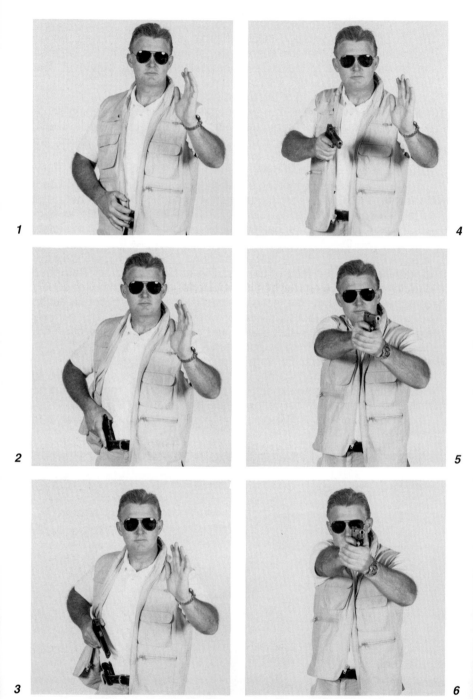

Drawing from the appendix position

1

4

2

5

3

6

Drawing from the Eagle weapon fanny pack

ADVANCED TRAINING

Once shooting fundamentals have been mastered and the shooter has achieved a well above average standard, he must then look beyond the conscious mechanics of **sight picture/trigger squeeze** and strive for a level where shooting becomes more natural and reactive. With enough shooting, one reaches a level where the weapon becomes an extension of the body; muscle memory brings the weapon to alignment instantly; the eye registers the sights without conscious thought; and the trigger releases when all conditions are correct. It is the same coordination, skill level and reflex action enjoyed by top competitors in any sport. This is what separates the champions from the masses, and in gun fighting, there can be only winners since there is no second place. Not alive anyway.

This conditioning will be recognized in practice when one draws, engages multiple targets, scores all center hits, but does not recall actually seeing the sights. In reality, one is subconsciously seeing the sights and registering all the other information through increased awareness and visual acuity. This is much the same as the ping-pong player who hits fast balls more by feel than conscious effort.

Fast, accurate shooting and good conditioning should not be confused with what some call Instinct Shooting. Man is not born with the "instinctive" ability to handle a firearm or shoot. An individual may possess exceptional eye sight, reflexes, coordination and aptitude for firearms handling, but NATURAL POINT SHOOTING is a learned skill. There are individuals who will have people believe that they are instinct shooters, but in actual fact they are incorrectly labeling their style of shooting.

Point shooting, without use of the sights, can be mastered through constant repetition of a given movement until muscle memory develops. If a weapon is brought to the aiming position, eye level, enough times, eventually it will return to that position even if focus is maintained on the target. This is not instinct but simply a combination of concentration and muscle memory, and a by-product of repetition and positive reinforcement.

Any shooter who has done enough aim-fire and combat shooting has a high probability of hitting a target, even if the sights are not visible. It is often referred to as "getting in the grove", and is a valid form of point shooting, without the necessity of learning a different technique.

Speed is another area worthy of discussion. Many firearms instructors place too much emphasis on speed shooting only, requiring their trainees to achieve certain goals based on time alone. This can severely hinder the progress of a new shooter who, instead of working on a smooth draw, correct form and guaranteed hits, is simply trying to get all shots off in the required time limits.

The speed with which one shoots should be dictated by the SIZE of the target, the DISTANCE to the target and most importantly, personal ABILITY. With that in mind, every BG should set personal standards that require shooting under stress and within strict time limits, but these should be realistic standards that are some what immaterial during initial training. The initial emphasis must be placed on accuracy and GUARANTEED HITS. Only with the confidence that comes with repeated center-of-mass hits, can the shooter begin to push the envelope and develop more speed without sacrificing acceptable combat accuracy.

In an actual gunfight, speed will be a natural by-product of fear and adrenaline. The most important consideration for the shooter is the conditioning that will guarantee the first hits, not the fastest misses.

TEAM TRAINING

Once the BG has mastered the skills necessary to be a dependable individual shooter, he must then seek out the opportunity to integrate those skills into more advanced team drills.

The purpose of the team drill is to replicate actual situations that a team of two to six bodyguards may find themselves in with a client. The number of these drills is only limited by the participants' imaginations but should always reflect reality without compromising safety.

The most basic team drill and foundation of all others is the **cover** and **evacuate** drill, which is the immediate response to an attack or gun fire. The BGs closest to the attacker or direction of attack will draw weapons and either cover or engage hostile targets. Simultaneously, those BGs closest to the principal and away from the attack will take physical control of the principal, forcing his head down and evacuating the kill zone.

Federal agent practices vehicle ambush drills.

These drills depend on everyone being on the "same sheet of paper" and knowing their individual roles under a variety of attacks. The simplest way to replicate this on the range is to set up a "crowd" of movable, man-sized, color-coded targets, and then with one BG playing principal, walk the team through the crowd. At any time, an instructor or observer calls a direction and a color, for example, "blue, right!". The team immediately responds to this command by covering that target and moving the principal to a safe area. If the target had a simulated weapon then the nearest BGs could engage the hostile target, taking care not to hit bystander targets or each other.

Although realism is an important aspect of team training, safety is still the single most important consideration. When practicing team cover and contact drills, there is always a potential for cross-fire situations. These must be avoided at all cost by constant re-evaluation of the problem, awareness of the other shooters and the pre-determined decision to cease fire if unsure.

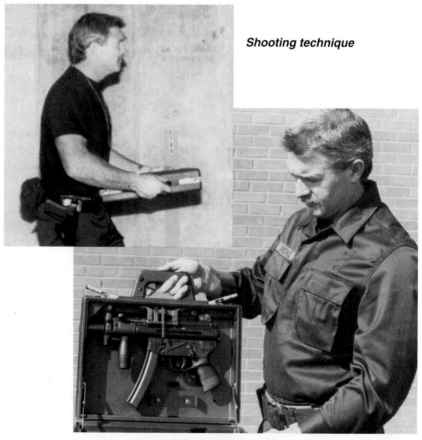

Shooting technique

H&K MP5K in a briefcase

MENTAL PREPARATION

Also known as mind set, mental preparation is an important part of accurate, controlled shooting. Whether in training or on operations, a shooter needs a relaxed, positive mental attitude if he is to function efficiently. Excessive anxiety will adversely affect performance, and unfortunately is a by-product of working high risk protective details where there is no way to predict the time or place of an attack.

During initial combat weapons training, the shooter must be carefully coached and encouraged to get the maximum performance possible. Calm instruction, patience and positive reinforcement will boost the trainees' confidence and produce better results than negative criticism and an overbearing attitude on the part of the instructor.

A dedicated shooter will eventually push himself to greater levels of speed and accuracy, when he comes to realize that this training is for real, and that operationally, his life and that of his team may come to depend on his ability. This is a significant stressor, and one that can have very positive side effects on a motivated individual.

Even in training, in the face of self induced pressure, peer pressure and the need to meet team standards, a shooter can be subjected to a lot of stress. This stress, real or perceived, has a wide variety of effects on different individuals, enhancing performance for some, but causing a drop in performance levels for others. Each shooter must make a conscious effort to channel this stress into a positive force by mentally calming himself and concentrating on the task at hand, prior to engaging in any shooting exercise.

A shooter or trainee that cannot control stress on the range, and is unable to score well because of peer pressure, is a liability in the street. If the minimal pressure of range training stresses an individual, the very real pressures of actual operations may cause that same person to freeze or react illogically.

When confronted by the prospect of being deployed on a high risk detail, new BGs will often ask, "What is the difference between training and the real thing?" The answer is "None, but in the real world you just don't get any more mistakes."

If the training drills were based on reality, then the operation should be just like one more go round on the range. Granted, the location and targets may be different, but the team drills and shooting are the same. Often times, operations are far less complex than some of the hellish training exercises dreamed-up by fiendish instructors.

The BG must also come to grips with the thought and reality of possibly having to terminate another human being's life. Police officers are taught to "shoot to stop", or "to incapacitate", or "neutralize the threat", but these are just polite euphemisms. It all comes down to the same thing—when the shooting begins, some one is going to get hit, with a high probability of death. So what should be the thought process for an individual first confronted with this eventuality?

Understanding the possibility of gunplay before the BG takes a job, requires that he have a certain level of confidence in his ability to handle it. Not the cocky "I am Superman" attitude, but a more mature confidence brought about by a realization that he is a trained, well equipped individual.

Now to the probability of killing. It is just a job. He should be trained for it, equipped for it, and hopefully psychologically capable of it. He is not going in with the sole purpose of killing. He has dedicated himself to protecting the lives of others and will do whatever is necessary to ensure their safety. When threatened, and deadly force is warranted, he shoots TO STOP—to stop whatever action threatens the lives or safety of the protectee(s).

The action of shooting (killing), becomes a conditioned response to an external stimuli, that may not require conscious decision making. The shooter should have certain ingrained responses conditioned into his psycho-motor memory as a result of realistic training. When confronted with an armed target, he shoots. When confronted by a surrendering target, he covers but does not shoot. When confronted by an unarmed attacker, he physically blocks the approach. These are conditioned responses brought about by the programming of the brain to stimulate an immediate response (reflex) to a given set of circumstances.

If a shooter does not have a fast, reflexive response to imminent danger, he may react too slow to survive. Conversely, for the BG with a correctly conditioned response, any attacker or gunman that dies has brought it on him or herself. The criminals or terrorists knew the rules. When they made the decision to attack, they took away the bodyguard's options by choosing a path which led directly to their death.

The BG, if carrying a gun, must accept that gun play is a possibility, and if confronted, he is prepared to respond with deadly force. A BG who hopes or expects that it won't happen, will be caught flat-footed when it does. He will have to suddenly overcome the shock of reality, recognize the danger, make a decision to draw, actually draw, align his weapon and make the conscious decision to shoot. By this time the gunman may have already pumped four rounds into him and killed the client.

Mental acceptance of the possibility, and preprogramming for danger, will greatly reduce the shock and reaction time when the inevitable occurs. The BG should never under estimate an adversary or try to predict how a gunman will react to the threat of death or capture.

The ability to function efficiently is hindered by excessive emotion. Unlike a football team that psychs-up for a game in the locker room, the BG must psych himself down prior to going on the street with a client. His actions must always be calm, calculated and precise.

Another mental aspect of BG work and close quarter shooting is FEAR. Fear that we may be killed or injured; fear that we may make an error that costs our partner his life; fear that we may shoot an unarmed man; fear that we may hit a hostage. All are very real fears that have been experienced by most professionals at some time in their careers.

The man that shows no fear is deluding himself and the man that has no fear is probably psychotic, and has no place working as a BG or on a DVP team.

Fear is a healthy reaction to a dangerous situation. It may advise caution or give us the strength and speed to overcome the danger. This is known as "the **fight** or **flight**" syndrome. When harnessed correctly and combined with mature judgment, fear may well be the deciding factor in a confrontation. The shooter will experience heightened awareness, increased speed, increased strength and an increased ability to absorb pain and injury.

Again, the BG must recognize fear for what it is, and when present, consciously calm and reassure himself, mentally rehearsing the plan and reviewing options. This problem solving mode will distract the mind from the initial fear.

Time on the job coupled with experience on the live-fire shooting range, confronted with numerous realistic shoot / no-shoot scenarios, will better prepare the BG for the split second decisions he may be required to make. Reality in training builds confidence. Confidence can turn stress and fear into positive forces.

Cover and evacuate drills are the foundation of all team live-fire training.

GUNFIGHT SURVIVAL

The subject of gunfighting and gunfight survival, although interesting, is a broad subject that could fill several books. Keeping in mind the small role that guns play in BG work, an in-depth study is beyond the scope of this book. However, the subject does warrant brief discussion. The following tips will help the BG better understand just what it takes to survive a gunfight.

Will to Survive—First and foremost, when confronted, fired upon or even hit, the BG must hold onto life with a fierce determination and fight back with controlled aggression. It is OK to feel anger towards an attacker.

Physical Conditioning—All too often BGs, like police officers, let their personal fitness deteriorate after leaving the academy. Good physical condition will increase speed and strength; improve reflexes and the ability to handle stress; reduce recovery time if injured; and greatly improve survivability.

Firearms Proficiency—A fast draw and fast first shot is absolutely useless if one does not hit the intended target. No one was ever stopped by a fast moving noise. Accuracy of fire will also eliminate misses that may result in the accidental shooting of bystanders.

Mental Preparation—The more cerebral side of gunfighting includes fight anticipation, recognition of danger areas, mental rehearsal of reaction drills and general alertness. Also the acceptance that it actually could happen and at any time.

Quick Aggressive Response—Gunfights are not the place for indecision or timidity. The BG must move quickly, make use of cover and return fire accurately. Fight for life!

Lastly, it is important to understand that the BG, by his very nature and suitability to BG work, is a somewhat caring and protective individual. He is therefore handicapped in a confrontation with a determined killer whose criminal survival instinct is to fight without thought or compassion and to react without logic. This gives the criminal an obvious advantage over the law abiding individual who is less comfortable with violence. However, this can be overcome with adequate, realistic training, superior weapons skills and a calm, aggressive, professional response.

14

DRIVER TRAINING

Even though it is difficult to get accurate statistics on past attacks on VIPs or corporate executives, one reliable source indicates that approximately 95% of kidnappings occur between the home and the office. This makes driving and vehicular security one of the primary areas of concern for the bodyguard.

Some of the more common driving related duties required of a BG could be as simple as driving a client around town for shopping or meetings; making an airport pick-up of a visiting VIP; driving a chase car as the CEO travels to and from his corporate office; or setting up the security and motorcade for a high profile delegation .

The BG's first responsibility for any movement is the security of the principal and not necessarily the actual driving. However, this brings up the point of whether the BG should actually be doing the driving, or whether this only hinders his ability to function as a bodyguard. Many organizations try to save money by training their drivers to be bodyguards or their bodyguards to be drivers, but this is not smart management.

Firstly, an individual who takes a position as a chauffeur or has worked all his life as a professional driver probably does not have the aptitude for BG work. Nor can he receive adequate BG training in a few days or even a few weeks. Similarly, a professional bodyguard who is well trained and physically active will become bored and restless with just driving. Driving also puts the BG in the position where he must constantly deal with the car, traffic and parking, detracting from his ability to concentrate on early threat recognition and protection of the principal.

That said, in the real world of compromise, the BG will at some time in his career be required to drive. Some more often than others. Considering this, both bodyguards and chauffeurs will benefit from high performance driver training. The bodyguard to gain skill and better understand vehicular ambush scenarios, and the chauffeur to recognize the signs of an ambush and to have the opportunity to drive more aggressively under controlled conditions.

Driver training for bodyguards is more than just being able to drive fast or execute tire-smoking bootleg or J turns. It includes learning about vehicle selection, essential modifications, handling characteristics of limos and armored vehicles, searching for explosive devices and car bombs, road side repairs and maintenance, and most importantly, developing the ability to drive SMOOTHLY and SAFELY.

One of the essential prerequisites of a professional bodyguard is not a file full of certificates from high performance driving schools or a lead foot, but a relatively clean driving record. So much so that a clean driving record is almost a necessity with many corporations. Corporate administrators and insurance brokers will require that employees with poor driving records, accidents or too many traffic violations, be dropped from corporate policies and not permitted to drive company vehicles. This is much the same as police departments and federal agencies who now refuse to hire or even consider applicants with too many traffic violations or accidents.

On a more personal level, clients will not have much faith in a BG's driving ability if he has a bad driving record, especially if that same BG is responsible for driving their kids to and from school. Clients will be further unimpressed with a driver who is constantly on and off the gas, changing lanes, diving on the brakes or generally giving them an uncomfortable ride. Even though a BG may not aspire to be a chauffeur, he or she should still exhibit all the skills of a professional driver.

Driver training for a BG can be broken into three categories: **defensive** driving, **evasive** driving and **offensive** driving. Defensive driving covers the skills necessary to avoid accidents and become a good, safe, considerate driver. This is not unlike the training received in high school drivers' ed class and what may be State required to get a traffic violation off of one's record. Having defensive driving skills has application to the bodyguard in that no one wants to be damaging their own car or that of the client unnecessarily. In addition, any minor fender-bender while working will require that the BG stop to exchange information with the other driver, causing unnecessary exposure, delay and inconveniencing the client.

Evasive driving is best learned at a high performance driving school and covers the more aggressive maneuvers necessary to evade ambush. Offensive driving, even more aggressive than evasive driving, is also taught in some schools and involves the use of the motor vehicle to ram or destabilize an attacker's vehicle.

DRIVING SCHOOLS

Like firearms training, high performance evasive driver training is one of those skills that is essential to have but hopefully will never be needed. There is however, a much greater chance of putting one's driving skills to the test in BG work than in testing one's abilities in a gunfight.

Bob Bondurant, Tony Scotti and BSR run some of the best known schools in the United States and have also taken their courses on the road to several other countries. These schools offer a variety of standard and custom programs at their base facilities or through their mobile training teams.

Driving schools that cater to the law enforcement and security industry should offer four types of training:

1. Lecture and classroom programs covering most aspects of executive protection as it relates to vehicles, attack recognition, danger zones, ambush theory, car bomb recognition and counter surveillance.
2. Lecture and classroom discussions on actual driving dynamics covering emergency control, weight transfer, brakes and braking, tires and traction, speed and road use theory.
3. Hands-on driving course designed specifically to improve the drivers high performance driving skills, track use, braking and shifting, cornering, apexing, and race strategy.
4. Evasive driver training for chauffeurs and bodyguards where the participant gets actual wheel time in high speed driving, braking and turning, bootleg turns, J turns, slides, skid pans, night driving and reactions to vehicle ambush.

On many executive protection programs, the student begins with basic driving theory and practice, then moves up to counter terrorist theory and finally actual evasive driving. These courses can vary from two to five days in length with additional advanced programs available on motorcades, advance work, pursuit driving, surveillance and counter surveillance and instructor level training.

Now a word of warning. There are schools that offer all of the above but do not even come close to meeting the requirements of the bodyguard.

Author's Note: In 1988 I attended a four day course advertised as an intense Anti Terrorist Executive Protection Driver Program. The course was neither "intense" nor related to "terrorism" or "executive protection". What I ended up in was a four day high performance driving school where not one of the instructors had any knowledge or experience in tactics, counter terrorism or security work. In fact the class was never even told the instructors' driving credentials, most dressing more like mechanics than professional drivers or instructors.

These schools are not cheap, running around two thousand dollars for four days, not including travel or accommodation costs. For a BG on a career track, it is important to pick a reputable program since the name of the school on the graduation certificate is almost as important as the training.

Firstly, a novice driver should be suspicious of any school that does not have some form of race track as a base of operation. Secondly, be wary of any school that requires the participants to bring their own car or a rental car. Finally, check the credentials of the instructors, not just in driving but also in executive protection and counter terrorism. It is not enough that the owner of the school has a good reputation since, all too often, the owner does not even teach the program. If possible, talk to recent graduates to see if they are satisfied customers.

Ramming is an advanced maneuver that should only be attempted when there is no other option. Photo: Direct Action

Bondurant instructor's modified Ford Thunderbird

Professionally setup training cars

An armored limo handles very differently to a normal sedan so the BG should try to get in some track time in this type of vehicle.

VEHICLE SELECTION & MODIFICATION

A lowly bodyguard may not have much input into the selection of a client's car, but if his opinion is asked, he should be able to make an intelligent choice of vehicle. There is no doubt that some vehicles are more suited to executive protection than others, depending on the location and nature of the assignment.

If the threat is real, it is important that the car blend into the local scenery and not draw unwanted attention. This is especially true in foreign countries. In most cases a good solid four door sedan with a powerful engine is the ideal. Obviously this eliminates small sports cars with convertible tops and minimum ground clearance since they afford almost no protection to the driver.

The color of the car should be non-descript, definitely not bright yellow or red and probably not black. In most countries a black sedan or limo is an indication of a government official or someone of importance.

The factory installed options should include:

• The most powerful engine available
• A high performance handling package with heavy-duty suspension
• Steel-belted radial tires
• Power disc brakes and/or ABS braking
• Power steering for ease of handling
• Air-conditioning so that windows can be kept rolled up
• Dual external rear-view mirrors with internal power adjustment
• Power window and door locks
• Trunk and hood locks to prevent theft and placement of bombs
• A locking gas cap to prevent tampering
• Rear window defrost for counter surveillance
• An anti-disturbance alarm system that works off both voltage drop and vibration.

In addition, the following options could be added:

• Heavy duty bumpers or grill guard
• Additional high intensity headlights
• Radio and cellular telephone communications
• High intensity reversing lights for emergency maneuvers
• Under grill mounted PA system and/or flashing lights
• A bolt through the exhaust pipe to prevent tampering

Two other electronic features that have merit are:

• A remote radio-controlled ignition start which can prove the safest way to check for bombs wired to the ignition system.
• A silent pager type alarm system that will notify the driver if someone attempts to tamper with an unattended car.

The rest is common sense. The driver should carry a spare set of car keys at all times; there should be an emergency road kit with spare tire and tools in the trunk; and a trauma kit in the passenger compartment for any immediate injuries resulting from an attack.

Where conditions dictate snow tires should be added or a four wheel drive vehicle may be more appropriate. In fact, many security teams opt for 4WD trucks like the Range Rover, Chevy Suburban, Ford Bronco and Chevy Blazer for both escort and principal vehicles. Their higher driving position and ample interior room, combined with increased ground clearance, powerful engines and the 4WD option make them an excellent choice for most operations. They do however suffer in the high speed handling department, being somewhat top heavy and not designed for fast cornering.

Note extended running boards for Secret Service protection detail.
(Photo: Secret Service)

ARMORED VEHICLES

The concept of a bulletproof car would seem very attractive to most people, especially bodyguards and individuals who find themselves in the high risk bracket. Unfortunately, there is no such thing as bulletproof, only bullet resistant. The laminated bullet resistant glass being the most vulnerable area will eventually be defeated by more powerful rounds or multiple impacts in the same area.

In addition, armoring a vehicle is an expensive undertaking that adds considerable weight to a vehicle. A luxury sedan, totally armored to an acceptable standard, will run seventy to one hundred and twenty thousand dollars on top of the cost of the car. To just armor the passenger compartment to a medium threat level will cost thirty to forty thousand dollars installed on the client's car.

The armor in a full-sized sedan package can add about 800 to 1000 pounds to the weight of the car, adversely affecting handling. This can only be off-set by a more powerful engine and heavy duty suspension but all to no avail if the added weight is not distributed correctly.

Vehicles can be designed and built for various threat levels, all depending on the thickness, number layers and weight of the armoring material. Different companies use different materials or combinations of materials in their vehicles, but the most common ones are steel, aluminum, aluminum ceramic, ballistic nylon, reinforced fiberglass, DuPont Kevlar, Spectra Shield and a combination of glass and transparent polycarbonate laminates for the windshields.

The challenge in the ballistic armor business is to develop materials that weigh less but stop more. Kevlar and Spectra being the lightest but most expensive. For the BG, the challenge is to match the type of armor and level of protection to the client's anticipated needs.

Underwriter's Laboratory has established basic standards for evaluating the bullet resistance of various materials. In addition, manufacturers and installers of bullet resistant material will issue guidelines as to what specific calibers, projectiles and muzzle velocities have been tested on their products. The following should be used only as a general guide and not as a substitute for further testing.

Level I Is intended to defeat smaller handgun rounds but is considered too light even for personal body armor.

Level II Defeats most medium power small arms in the 9mm to .357 Magnum range, ie 124 grain 9mm FMJ at 1120'/sec.

Level III Defeats most powerful small arms in the .44 Magnum range, up to an including 12 gauge solid slugs and .30 Carbine 110 grain ball at 1900'/sec.

Level IV Is designed to defeat most high powered rifles in the .223 to 7.62 NATO range, up to and including 30-06 220 grain SP at 2410'/sec. Some will stop 30-06 M2 166 grain AP at 2850'/sec

Level V Should stop .50 AP M2 708 grain at 2400'/sec

Most manufacturers of armored vehicles have their own threat level data based on the type of bullet resistant material utilized and the method of installation. This data is usually listed in their brochures but can be verified on test samples if necessary.

The higher the threat level that a vehicle is designed to defeat, the greater the weight and cost. As an example from one company that utilizes Spectra and ceramic compounds, Level III material weighs 4.3 pounds per square foot while level IV goes 8.4 pounds and Level V weighs in at 11.9 pounds per square foot.

For the client or corporation who does not consider themselves a target for assassination and does not wish to invest in a fully armored car, there are several more cost effective options. Some celebrities and wealthy individuals, more concerned with random street crime than a terrorist attack or kidnapping, have taken to armoring just the passenger compartments of their cars against small caliber weapons up to and including nine millimeter. This modification to a BMW or Mercedes will cost around thirty to forty thousand dollars and add less than a couple of hundred pounds to the car.

Since most random attacks target the windows, or the occupant through the windows, even up-grading the windshield and side windows with a polycarbonate/glass laminate would greatly improve survivability. Another alternative, if the client drives him or herself, is to simply armor the drivers side door and window. The door will be the attackers' primary concern in trying to get to the driver and should delay the attacker long enough for the client to start the car and drive off. Or at least delay the attack long enough for the BG in the chase car to react.

Another negative feature of armored cars, apart from weight and handling, is the quality of the glass work. To be effective, glass must be bonded to a polycarbonate and manufactured thick enough to stop bullets. The flat laminates that are cheaper and easier to manufacture have applications in banks and armored trucks, but they are not suited to a sedan that must appear to be unmodified.

Armored sedans require the use of curved laminates but they are more difficult and more expensive to manufacture, and if not done perfectly, will have optical distortions in the glass. These flaws can be a safety problem, but more importantly, they can give the driver blinding headaches as his eyes try to compensate for the distortions. Any indication of optical distortion or delamination will require that the glass be replaced before the car goes into service.

In addition to the problems one can have with the windshield, the side windows may be so thick that they cannot role up or down. The easiest and least expensive solution is to simply install fixed windows, but one must then consider what happens at toll gates and private parking entrances that are card controlled. The driver will be unable to roll down the window to pay the toll, take a ticket or insert a coded card.

Whether the windows roll up and down or not, in most cases the windows will be kept up to prevent anything being tossed into the car. This requires that the car be equipped with a reliable air-conditioner and possibly a second heavy duty battery to supply power even when the car is parked. No principal will want to get into a hot car that has been sitting in the sun for any length of time.

Author's Note: In the early eighties the security officer, a navy Seal Commander, at the US embassy in San Salvador, found his car's air-conditioner to be inoperable. To be able to wind the window down and get some fresh air, he had to remove the ballistic laminate attached to the inside of the car door. Sure enough on the second day, picking his girlfriend up from the university, he was shot and killed through the open window by local terrorists.

Apart from the normal maintenance associated with any car, armored cars have some unique requirements. A new vehicle that was not assembled with adequate quality control can arrive with several noticeable defects, or the car may be fine at the time of delivery but develops problems with time and use.

The first noticeable problem may be noises or rattles in the coach work. This is an indicator of ballistic panels that were either incorrectly installed or have vibrated loose.

Another problem can occur with the way the doors hang or close. Because of the added weight in the doors from both the glass and the hidden panels, the hinges will wear, weaken or loosen prematurely. This is a design or installation problem that needs to be fixed at the first signs of trouble.

Because of the overall weight of the car, the engine, suspension, transmission and brakes are all subjected to additional loads and wear. This may also cause the car to overheat. The tires must also be checked to see if they are rated to take the additional weight at the prescribed pressure. This is written on the tire but does require that the driver know the car's weight. No more than fifty-five percent of that weight should be on the front wheels in a standard front engine car with rear wheel drive.

Lastly, armored cars do not hold their resale value very well. Since most wealthy people prefer to drive new cars, they are not going to invest in a two or three year old model, even if it is already armored. To compound the problem, these heavy cars wear and age much faster than regular cars. So much so that it is often possible to pick up a used armored vehicle cheaper than a comparable model of the same year without armor.

In conclusion, it is better to be invisible than bulletproof, since we have already established that there is no such thing as totally bulletproof when it comes to cars. An armored sedan only has value if no one knows that it has been modified. If the bad guys know a car is bullet resistant, they will only wait for an opportunity when the client is out of the car to strike. Even with an armored vehicle, one should still practice good counter surveillance, travel at irregular times, and alternate routes between frequently visited locations, such as home and work. "If they can't find you—they can't get you."

Mercedes 560 SEC with armored passenger compartment

The first step in armoring a vehicle is to completely strip the interior and glass

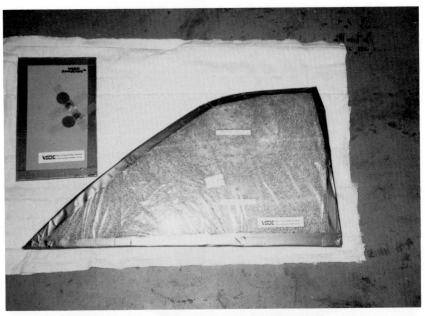

Random armor panels tested by actually shooting them

It is important that when the car is reassembled one cannot tell that it has been modified.

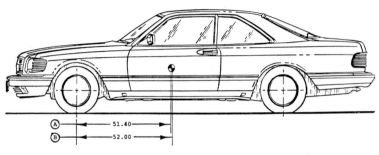

MERCEDES-BENZ
560SEC

CURB WEIGHT AND LONGITUDINAL CENTER-OF-GRAVITY SUMMARY

Gross Axle Weight	Front	Rear	Gross Vehicle Weight
GAWR (Lbs)	2260	2435	4695 (GVWR)
(A) As received	2120	1800	3920
(B) Armor conversion	2130	1840	3970

(A) ◄—— 51.40 ——►

(B) ◄—— 52.00 ——►

MODEL: 126C

VSDC VEHICLE SYSTEMS DEVELOPMENT CORPORATION
P.O. BOX 366-UPLAND, CALIFORNIA 91785-U.S.A.

Change in weight and balance chart for an armored 560 SEC

GSG-9 modified 4WD with ballistic windshield and gun port
(Photo: H&K)

DRIVING TECHNIQUES

Just as the old saying of "An ounce of prevention is worth a pound of cure" applies to first aid, it also applies to BG driving. If a BG driver can recognize danger zones and potential ambush locations, and avoid them, he will not have to risk the principal's and his own life in a wild evasive maneuver. Only when the ambush comes by surprise will the driver have to react with all his training. Even then, it is hoped that there was some early recognition that gave the BG time to react and limit damage or injury.

BG driving begins with common sense procedures like wearing seat belts, keeping doors locked and windows rolled up, staying alert, watching the traffic flow ahead, knowing local bottle necks and avoiding the rougher parts of town.

The driving skill that the BG must master is more closely associated with precision driving than evasive driving. The driver must know exactly where his wheels are on the road and develop a good sense of the size of his vehicle as it moves through traffic and obstacles. The driver must also become intimately familiar with the acceleration, braking, steering control and turning radius of his car. This will allow him to maneuver and react with minimal hesitation and maximum control at all times.

The more advanced mechanics of performance driving like the applications of weight transfer, trail braking, when to down shift, late apexing in corners and emergency stops will all be learned in the driving school and practiced under controlled conditions.

An important skill that must be mastered by the BG is high speed reversing. An emergency stop and aggressive reversing is a fundamental skill and simple tactic necessary for escaping a road block ambush. The difficulty in maintaining control in this exercise is deceptive, illustrated by the fact that it is much easier to flip a car in reverse than when moving forward.

Once reversing has been mastered, the BG can try a J Turn or reverse 180. This requires the driver to get the car moving in reverse and then when at speed, turning the wheel sharply. This will cause the car to spin 180 degrees and as the front of the car is coming around, shift into drive and accelerate out of the ambush.

The other popular maneuver is the Bootleg Turn used when driving forward and wishing to exit in the opposite direction. While moving forward at speed, the driver turns the wheel and sharply stamps on the emergency brake. This will cause the back to slide around until the car has done a forward 180. Barring any unforeseen circumstances, the driver then simply releases the brake and accelerates away in the opposite direction.

These maneuvers should not be attempted without professional instruction and supervision. If the conditions are not right or the car not set-up correctly, it is all too easy to roll a tire right off of the wheel rim and flip the car. Even without flipping, any loss of control could endanger life or property.

1. Reverse quickly

2. Turn wheel sharply

**3. Turn into slide,
   shift into drive**

4. Accelerate away

"J" turn—reverse 180°

3. Release brake and accelerate away

2. Let the rear end slide around

1. Turn wheel sharply, stamp on emergency brake

Bootlegger's turn—forward 180°

*Scene of the kidnapping and subsequent murder of
former Premier Aldo Moro, Rome, 1978*

COUNTER AMBUSH DRILLS

The primary reason for high performance evasive driver training is to arm the driver with the necessary reflexes and skills to exit the kill zone of an ambush.

The first counter ambush principle is **avoidance.** By studying past ambushes, attacks and kidnappings, the BG should learn to recognize the danger zones and potential ambush sites and make every effort to avoid them.

If an ambush cannot be avoided, the driver should stop prior to the road block, reverse and exit the kill zone. If he has room, he may not need to stop and simply perform a forward 180 bootleg turn. If there is no actual road block and no reason to slow down the driver may choose to just punch it and accelerate through the ambush. The down side of this maneuver is that his path of escape takes him directly through the kill zone. The area of greatest danger.

Just because the car comes under weapons fire is no reason to change tactics or slow down. A car with flat tires is still driveable and even with a bullet riddled radiator, a car can run up to ten miles before totally overheating.

Most armored cars and limos will have special run-flat tires, armored battery box, and explosion proof gas tanks. Some are even equipped with armored radiators, although these tend to cause overheating, and smoke or gas ejection ports to confuse the enemy and cover the escape.

If blocked by another vehicle, the driver may elect to ram his way out of the kill zone. If this option is taken, it is best to ram the trunk end of the blocking vehicle, making it rotate around the heavier engine end of the car.

Only at a last resort, if the principal vehicle is stopped and disabled should the BG consider shooting their way out. If this option is taken, it is best to exit the car from the side opposite the ambush and make maximum use of the engine compartment for cover. It is also recommended that the driver or principal get on the cellular phone or radio at the first indications of trouble to notify authorities and mobilize assistance.

See Chapter 17 for information related to car bombs and Chapter 22 for additional tips on driving on the job.

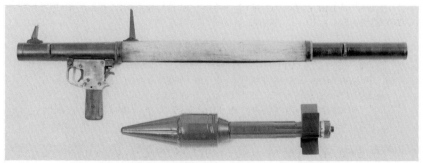

RPG-2 Anti-tank launcher and rocket-propelled grenade

15

KNOWING YOUR ENEMY

Just as opposing football teams study each other throughout the season, not just the week before the big game, the professional BG must identify and study a variety of potential adversaries, even if they do not pose an immediate threat to a specific client. Having a working knowledge of the methods and motivations for the various terrorists, criminals and crazies that the BG is most likely to encounter, will better prepare him for the tasks of first identifying and then formulating counter-measures, should the need arise. This endeavor should not be confused with threat assessment.

Threat assessment, covered in more detail in Chapter 16, is a detailed study of the specific threats to a client, corporation or government entity. Knowing one's enemies is more of a broad based overview of the unsavory players with whom we share this planet. The same individuals that the news media tend to lionize, but who street cops lump together as "scum-bags". For the BG, they cannot be lumped together and must be studied as sub-groups with specific commonalities.

The concept of studying one's enemy is not a new one. It was the Chinese philosopher Sun Tzu's book, The Art of War, written 500 BC, that recorded the importance of not only knowing one's own strengths and weaknesses, but knowing those of your enemies.

> "Know the enemy and know yourself; in a hundred battles you will never be in peril.
> When you are ignorant of the enemy but know yourself, your chances of winning or losing are equal.
> If ignorant both of your enemy and of yourself, you are certain in every battle to be in peril."

Although many novice bodyguards harbor romantic visions of themselves gunning down ski-masked international terrorists on the streets of

Rome, the most frequent threat will usually come from disgruntled ex-employees, jealous family members, common criminals and obsessive fans. This is not to say that terrorism is not a real problem for those traveling in Europe, South America, Asia, Pacific Rim countries or the Middle East. It must simply be kept in perspective.

A ski-masked terrorist with a gun in his hand is not difficult to identify, the threat that he poses being quite obvious. However, the threat from the "trusted inner circle" of friends, family and associates is more insidious, harder to identify and more difficult to protect against.

The following groups are covered in the order that a bodyguard is most likely to encounter them. Although not all are perceived to outwardly exhibit the same propensity for violence, all carry the potential to cause harm to a principal.

FAMILY MEMBERS

Much as one would like to assume that the threat always come from without, time and statistics have proven that the assailant is often known to a victim. A large percentage of violent crime involves crimes of passion or revenge, perpetrated by enraged spouses or jilted lovers. Theft and embezzlement are also most easily accomplished from within an organization by key management personnel and trusted employees.

A sudden change in wealth or social status can create jealousy and envy with those less successful. So it is only logical that the protection professional look first to those who would most benefit by the demise or disappearance of the principal, usually a family member, ex-wife or husband or business partner. The Menendez brothers killing of their own parents in Beverly Hills being a good example of this.

It is not uncommon for a BG to be retained to protect a female celebrity going through an ugly divorce, especially if there is a prior history of spousal abuse by a husband prone to violent rages. Similarly, a principal may fear attacks on his new wife or girlfriend from her ex-lover or a spurned ex-wife.

In the late seventies and early eighties, the Red Brigade turned kidnapping for ransom into not only a method of intimidation but also a very lucrative business. However, terrorists are not the biggest perpetrators of kidnapping, so in dealing with this type of threat, the bodyguard must first look to the obvious. Most kidnappings are of children and the direct result of a custody dispute between estranged couples. This is a particularly serious problem when one party, usually the father, is from another country. However, the guilty party may still try to shift blame to some nebulous terrorist or criminal group.

EMPLOYEES & ASSOCIATES

There are numerous reasons for an employee or ex-employee to harbor ill feeling toward an employer, company owner or CEO. This applies to both corporate employees and domestic staff, and is often a direct result of termination.

The dissatisfied or disloyal employee may have no problem skimming funds, falsifying expense accounts or ripping off valuables from the household. That same disloyalty can result in disclosure of confidential information, the sale of high technology, the destruction of computer records, industrial sabotage or even direct action against the owner. The ex-employee, laid off several months earlier in a reorganization, or for drug abuse or sexual harassment, may come back to vent his or her anger on the President or CEO. This character may have lost his job two or three years prior, in a hostile take-over, and since then been unable to find a comparable job. Unemployment resulting in depression, which then leads to drinking, the break-up of a marriage, foreclosure on a mortgage, eviction, etc—all fueling the fire of frustration and anger.

From this low point, the disgruntled ex-employee, finding it difficult to direct hatred towards a large, impersonal organization, will redirect his or her hostility toward a high profile representative of their frustration. Usually the owner, CEO or a managing director.

The pre-indicators of this type of threat are: an angry outburst at the time of dismissal; pleading or threatening letters on file; interviews with the press expressing anger and dissatisfaction; appearance of the suspect on picket lines; anonymous letters from the suspect's postal zip code; or threatening phone calls identified through Caller ID technology.

The same is true in the political arena where careers can be made or lost at the stroke of a pen. In addition, politicians are notorious for there dirty in-fighting and willingness to destroy an opponent's reputation or career. In some countries, this type of political rivalry can escalate to open hostility, civil unrest and ultimately, kidnapping and assassination. The BG working the political circuit must always consider the fact that for every party in power, there are others on the outside looking in, some with evil intent.

The threats from within an organization will be addressed more in the chapter on threat assessment. However, the key to the puzzle will always be, "Who has the most to lose or to gain?" Law enforcement investigators have long known that money is the root of most evil, so it is no coincident that most FBI agents have degrees in law and/or accounting. They have learned from experience that to solve a crime, first study the business records and accounting files of the victim. Put more simply, "follow the money—find the culprit".

CRIMINALS

The rich and famous have historically been the targets of not only free-loaders, over zealous fans and opportunists but also the common criminal. Thieves, burglars, purse snatchers, carjackers and muggers know that the best return for their effort will come from affluent neighborhoods, nice houses and wealthy individuals. Assaulting the rich carries the same punishment as assaulting the poor, and the value of the take has little impact on the penalty for the crime. Any criminal also knows that expensive name-brand items are easier to sell than generic junk—

the Rolex Bandits who preyed on Beverly Hills in the early nineties best typifying that mentality.

The more material possessions that people amass, the more they become targets for the criminal element. With increased crime, comes increased fear and paranoia in the wealthy communities. This was never more evident than during the LA riots of 1992 when the Beverly Hills elite all but barricaded themselves in their residential enclaves.

The prime motivation for most criminal activity directed against the wealthy is money. The obvious being the simple street hood intent on robbery. He will generally be young, aggressive and predatory in nature. He will stake out a location such as a shopping center or parking lot in an affluent part of town and proceed to profile potential victims.

The robbery will occur in a parking lot, public bathroom, secluded doorway, or at a traffic intersection. He may choose to jump in the car with the victim, follow her home, or at least follow to a quiet residential side street. Out of public view, violence and intimidation become his tools.

The perpetrators of this type of crime probably have a long list of priors, often work with a partner, and come from "the wrong side of the tracks". In Los Angeles, as in many large cities, there is often also some gang affiliation.

Even though comfortable with violence, these individuals are looking for an easy target. A woman alone, with nice clothes, expensive jewelry and a convertible Mercedes would rate high on their list. Fortunately, these scum will be deterred by the mere presence of a bodyguard or the appearance of any security awareness on the part of the intended victim. They are cowardly scavengers and not looking for a challenge. However, armed robbery does carry some status with the other inmates in the prison system, so the prospect of merely getting caught is not in itself necessarily a deterrent—a bodyguard is.

The next type of criminal is the burglar. Again, if one is in the breaking and entering business, it is only logical to hit houses that contain money or objects of value. The B&E types are generally not the cat-like professionals seen on television circumventing elaborate alarm systems, picking locks, or blowing safes.

The more common MO is over the back fence, jimmy a window (or find an unlocked door), hit the master bedroom for cash, jewelry or a VCR and scamper. These individuals work the same hours as most people: hitting houses between 8am and 11am, taking a break for lunch less the owners come home, and then working again from 2pm to 4pm. The only time they work at night is when they know the owner is out of town or the house is unoccupied.

Just another example of the vermin who are too lazy to work and choose to prey on the wealthy. Unfortunately, the affluent make their job all too easy by leaving doors and windows unlocked, failing to close gates or garages, general lack of awareness, and the biggest sin of all, failing to believe that it could happen to them.

Even minimal fencing, dogs or alarm systems will deter this individual. It is not necessary to turn a house into Fort Knox but simply make it a harder target than another house on the same block. The easiest target will be the one hit.

If a burglar does fit the popular Hollywood profile of a sophisticated jewel thief, he will more than likely save his talents for a more rewarding target like an inner city gold exchange or gem merchant. Either way, he is not interested in confrontation or violence. He simply wants in and out with the least fuss, and fence the goods.

The next level of escalation is the direct or indirect threat of physical violence for the purpose of intimidation. It is not unheard of for one party to hire thugs to threaten another in the world of high finance, construction, politics and even entertainment—especially when lucrative contracts may be at stake.

It is the thug or attacker who is the immediate threat and again, his motivation is money. Someone is paying for this "service". The attacker will want to select a time and a place where there are no witnesses, no unwanted intrusions and no assistance available to the intended victim.

Not wanting to get caught or identified, any appearance of a bodyguard or security will deter the confrontation. However, since this may be a violent and motivated individual, willing to stake out a target for several days, there can be no break in the security coverage that would provide an opportunity for the attack. The advantage that the intended victim has is one of early warning. There is usually a request, then a demand, followed by a threat of violence for non-compliance, before the actual attack.

From intimidation the level escalates to kidnapping. Not the domestic type found in custody disputes, but kidnapping for ransom, possibly of the principal but more likely a family member.

A kidnapping serves one of two purposes—coercion or money. For either reason, kidnappings are quite complicated capers since, although quite easy to snatch a victim, it is more difficult to make the exchange for the money. Many kidnappers do not have the intelligence or sophistication to orchestrate a successful exchange, as seen in the 1981 kidnapping of General Dozier by Italian Red Brigade. After 42 days of captivity, the General was successfully rescued, fortunately before the kidnappers became too frustrated and killed him.

Apart from the difficulty involved in executing "the back end" of a kidnapping, the kidnappers also risk long term exposure to the kidnap victim and the potential for future identification.

As stated earlier, the principal is not always the victim. The primary reason for not kidnapping the actual principal being that he is the individual most capable of responding to demands or coming up with the ransom. Unless some prior arrangement has been made, like kidnap insurance, no one else in his family or organization may have access to the necessary funds. Better to kidnap a loved one of a wealthy man (the wife not always being the best choice) so that the principal is free to raise the ransom and negotiate the release.

From kidnapping, the criminal graduates to murder for hire. The shady contract where an individual is simply paid to kill another. Again, one must look to the money, knowing that the killer is being paid by someone, and that person stands to gain something from such a radical and risky action.

It should come as no surprise that very few contracted killers ever succeed. Many of the clowns that offer their services in this area are not rocket scientists. Some even advertise their availability in mercenary magazines. "Merc for hire—Anything, Anywhere, Anytime" or "Ex-Special Forces—Dirty jobs done dirt cheap". These are the same yo-yos that placed a grenade under one person's car but forgot to pull the pin; then in frustration, tried to shoot the intended victim but missed the mark completely.

Further contributing to the potential for failure is the fact that the individual putting up the money for the hit is also probably an amateur in such things. Most contract killings, outside of the mob and the drug cartels, are a one time deal between an individual with little experience in this dark world, and some wanna-be mercenary who will do anything for money. Fortunately, professional hit men are rare and are even harder to find, so the amateurish jobs are usually bungled.

For a case study in "amateurs at play", look at the comedy of errors that made up the attack on Olympic skater Nancy Kerrigan by her competitor's so called bodyguard and boyfriend. *NOTE: My sympathy to Nancy, but if brains were dynamite, her assailants wouldn't have enough to blow their noses. As for Tanya's bodyguard, his only value would have been be as a large slow moving barricade. Another case study of the bozos often attracted to the personal protection industry.*

The key problem with most attempted "hits" is that the assailant's first concerns are escape and self preservation, not success. This, coupled with inexperience, lack of training and poor planning sets the stage for failure. What usually happens, after a good dose of liquid courage and a predictably bungled attempt, is that both parties get nervous, lose heart and give up. Or are apprehended during a second, equally amateurish effort.

This is not to say that there are not a few competent, experienced professionals out there, but as stated earlier, they are expensive and hard to find.

All in all, it is not necessary for the BG to study individual criminal profiles, but more criminal methodology in general so as to be able to pre-empt any attempts. The key commonality is financial gain. Criminals are not looking for a challenge, they are easily deterred and, unlike a terrorist, are not willing to give up their lives or freedom for a few bucks.

One sub-category of criminal that does not fall into the above groups and can be a little more dangerous is the dope fiend. The heroin or crack addict in need of a fix will rob or burglarize for money or stalk doctors and pharmacists who have access to prescription drugs. Either way, this individual is particularly dangerous since he is already strung out and probably not thinking logically. His propensity for violence is directly proportionate to his need for drugs, or money to buy drugs. He may not be deterred by a security system but he can be physically stopped by a competent bodyguard (and a few well placed hollow-points if necessary).

CRAZIES & STALKERS

The obsessed fan or psychopath is by far the biggest area of concern for bodyguards working the entertainment industry. In fact, anyone in the spotlight of public attention such as politicians, religious leaders and even sports personalities will attract their share of crank mail, weird calls and the occasional stalker.

Stalking is not a new problem but it is only in recent years that is has been identified, studied and labeled. John Lenon was stalked by Mark David Chapman for months before he was shot in 1980. Actress Teresa Saldana was stalked and stabbed by Arthur Jackson in 1982. John Hinckley Jr. had followed Reagan's movements for some time before his attempted assassination. However, stalking, as we now know and understand it, was first identified as a problem in Hollywood with fans of stars turned fanatics. Such notables as Brooke Shields, Cher, Vanna White, Sylvester Stallone, David Letterman, Johnny Carson, Michael Jackson, Michael J. Fox, Madonna, Olivia Newton-John and Debbie Gibson have all had problems with stalkers.

However, not all stalkers come after celebrities. One report indicates that there are over one million people currently being stalked, most commonly by an ex-lover or spouse. There are also an estimated 100,000 people who have stalked public officials.

From a professional standpoint, the protection specialist divides the threats into two groups. 1/ General threats by a number of individuals toward what a client represents. 2/ Those that are made by a specific individual against a specific celebrity. The later being the more potentially serious, especially if there is a pattern of escalation.

To combat the stalker, he or she must first be identified. One study by noted Forensic Psychologist, Dr Park Dietz, indicates that over one third of the individuals who have stalked a Hollywood celebrity have also stalked some other famous person. The same is true for the subjects that have stalked a member of the US Congress. This makes for a lot of people leaving a lot of trails and clues.

There are some common points about stalkers, both men and women, that can be noted here.

The stalker:
• Sets his or her mind on a specific person to pursue
• Wants control over that person
• Seeks intimate involvement with the victim
• Is uncompromising and will not take "No" for an answer
• Will ignore all obstacles in the way, both legal and physical

To identify and track the stalker requires the study, logging and cross-referencing of all fan mail, letters, notes and phone calls made to a particular celebrity. Then by carefully cross-referenced files for commonalities in each communication, the investigator may identify one particular potential threat. The common points used in cross-referencing could include:

• Form of communication—card, letter, gift, phone call, etc
• Nature of threat—obsessive, loving, hateful, threatening physical harm
• Nature of the relationship that the writer perceives with the celebrity
• Origin of communication—state, city, postmark
• Name—real or assumed
• Type of writing in letters—typed, hand written, color of ink
• Accent on the phone—male, female, angry, threatening, stoned
• Indications of specific knowledge or observations of the celebrity
• Knowledge based on tabloids, news reports or actual observation

The more data collected and analyzed related to one celebrity or a group of celebrities, the greater the potential for identifying an obsessive fan or potential stalker. There is also a computer program, developed by an LA security consultant who tracks nearly 15,000 stalkers, called Mosaic II. This system, in use by LAPD and several federal agencies, is a threat assessment tool that aids in assessing and managing known threats. The program creates a profile on potentially dangerous persons by cross-referencing twenty-four questions related to the threatening communication, the writer, and how he or she views or describes themselves and the victim.

If the celebrity is a radical religious or political leader, a large volume of both supportive and negative mail can be expected. With movie stars and entertainers, the communications are more those of undying devotion and love, periodically taken to an unhealthy extreme. For both groups, the volume of mail and telephone communications can run into the thousands.

The most significant case in Los Angeles was the 1989 stalking and murder of television actress Rebecca Schaeffer, by nineteen year old Robert Bardo. Bardo was a high school drop-out, twice confined to a mental institution, who stalked Schaeffer for two years. He first turned up at the Warner Studios lot in 1987 with a large teddy bear. The second time with a knife. On both occasions he was unable to get past security at the studio gates.

Frustrated, he did not give up. He remembered a case in 1982 when stalker Arthur Jackson had hired a detective agency to get the address of actress Teresa Saldana—after which he had stabbed Saldana ten times almost killing her. Bardo contacted an agency in Tucson who, for $250, accessed the California DMV records and supplied him with the Schaeffer's address in Los Angeles.

Bardo went to her apartment building, camping out all night in front. The first time he rang the buzzer in the morning, she came down to the main door herself, since the intercom was not working. Not expecting to see her in person, Bardo was surprised and intimidated so left. He came back about a half hour later to try again.

This time Schaeffer came to the door expecting it to be the script for an up-coming project, which were usually left on her doorstep. Bardo grabbed her by the arm, pulled a .357 Magnum from his belt and shot her directly in the heart, killing her.

He was successfully prosecuted for murder in the first degree, with premeditation, by Assistant D.A. Marcia Clark and is currently serving time at the California State Prison at Vacaville. Clark said that his motivation was "his quest for fame ... he wanted to be famous", and this was the easiest way to the top.

To get more insight into how a stalker operates, it is interesting to note that Rebecca Schaeffer was not Bardo's first choice. He had considered and written letters to Schaeffer about Dyan Cannon; he had also considered Madonna and rejected her. He had stalked Tiffany but rejected her when he went to her concert but noted that security was too heavy. He had tracked Debbie Gibson all the way to New York but found her to be inaccessible. So settled on Rebecca Scaeffer.

When interviewed at Vacaville, Bardo indicated that by watching the stars on television, reading about them in magazines and learning about their families and road to fame, that he felt he was part of their lives. They were not strangers to him and the relationship was real in his mind.

As a direct result of this case, the LAPD formed the specialized Threat Management Unit in 1989 to deal specifically with the stalker problem in Los Angeles. This unit was the only one of its type and has gone on to successfully investigate and prosecute many stalkers with the assistance of California's relatively tough new anti-stalking laws. Forty-three states now have anti-stalking laws with more to follow—the LAPD unit having helped to draft federal legislation against stalking.

The obstacles in legislation and enforcement are those of protection of the victim versus the constitutional rights of free speech and freedom of movement for the stalker. Many would say the victim's life is more important but knee-jerk civil libertarians will say otherwise.

In studying threats and attacks on daytime soap opera stars, it became evident that there are some sick puppies out there who, in their warped sense of reality, actually identify with what happens in the soap episodes. For instance, if a male actor abuses a favored female player, the actor may find threats of revenge from the female's obsessed fans. Another case involved an obsessed fan who was disgusted when his favorite actress slept with another character on the show. The fan wanted to first come to LA to rescue her, then simply decided to kill them both. It didn't happen, but the threat was taken seriously until this individual was tracked to an apartment on the East coast.

One interesting case that I worked on was a death threat left on a film producer's answering machine. The caller claimed to have Arab affilia-

tions and was incensed at a recent movie that the producer had released portraying Arabs badly.

Taken on face value as a serious political threat from a possible terrorist organization, we went into high gear, but ultimately tracked the caller to San Francisco, only to find a wacked-out transsexual who believed the movie actually plagiarized his/her life story. This was hard to believe since the storyline was about a sixteen year old who flies an F-16 to the Middle East to rescue his father.

As stated earlier, not all stalkers are unknown obsessed fans or total strangers. In the most common cases of stalking, the stalker is an acquaintance or ex-lover of the victim. A good example of this is the case of Tina Sinatra, daughter of Frank Sinatra. After having her life totally disrupted by repeated fax and phone threats from her ex-husband James Farentino, Ms Sinatra first filed for a restraining order based on police crime reports. She then succeeded in having him charged with two counts under the stalking laws.

This illustrates how stalking is very much a victim problem, not a police problem. Because it is a long term problem, the police do not have the resources to protect every victim twenty-four hours-a-day. The victims must take measures to protect themselves. This will mean looking at the options. Is there enough evidence to have the stalker arrested? What is the cost in time, money and bureaucracy? Will action further anger the stalker? Is it possible to move or change identities?

For those who can afford it, it may mean increased security, a bodyguard, and professional assessment of all mail, phone calls and threatening communications.

The most important part of the process for the bodyguard who is called in to protect a frightened celebrity is to evaluate the public's accessibility to this particular celebrity. Most often, celebrities' addresses are not common knowledge, their numbers are not listed and their work day is usually within the security of the studios. If however, the perpetrator has given some indication in a letter or call that he has actually observed the celebrities movements, then security must be stepped up.

If the residence is known, then locks and alarms can be up-graded, but a better alternative is for the celebrity to move into a hotel or with a friend until the stalker is found. A change in car may also be called for along with increased awareness on the part of studio security. Bodyguards should still be utilized for the movement to and from work, at work and during any public appearances.

Unfortunately, the problem does not end with the arrest or institutionalizing of the stalker. One day he will be released and Kathleen Batey, wife of Miami Dolphin Greg Batey and campaigner for more stalker legislation, knows first hand. Her stalker, Larry Stagner, an acquaintance from high school days, stalked and harassed her for eight years before almost killing her.

The first time Stagner was arrested he was released after just a 48 hour psychiatric evaluation, even though he was in possession of a weapon and ammunition at the time of arrest. He then returned and attempted to kidnap her at knife and gun-point but luckily the police had been alerted. As the police made their move, Kathleen escaped but Stagner was only taken into custody after a prolonged SWAT stand-off.

The problem is that even though Stagner was tried and sentenced, he was due for release in December of 1994. All, including Kathleen are convinced he will try again.

So for the protection specialist, this requires that the stalker be tracked in the legal or mental health system so that the principal can be notified of his pending release. Upon release, additional security and further investigation will probably be in order.

TERRORISTS

Terrorism has never been a big problem in the United States, but all bodyguards, and particularly those working internationally, still require a solid working knowledge of terrorist motivation and methodology. This will require an active interest in current world news, geo-politics and the dynamics of sub-national conflict.

Terrorism, by definition, is the use of violence to create change—usually on a political level. The acts of violence are a manifestation of a subversive group's frustration with the established order and their commitment to destabilize that government. If they do not have the power to defeat the government outright, they will adopt the guerrilla approach and at least try to destroy the people's confidence in the government's ability to protect them.

The level of violence is often directly proportionate to the terrorists' level of frustration with their inability to bring about change. The best examples being the Palestinians in Israel and the Armenians in Turkey. This frustration is something that we have all felt, to a lesser degree, when required to deal with any bureaucracy—only taken to the extreme by terrorists.

It is frustrating enough trying to effect change or bring attention to an injustice with a democratic bureaucracy, but with a corrupt regime, it is enough to drive any red blooded man to violence. Keep in mind America's own history and that the early settlers, who resisted English rule and ultimately won independence from the yoke of imperialism, were also considered terrorists by the British authorities of the time.

Corruption, injustice, oppression, lack of response to the people's wishes, inertia in the areas of social or economic reform can all result in a popular uprising that when crushed by government forces, will drive the freedom fighter underground and into the world of guerrilla warfare and terrorism.

The objective of the terrorist is to disrupt the status-quo, bloody the nose of the authorities and destroy the people's confidence in the government.

There was an influx in terrorism in the seventies and early eighties, due in large part to television and the efficiency of the international news media. Every violent act could be flashed around the world and into the very living-rooms of world opinion. Not surprisingly, acts of terrorism in the early to mid eighties had to increase in both violence and magnitude just to get air time and compete with already violent television programming. Terrorist acts became carefully planned and choreographed events, staged for the news media, who often received prior warning so that they could get the most spectacular footage.

Terrorist motivation can be a complex and often confusing subject, so the bodyguard should concentrate his efforts more on the study of their methodology. Learning to recognize the proverbial "fingerprint" or "signature" of various terrorist groups. The chosen tactics of the terrorist are founded on those of guerrilla warfare and based on the written works of such revolutionaries as Mao Tse-Tung and Che Guevara. Skills learned in the training camps of Libya, Yemen and the Eastern bloc countries; taught by North Korean and Cuban advisors; and passed from man to man in dark basements and remote locations.

Seeing himself not as a terrorist but a freedom fighter, the guerrilla fighter becomes a "small fish in the sea of the populace." Practicing his hit and run trade then melting back into the sea of humanity—protected and supplied by an essential sympathetic but passive network of supporters.

His weapons are intimidation and violence, demoralizing the police and military through fire bombing, sniping and ambush. He attacks those that have power and money, knowing that money drives corrupt governments. He kidnaps the rich and famous to finance his operations and to create an atmosphere of fear, forcing the politicos to retreat into their fortified "castles". By making the people with influence change their lifestyle, he wins a small victory.

In addition to methodology, the BG must learn to profile his adversary. To know what his enemy looks like and thus recognize the early signs of an operation. The BG must practice counter-surveillance so as to spot the pre-operational surveillance, used by terrorists to establish patterns of movement and predictability. For the fisherman to be successful, the fish must first swim into the net. This requires that the fisherman first know where to cast his net, or in this case, set his ambush.

When factoring the client into the formula, the BG must study the political or financial impact of his principal's death or kidnapping. How can the terrorists profit, either financially or ideologically, from an attack on him? Do they need money to finance their operations or do they just want to send a message?

The US diplomat or business man is a symbol of capitalism and the US government interference in foreign politics. By targeting US interests abroad and US embassy staff, the terrorist brings pressure to bear on the United States government. He does this knowing that the US has the power to bring even more pressure to bear on corrupt or non-democratic regimes. The US hostages taken in Iran and Beirut were taken for the sole purpose of bringing pressure to bear on the Israelis and to get the US armed forces out of Lebanon.

To conclude, the international bodyguard, just like an intelligence officer, must aggressively go after current information on this topic. There are several books listed in the appendix of this book that are directly related to terrorism and security, but for more current events, the BG should follow television shows like CNN and subscribe to magazines like Time or Newsweek.

For additional information, there are numerous courses, lectures and seminars available through a variety of police and military intelligence organizations, as well as associations like the Tactical Response Association and COPEX. For the more academically inclined, some colleges, such as Georgetown University in Washington, DC and the Jaffee Center of Strategic Studies in Tel Aviv offer more formal courses in terrorist studies. The Rand Corporation in Santa Monica, California also supports a terrorism related think-tank that has published several booklets on sub-national conflict and the problems faced by US interests doing business abroad.

Author studying terrorism in Israel, on the West Bank, 1985

AK-47

Scorpion machine pistol

RPG-7 rocket propelled grenade

16

THREAT ASSESSMENT

"Knowledge is Power"

Threat assessment is the process by which a protection specialist tries to best determine the potential for harm to a principal or corporation. It is only when the threat has been identified and evaluated, that a suitable response can be prepared. The nature of the threat will also impact on the cost required to combat it. The threat assessment is also intended to differentiate between the serious, specific threats and those that are of less significance.

Being able to prepare a comprehensive and accurate threat assessment is a valuable skill, but often considered beyond the capability of the lowly bodyguard. There are security consultants, usually ex-government or intelligence types, who specialize in nothing but threat assessments. The consultant can further capitalize on the contract by recommending and/or brokering the actual security services best suited to ensure the safety of the client. This however should not stop the independent bodyguard from learning how to do his own assessments, for only a fool would take on a contract without understanding the type and level of threat associated with the principal.

For the aspiring BG, being able to perform a valid threat assessment should be viewed as the calling card of a security professional. It will not only better acquaint the BG with the nature of the contract, but it will show the client that he is dealing with an intelligent, thinking professional. However, if the BG is not absolutely confident that he can do justice to the assessment, he would be best advised to concentrate on close protection and leave the technical stuff to those who can.

A threat assessment will indicate to a BG whether he should even consider a specific contract. As covered in Chapter 5, a BG must know his limitations as to the type of contract and the specific threat level for which he is trained and equipped. A well researched threat assessment should indicate the level of risk involved with a client and provide the BG with sufficient information to decide if he has the skills and experience to take on that contract. For example, protecting a US businessman at his corporate office in Newport Beach, California is considerably less risky than escorting that same individual to his manufacturing plant in some semi-third world country that has strong anti-American feelings. Similarly, protecting a judge in San Diego would not require the same level of experience and expertise as a judge in Columbia or Peru where the courts are plagued with drug related assassinations. Where the former may be handled by one or two BGs, the later in both cases would require larger close protection teams, extensive planning and big budgets.

The complexity and depth of the threat assessment will be somewhat dependent on the type of client, his business activities, public exposure, lifestyle and location. An assessment could be as little as interviewing the client, visiting his house and office, reviewing his business profile, reading current news articles, and looking at local crime statistics. At the other end of the scale, a comprehensive risk analysis may entail many weeks of interview, research and study into all aspects of the client's personal and professional life.

Threat assessments are more than just a matter of time and energy, requiring some diplomatic maneuvering since they do not always go unresisted. If the purpose of the assessment is to identify threats and reduce the risk to both the principal and the security team, then it must also bring about change. Both individuals and organizations can be resistant to change, especially if that change involves inconvenience to their well organized and comfortable lifestyle.

There are several steps involved in the threat assessment process, the first few being related directly to the threat, followed by a feasibility study for risk reduction. The latter considerations are dependent on the client's financial resources and willingness to make change.

Threat Assessment Progression:
- Identification of potential threats
- Evaluation of identified threats
- Prioritization of threats by relative risk
- Evaluation of the client's public life
- Evaluation of the client's personal life
- Evaluation of residences and offices
- Evaluation of existing security procedures
- Recommendations for risk reduction
- Allocation of security resources
- Implementation of new security procedures

In addition, the threat assessment must consider not only the present situation, but past threats and future risks based on changes in both business and lifestyle. For example, an individual who was considered a threat in the past may have been recently released from prison or a mental hospital, making him or her a future potential threat worth tracking. Similarly, a client who experiences a sudden change in wealth, restructures a business or makes a significant political decision could open the door to a whole new range of threats.

INITIAL THREAT ASSESSMENT

Security planning is usually based on a worst case scenario, so the threat assessment should also begin with the most serious risks. Taking into account those acts of greatest probability, the following are the five most common threats usually considered by a protection specialist:

1. Assassination
2. Kidnapping
3. Assault
4. Extortion
5. Terrorism

The three most common areas of vulnerability being:

* The home
* The work place
* In Transit

Fortunately for the bodyguard, number one on the list, assassination, is seldom the prime threat in the protection business. This is in part due to the fact that there is little value in killing the principal or a member of his family unless it is to make a political or religious statement.

For the wealthy, the greatest danger is usually number two, kidnap for ransom. For the political leader it is kidnap for intimidation and to bring about change. For the celebrity it is kidnap or assault out of misguided infatuation or obsession.

Number three, assault, which appears in two forms, is a more common problem and a constant fear of the rich and famous. An assault can be a **deliberate** act against a principal or merely a result of **random** violence. Celebrities, because of their public status and easy recognition, live in constant fear that they will be assaulted by a crazed individual or obsessed fan if they venture out in public. However, in reality, modern urban life carries with it an element of danger for everyone, so the BG must also factor this into his assessments.

On a daily basis, we run the risk of becoming victims of random violence, rape, robbery, carjacking, gang wars, drug wars, race riots, etc. The level of risk is usually predicated by geographic location, either neighborhood, city or country. In some countries such as Israel, Bosnia, Lebanon, Columbia or East Africa, the people live under the constant threat of violence, insurrection, terrorism and civil war. Yet life goes on, often with almost a fatalistic appearance of normalcy.

Without discounting the danger presented by street crime, for the BG, the risk analysis is more oriented toward the threats that an individual or organization faces because of status, lifestyle, travel or business activity.

On a more specific level, each type of client, celebrity, politician or businessman, carries with him or her some inherent dangers commonly associated with that occupation or position. Entertainers must always be conscious of the danger posed by obsessed fans; the wealthy will always be targets for kidnappers and extortionists; super models must be wary of stalkers; and rich philanderers must always fear the wrath of their wives (and their wive's attorney's).

In the political and religious arena there will always be diametrically opposed views that result in violence. In fact most of the bloodiest conflicts in history have been fought over religious beliefs, up to and including the Islamic Jihad of this decade.

A good example of the violence generated by opposing social views has manifested itself with the abortion issue. Several years ago one could not conceive of the rational behind killing doctors, and yet now the more radical anti-abortion activists seem to publicly support the shooting of doctors and the fire bombing of clinics.

The threat assessment begins with a meeting with the client and/or his trusted representative. This should be a face to face meeting in a comfortable environment, since it will take at least two to three hours initially. The client should have already been supplied with the BG or consultant's credentials and background experience prior to the meeting, so there should be no need for long personal introductions.

Note: Prior to a meeting and along with my personal bio, I like to supply the potential client with a fill-in-the-blank type questionnaire. This covers all the mundane but necessary information such as: personal data, family members, residences, addresses, phone numbers, cars, clubs, personal habits, personal secretaries, charities, political and religious affiliations, etc. Having this information on hand saves time and allows me to formulate a better overview of the threat potential for a specific client.

The professional will have already done some homework prior to the meeting and will be prepared to offer suggestions if required. However, a warning. The most common mistake made by amateurs in the security business is their eagerness to let everyone know how much they know by immediately making suggestions. The wise man is the one who has learned how to sit and listen, before opening his mouth.

Keeping in mind that something probably already occurred to require the presence of a security specialist, the BG can simply ask the principal to expand on his reasons for wanting an evaluation or up-grade of his own security. Was there a specific threat or are they anticipating one in the near future?

From this point, and only after the client has had his say, is it recommended to continue with a prepared interview format, complete with written questions and checklists suited to the client's status. The initial questioning can be divided into three areas—personal, business and travel—starting with general questions and becoming more specific. The following sample questions should be used only as a guide.

Personal—
- Who is the client and where did he come from
- What is his current position or status
- Are there known specific threats
- Is there a prior history of threats or attacks
- Are there samples of threatening mail or communications
- What are the religious and political affiliations
- Is his lifestyle high or low profile
- Do the tabloids show an interest in him or his wife
- Does his picture appear in newspapers or magazines
- What is the location of his residence(s)
- Are there existing residential security procedures
- How many employees at the residence
- Does he drive himself or have a driver
- Where do his children go to school
- How do the children get to school
- Has he ever received special training himself
- Who most benefits by his demise

Business—
- What type of business(s) is he involved in
- Who are his competitors
- What is his business philosophy or strategy
- Is he involved in hostile take-overs
- How many employees does he have
- How is he viewed by employees
- What is his annual staff turn-over
- Are there union considerations or opposition
- Is there access control to his office
- Are his calls and mail screened
- Where does he park his car
- Are there parking attendants

Travel—
- Does he have businesses or residences out of state
- To what countries does he frequently travel
- Is there significant terrorists or criminal activity
- How does he travel, commercial or private
- Who does his travel planning
- How many people know his itinerary
- Are public appearances scheduled in advance
- What hotels does he use
- Does he carry a lot of cash
- Does he visit casinos or nightclubs
- . . . and the list goes on.

Each question should in some way be related to the client's exposure and should give the BG that much more insight into the real or potential threats.

At the end of the meeting, the protection specialist can make a few observations, but before getting too committed, should explain the need to first visit the residence, his place of business and to interview key personnel at both places.

The evaluation of the residence begins at first sight as the BG approaches. Is there sufficient evidence of security to deter a common criminal? Is the gate closed? Is there access control by way of a speaker box, camera or security guard?

The evaluation of the residence is divided into four areas:

- The house
- The perimeter
- The family
- The staff.

The house must be inspected for physical security measures, doors, locks, windows, etc; safety equipment like intrusion and smoke alarms, fire extinguishers, fire escapes and panic buttons; and general structural integrity in the event of natural disaster.

The perimeter survey begins with the condition of physical barriers such as fences and gates; the positioning and effectiveness of existing intrusion systems; the positioning and application of CCTV surveillance systems; and the correct use of the access control system.

The family must be interviewed for knowledge of threat recognition; general security awareness; and to better understand their daily routines. The family must then be observed to see if they show a level of security consciousness when it comes to access control and visitor verification.

The staff must also be interviewed to ascertain their familiarity with general security procedure and awareness. It is also important to establish if they are happy in their work and how they feel about their employers. If there is a security staff, they must be interviewed at some length to establish their knowledge of procedure, training and level of professionalism.

The evaluation of the corporate office or place of business is similar to the residence in that first impressions are important. Is there perimeter security or access control gates? Are there vigilant security guards or parking attendants? Is the reception area monitored? Are the receptionists politely suspicious of visitors? Are unaccompanied visitors restricted to the lobby?

Just like the residence, the evaluation will cover perimeter, office structure and staff. Particular attention must be given to the administrative assistants' knowledge of basic corporate security procedure (Chapter 21), access control, phone discipline, and information dissemination. There should also be a review of hiring practices as they relate to background investigations and personal security checks.

After all this, and a complete investigation of anything that would be considered potentially threatening, the protection specialist is ready to make an educated threat assessment. This along with recommended changes in the client's lifestyle and security.

ON-GOING THREAT ASSESSMENT

It is the security manager or BG's duty to continually re-evaluate the client's exposure based on specific threats, changes in his lifestyle, news coverage, business moves or foreign travel. Threat assessment is also a day-to-day process, especially when a client is moving in public. The BG must constantly be aware, scanning the crowd looking for anyone that meets the profile of a terrorist, criminal or crazy. The same is true in trying to spot surveillance while driving the principal between frequently visited locations.

Lastly, as threats to the principal are identified, they must be graded just like the intelligence officer grades product as rumor, hear say, witnessed, corroborated, independently verified, hard fact, etc. To assess a threat, the BG will need to consider the following:

- What is the threatened act?
- Who is the target of the threat?
- How was the threat received?
- Is the threat verified by a reliable source?
- Is the threat practical or feasible?
- Does the threat pose a real concern to the principal?
- Does the threatening party have access to the principal?
- Is this threat similar to past threats?
- Is there a pattern of threatening behavior?
- Are they capable of carrying out the threatened act?
- Have they a prior history of violence?
- What should be the response?

In conclusion, even when a principal has a BG or a protection team, it is still beneficial to periodically have a professional, independent security advisor brought in to work up a current threat assessment and to evaluate the existing security procedures. Any procedures that remain unchanged and inflexible for too long will eventually become known to the enemy. With periodic restructuring it becomes more difficult for the enemy to find the weakness in the system or to plan an attack.

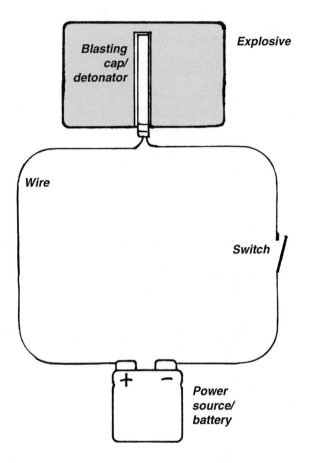

Explosive

Blasting cap/ detonator

Wire

Switch

+ **–**

Power source/ battery

All bombs and explosive devices are made up of five basic components: an explosive compound, a detonator, wire, a power source and a switch of some form. However, the size and design of an explosive device is only limited by the training, skill and imagination of the bomb builder.

17

EXPLOSIVE IDENTIFICATION

"There's no revolution possible without terror."
—Lenin tells the Politburo, April, 1922.

The bomb is a weapon of terror that can be used to kill, maim or intimidate. Bombs are cheap, easy to conceal, easy to transport and offer the user considerable flexibility in their application. Because of its inherent power, the bomb is both terrifying and intimidating. From a public exposure view point, the destruction and death resulting from the explosion virtually guarantees the terrorist prime time news coverage. So much so that some radicals have even been known to claim responsibility for bombings by other groups.

During the late seventies and early eighties bombs were the weapon of choice for several terrorist groups, most notable the PLO and IRA. However, in the early nineties, as these groups began to seek international acceptance for their plight, they found that the use of bombs on the civilian population was counter-productive to their cause. It was only in late ninety-four that radical Palestinian factions, dissatisfied with the peace agreements between Israel and the PLO, have returned to targeting Israeli civilians with a variety of bombs.

A bomb, built and placed by a trained professional, is a precision weapon, but in the hands of many terrorists it is a crude and indiscriminate device, on occasions killing the bomber before it is even placed.

For the bodyguard, the type of bomb one can expect will be dictated by the nature and location of his client, and this goes back to threat assessment. Is there greater value in killing or kidnapping the principal? Does he represent a government or organization that is being targeted by terrorists? Does he reside or travel in countries known for prior bombings?

On a domestic level, bombs have been utilized by organized crime and narcotics traffickers to eliminate competitors, and to kill or intimidate prospective prosecution witnesses in pending court cases. Bombs have also been used to intimidate businessmen who have affiliations with foreign countries.

The Bureau of Alcohol, Tobacco and Firearms' (ATF) U.S. statistics show several hundred criminal incidents each year involving the use of explosives. When broken down by motivation they range from vandalism, revenge and protest to extortion, labor related sabotage, insurance fraud and homicide. The targets include government offices, banks, aircraft, military installations, educational facilities, vehicles, commercial structures and residences. The containers used for the destructive devices include pipes, bottles, dynamite sticks, and boxes made from both metal and cardboard.

Since bombs have played such a significant role in the security industry's response to both domestic and international terrorism, the bodyguard should have a more than cursory knowledge of explosives in general and improvised explosive devices (IEDs) in particular.

Author's Note: In this chapter I have gone into a little more detail than is called for, but I consider it important that the bodyguard have a firm grasp of the origins, terminology and relative danger of the more common explosive devices. The following is intended to give the BG direction for future study and should not be taken as a substitute for professional explosive identification training. The actual handling or disarming of devices is well beyond the capability of the BG and should NEVER be attempted.

INTRODUCTION TO EXPLOSIVES

"An explosive is a substance that when subjected to heat, impact, friction, or other suitable initial impulse, undergoes a very rapid chemical or physical transformation, forming other more stable products entirely or largely gaseous, whose combined volume is much greater than that of the original substance". Explosives are capable of rapid and violent action, accompanied by a sudden rise in pressure and temperature.

Classifications:
Class A—High Explosive—Dynamite, TNT, C-4, Tovex, etc.
   Can be detonated by a blasting cap when unconfined and are suited to cutting and shattering charges.
Class B—Low Explosive—Black powder, commercial fireworks, etc
   Tend to burn rapidly rather than detonate and are more suited to pushing, pounding or propelling charges.
Class C—Related products which contain small quantities of Class A or B explosives—for example: blasting caps, safety fuse, det cord in small quantities (less than 100 pounds), etc

Other Useful Definitions:
Blasting Agents—Materials that require a booster, such as uncontained ammonium nitrate/fuel oil mixture (ANFO)
Binary—A two-part mix that is not considered explosive until combined. Kinepak (oxidizer + sensitizer) is one example of a high explosive when mixed.

Safety Fuse—A slow burning fuse that contains black powder and should burn at a rate of not less than 40 secs / foot.

Nonelectric Blasting Cap—A sensitive detonator that has a base charge of 6,8,10 or 12 grains of PETN and a priming charge of Lead Azide or Fulminate of Mercury.

Electric Blasting Cap—An electrically fired detonator that also has a base charge of PETN and a priming charge of Lead Azide.

Detonating Cord—Det-Cord or "Primacord" is a fast burning (26,000 fps) initiator that has a white core of PETN.

Different explosives have varying properties such as: strength, velocity, density, sensitivity, water resistance, temperature resistance and stability. The military, for example, requires explosives that have high velocity (for power) and low sensitivity (for safe handling) that can be stored for prolonged periods under adverse temperatures (-65 degrees to +165 degrees).

C-4 is probably one of the best known military explosives with a detonating velocity of 26,500 fps. Also known as plastic explosive or plastique, C-4 is a whitish, odorless substance that is 91% RDX combined with non-explosive plasticizers.

TNT (Trinitrotoluene) is another widely used military explosive being stable, relatively insensitive, with a convenient melting point of 81 degrees C. and low cost.

Since TNT is so common, many other explosives are rated in comparison. TNT being the standard of 1.0.

Relative Effectiveness:

Ammonium Nitrate		0.42	
Ammonium Dynamite	40%	0.41	
	60%	0.53	
Straight Dynamite	40%	0.65	15,000 fps
	60%	1.0	18,200 fps
Military Dynamite		0.92	(RDX based / no nitroglycerin)
TNT		1.0	21,000–22,500 fps
Tetrytol		1.20	(75% Tetryl / 25% TNT)
Amatol		1.20	(20% TNT / 80% Ammonium nitrate)
Tetryl		1.25	23,400 fps
Pentolite		1.26	(50% PETN / 50% TNT)
C-3		1.34	25,000–26,000 fps
C-4		1.34	(91% RDX + plasticizers)
Comp B		1.35	(39% TNT / 60% RDX / 1% wax)
HBX 1	in air	1.48	(TNT / aluminum powder)
	in water	1.68	

SOURCES OF EXPLOSIVES

Explosives are neither expensive nor hard to obtain. In many cases, they are easier to procure than a handgun or assault rifle. They are also easier to transport and conceal, since to the untrained eye, they may appear to be no more ominous than a lump of putty, a bar of soap, a bottle of liquid or a bag of granules. The factory packaging or shipping labels being the only identifying features, both easily removed.

Commercial explosives, such as straight dynamite, det-cord and blasting caps, are not difficult to obtain. On a federal level, it may be difficult to get permits to transport or store explosives, but it requires no more than an ATF form for a farmer or certified blaster to purchase a sufficient quantity to blow some tree stumps.

On an illegal level, explosives are frequently stolen from quarries, mining operations, construction sites, demolition projects and military installations. Again, looking at the ATF statistics for explosives stolen in the United States, from 1987 to 1991 shows; almost 50,000 pounds of dynamite, 336 pounds of military C-4 and TNT, 3,691 pounds of primer, and 3,337 pounds of boosters—totalling almost 57,000 pounds of explosive. If that isn't impressive enough, add 66 hand-grenades, 31,199 pounds of blasting agents, 264,049 feet of det-cord and safety fuse, and 123,090 detonators.

Considering that it takes less than half a pound of explosive and one blasting cap to ruin your whole day, the thought of almost one hundred thousand pounds of product on the black market is truly scary—and that is just in the United States. In countries known for state sponsored terrorism like Libya, North Korea, Cuba, Bulgaria, and the old Soviet Union, supplies of modern military explosives were virtually limitless.

The military is a significant source of illegal explosives, either in pure form or as part of explosive projectiles, mines or loaded weapons systems. In the towns and cities neighboring large military bases, in both Europe and the United States, military ordnance can be purchased on the black market from serving military personnel. This was a major problem for bases in West Germany and with the collapse of the Soviet Union, in particular East Germany, the region became flooded with black market arms and ordnance.

However, potentially more hazardous than commercial or military explosives are the homemade varieties, also known as improvised munitions. These are still illegal but do not require a permit for the components and do not need to be purchased on the black market. With a minimal knowledge of chemistry and very little equipment, they can be brewed from unrestricted chemicals and in some cases household products.

There are a variety of black books on the market, such as Improvised Munitions and the Anarchist's Cook Book, which give detailed recipes, using both specific chemicals and household substitutes for such explosives as; nitroglycerin, dynamite, TNT, tetryl, black powder, mercury fulminate and blasting gelatin. They also give basic formulas for demolition and the placement of charges, and diagrams for the construction of explosive booby-traps.

Author's Note: Many of the formulas described in these books are either incorrect, require a good working knowledge of chemistry or are very sensitive and unstable when mixed. If the reader decides to read these texts, study them from the view point of learning to better recognize the devices that some nut-case may try to make or use. Under no circumstances try to make the explosives or compounds listed. Some chemicals are so unstable that they can explode just by mixing them together or with as little as a few degree change in temperature. Even professionally trained explosive ordnance technicians are hesitant to try and move or deactivate home brewed explosives because of their unknown sensitivity, unstable nature and unpredictable properties.

IMPROVISED EXPLOSIVE DEVICES

IEDs, also known generically as destructive devices, are the prime concern of the bodyguard. To be classified as a device, an explosive must have some form of initiating system or triggering mechanism. A stick of dynamite or a block of plastic explosive, like a box of ammunition, is in itself inert and not a real threat. It is not until the explosive is armed, or the ammunition chambered in a weapon, that it becomes a danger. Then, just as the trigger releases the firing pin and causes a round to discharge, so the bomb must have some triggering mechanism to initiate the explosive.

It is the method of construction of a device that most interests the protection specialist, since it is the parts of this arming or triggering mechanism that are most often the tell-tail signs of a bomb. Unfortunately, the number, complexity and application of explosive devices is beyond description, limited only by the training and imagination of the builder. However, there are certain commonalities to all devices.

First, a device requires a quantity of explosive, but since most explosives are designed to be transported and handled safely, they are usually somewhat insensitive. This insensitivity necessitates the use of a more sensitive initiator in the form of a blasting cap or detonator. To fire the blasting cap, an electrical impulse must be applied requiring both a power source and wires to carry it. To complete the circuit, the device must have some form of switch or electrical contact, otherwise the device would explode as soon as the builder hooked up the battery. Understanding all this, a variety of devices can be constructed from the following components:

1. An explosive compound
2. A blasting cap or detonator
3. A battery or power source
4. An electrical contact switch
5. Electrical Wire

Now although some blasting caps and explosives, such as black powder, can be initiated non-electrically, by use of safety fuse and a naked flame, these are not suitable for most devices. The burning safety fuse has very limited time delay capability, burning at approximately 40 seconds per foot, and would be easily detected by both smoke and smell.

Most devices used against people or structures are equipped with some form of timing mechanism, trip-switch or remote switch. This is to guarantee that the device goes off at the intended time or is tripped by the intended target. Burning fuses simply do not offer that flexibility or capability.

Explosives, detonators, wire and batteries are all rather basic, but the options for a triggering switch are endless. The trip switch could be any form of two contacts that, as a direct result of an action of the victim, are closed completing the circuit. This could be an actual switch as would be found in a car's ignition or a wall mounted light switch; or it could be improvised from two wires and a rubber band, two pieces of tin-foil separated by cardboard, or a clothes peg held open by some form of insulator. The electrical contacts on these types of switches can be closed by direct pressure or pressure release.

Timed devices and time bombs have been depicted frequently on television and are quite simple in function. In place of a manually operated switch, the device has a clock or timer that will close the switch at a given time. This is often as simple as two bare wires soldered to the body and the sweep hand of a cheap alarm clock. The time could be set for hours or minutes depending on which sweep hand is utilized. Lacking a clock, improvised time devices can be made using melting ice, water running through a small hole in a can, beans swelling in a can of water or the automatic timers found in exterior lighting or sprinkler systems.

Disturbance and anti-disturbance systems operate similar to a basic trip switch or booby-trap but are designed to detonate the device if someone attempts to move or disarm it. The most common forms of anti-disturbance switches are mercury switches that operate by means of liquid mercury rolling around in a tube; a ball bearing rolling between two contacts; or a system of wire contacts suspended inside a bare wire loop. Anti-disturbance systems are not popular with the amateur bomber since their innate sensitivity makes them equally dangerous for the bomber to handle. They usually also preclude any form of "make safe" contingency if the bomber changes his mind after arming the device. However, the potential for anti-disturbance systems is the prime reason that the BG should not attempt to touch or move a suspicious device.

Command fire systems are those that are initiated by the bomber at the most opportune time. These are often made from radio control units purchased from any model-makers' shop or even a remote garage-door opener. However, both these units tend to lack range so more sophisticated devices can be initiated by high frequency radio transmissions or cellular phone technology.

In addition to the above switches, there are more sophisticated initiating systems that can be operated by barometric pressure, oil viscosity, water flow, temperature, proximity to iron and magnetic fields and vibration, but they are still just switches. To become a device they only require an explosive charge, a detonator, wiring and a power source.

One booby-trap device that does not follow the above criteria and is not uncommon, is the hand-grenade. When a grenade is placed in a tin-can, jar or water glass, the safety pin can be pulled without the spoon releasing. If a trip wire is then rigged to the grenade so that the opening of a door or a person walking into it pulls on the wire, then the grenade is pulled from the glass or can, releasing the spoon and activating the grenade. The result will be the same if the glass containing the grenade is placed in such a way that it will be knocked over or broken, for example on or behind a door.

From an investigators stand-point, the way these components are assembled to make a device may carry the "fingerprint" or "signature" of a group. The bomber may do this intentionally to send a message, or unintentionally being that this is the only type of bomb that he knows how to build. Some terrorist networks have been known to exchange recipes or plans for bombs, giving the investigator further evidence of links between these groups.

The size, design and placement of a bomb will be dictated by its intended target. Some are designed to destroy buildings; some intended to kill one person; some to kill or maim a large number of people. In general, they are classified like land-mines as anti-personnel or anti-material.

An anti-personnel device designed to kill or maim one person need only be small and placed close to the intended target. Death may occur as a direct result of explosive over-pressure or from fragmentation injuries.

An anti-personnel device designed to kill or maim many people will be much larger and placed in either a crowded public area or in a meeting hall. The bomb will have built-in fragmentation in the form of nails, ball-bearings, nuts, bolts or metal fragments; or be placed to create a hail of secondary fragmentation from window glass, car-body metal and surrounding concrete.

In the case of the December 1988 bombing of Pan Am 103 over Lockerbie, Scotland, the intent was to kill a lot of people, but the bomb was directed against the aircraft. The actual plane crash killed the passengers, not the relatively small bomb that it took to bring the plane down.

An anti-material device is usually very large, often in the region of hundreds or even thousands of pounds of explosive. The car bombs directed against embassies and the truck bomb that demolished the Marine Barracks in Beirut are typical of the size of some of these devices.

CAR BOMBS

Since car bombing is popular with both terrorists and criminals, vehicle security becomes a significant part of executive protection. Unfortunately, the security systems and procedures that are routinely implemented at the home and office, are often neglected when it comes to cars and limousines.

Car bombs come in several forms, ranging from the small device placed to kill or intimidate the driver or occupant, to whole cars loaded with explosives for mass destruction. More specifically, there are four basic types of car bomb.

1. A booby-trapped car designed to kill a specific target, usually the driver, occupant or owner.
2. The explosive laden car left in a public area to cause maximum indiscriminate death and injury.
3. The large car bomb intended to destroy a specific structure, office or embassy.
4. The large car or truck bomb directed at a specific target by a suicide driver.

The recent vehicle bombing of the World Trade Center in New York is a good example of terrorists' willingness to bring their deadly trade to the continental United States. This was a bomb laden van parked beneath the structure, but for the private sector bodyguard, only the first type of car bomb is of real concern. This is the bomb placed in a client's car or limousine for the sole purpose of killing, maiming or intimidating the occupant.

This type of device is not restricted to countries with known terrorist activity or narcotics distribution. Even in the idyllic setting of the exclusive ski-resort town of Aspen, high in the Colorado Rockies, a witness in a drug related case in another state found himself the victim of a car bomb. The device had been attached to the underside of the car with the switch connected to the drive shaft. It was triggered when the car was placed in gear and the drive shaft began to turn.

When placing a bomb, the closer within the vehicle that this type of device can be placed to the intended target, the more effective it will be. A small device in the trunk may seriously injure the driver, but the same device placed directly under his seat is almost sure to kill.

There are a number of ways that these devices or bombs can be initiated, starting with the ones that are triggered by some action of the driver. Any part of the car that is moved as the driver or passenger enter the vehicle can trigger a device. These could include:

- Opening the car door or doors may pull a string or release a plunger.
- Sitting down on the seat may apply pressure to a pressure plate or simply push two contacts together.
- Turning the ignition key could close electrical contacts.
- Actually starting the car could feed power to a device.
- Any forward or reverse movement could wind a string or wire around the drive-shaft, tripping a switch.
- Driving over a bump in the road could close two contacts positioned in the suspension system.

Apart from all of the above, the device may be equipped with a timer and designed to explode at an opportune time. Or the bomber may chose to go with a radio-remote so as to command detonate the bomb only when he is sure the target is in the vehicle.

Considering all of the above, this gives the bodyguard some indication of where to search for a device. The most common places being, under the car, up under the wheel wells, on the fire-wall in front of the driver, or under the driver's or passenger's seat.

There are several vehicle related preventive measures that will make the bomber's job more difficult

1. Install locks on the hood and trunk
2. Install a lock on the gas cap
3. Place a bolt through the exhaust pipe
4. Put an anti-disturbance alarm on the car
5. Always park in a locked garage at the residence
6. Always park in secured parking areas at the office
7. Have the driver stay with or observe the car at all times
8. Use a remote ignition start for use before approaching the car
9. Search the car anytime it is left unobserved
10. Keep the door open as the car is started. This may help alleviate an over-pressure injury.

Author's Note: When travelling overseas or staying in hotels, I will usually have the doorman or valet parking attendant bring the rental car up to the front door. If the car is already at the door, I may call down and have the attendant start the car "to warm it up" for my client. If using limousines, then I will educate the drivers to never leave the vehicle unattended and to report any suspicious activity immediately to me. I emphasize that this is as much for their own safety as mine or the principals.

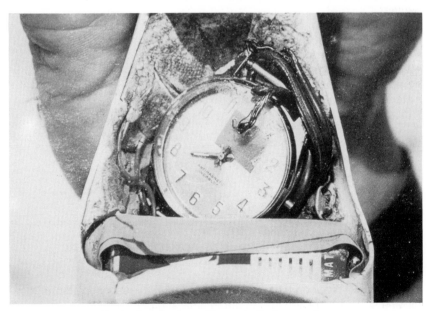

Explosive device with crude timing system

191

LETTER BOMBS

Some years ago, the mere mention of letter bombs struck fear into the hearts of many executives, ambassadors and diplomats. They were impersonal, far reaching and cost effective. They did not require personal delivery and were activated when opened by the addressee. One key problem that only served to increase the seriousness of the letter or package bomb, was that in many cases, the addressee was not the victim. Bombs were killing postal workers, delivery personnel, mail room staff, secretaries, minor functionaries, and most feared of all, family members.

As a direct result, many corporations, government offices and embassies modified their mail rooms, installed X-ray machines, supplied secretaries with metal detectors, and warned family members to accept nothing that was not expected.

In trying to detect mail bombs, without the benefit of high technology, the bodyguard should keep in mind that the letter bomb must still contain an explosive compound, a detonator, a battery, wire and some form of electrical contacts. Even with thin sheet explosive, a small flat watch type battery and the smallest blasting cap, the letter becomes quite thick, and more like a small package. Knowing this, anything over a quarter of an inch or fifty millimeters thick should be treated with suspicion, especially if the sender cannot be immediately verified.

With the rash of mail bombings in the late seventies and early eighties, the International Association of Bomb Technicians and Investigators (IABTI) put together an excellent guideline for corporate and government mail handlers. Any of the following points should create suspicion and caution.

Letter & Parcel Bomb Recognition Points:
- Foreign mail, air mail and Special Delivery
- Markings such as Confidential or Personal
- Excessive postage
- Hand written or poorly typed addresses
- Incorrect title of addressee
- Title but no names
- Misspelling of common words
- Oily stains or discolorations
- No return address
- Excessive weight
- Rigid envelope
- Lopsided or uneven envelope
- Protruding wires or tinfoil
- Excessive securing material such as masking tape, string, etc
- Visual distractions

If there is a real concern with any package, the local police bomb technicians should be called. In the mean time, the package should be isolated, preferably in a ventilated room with the windows open, and if available, the package can be placed in a bomb basket. Do not cover the suspected bomb with a blanket or anything else, since the bomb techs will only have to remove that before they can get at the device.

Note: Letter bombs are still a problem. In January, 1995 an individual was arrested attempting to send a mail bomb to the President of the United States.

C4 plastic explosive

Binary explosive (left)
Commercial dynamite (right)
Military blasting cap (upper left)

Various U.S. hand grenades

EXPLOSIVE COUNTER-MEASURES

General explosive counter-measures are much the same as the general security procedures that are covered in other parts of this book. Most are centered around common sense and access control.

1. Use non-descript cars whenever possible
2. Change cars whenever the threat level warrants
3. Do not use personalized registration plate
4. Do not identify VIP corporate parking spaces
5. Deny public access wherever possible
6. Use ID cards and access control systems
7. Run periodic bomb sweeps and searches
8. Run all corporate mail through a screening process
9. Keep maintenance closets and lockers locked at all times
10. Control access to executive washrooms
11. Make all employees familiar with bomb recognition points
12. Do not allow any bags to be left in lobby or closets
13. Teach all staff members to have a healthy suspicion of visitors, packages and strange occurrences
14. Make maximum use of trained bomb detection dogs if the threat level is sufficient
15. Screen all visitors, large packages and bags with x-ray and vapor detection equipment if necessary

In conclusion, the BG should learn as much as he can about explosives, bombs and improvised devices so that he can recognize the tell-tale signs. Upon identifying a suspicious package, the BG should disturb nothing, move nothing, evacuate the area, secure the perimeter and call the experts.

IF THERE IS DOUBT—DO NOT TOUCH IT!!

Access control and physical barriers are the foundation of any security system

18

SECURITY SYSTEMS

A threat assessment will usually indicate that the principal spends the bulk of his or her time either at home or at the office. Although the daily routine for different individuals may vary, most tend to leave for work in the morning and return to their residence late in the afternoon. There is also a high probability that they will be at their place of business, corporate office, or studio most of the day.

Protection specialists understand this potentially dangerous routine and with a little surveillance, the stalker, attacker or kidnapper would realize the same thing. There is a predictable window of opportunity twice a day, coming and going, from both locations.

The bodyguard should know to be extra vigilant approaching and leaving both the house and place of business when moving with the principal. Unfortunately, everyone tends to relax when safely in their own home or office. Of the two locations, both have threat potential but for different reasons.

The office is usually more accessible to the villain since the address can be obtained from the telephone directory and there is already some public traffic. However, there will always be people around, a receptionist to get by, hopefully some form of access control and probably uniformed security guards. The home address, on the other hand, may be harder to find but there will definitely be less traffic, fewer people and more privacy. The residence can be considered a sanctuary to the principal, but in actual fact, can also be an isolated, secluded environment for the perpetrator of a crime.

Understanding this predictable vulnerability and the natural tendency to relax one's guard at home or in the office, both targets should be hardened. Hardening a target can be broken into three levels:

• Improve physical security
• Install electronic detection systems
• Hire security personnel.

Each of the above has advantages and disadvantages for different applications, but all are designed with the four Ds in mind.

- To Deter by use of visible equipment and procedures
- To Deny access by use of physical barriers
- To Detect an intruder as soon as possible
- To Delay an intruder until a response can be activated

PHYSICAL SECURITY

The first step in hardening a target is to up-grade the physical security of both residences and corporate offices. Physical security refers to a structure's design, construction materials, doors, locks, windows, walls and fences, and their combined ability to deter intrusion and physically deny access.

Physical security begins at the outer property line and works inward. The first line of defense is usually a wall, fence and gate—all of which should be designed with security in mind.

The initial deterrent is a wall or fence that is of sufficient height and design so as to be not easily climbed. This physical barrier should also provide the occupants with a degree of privacy and deny the prowler or unwanted observer the ability to case the house or photograph the principals.

The gates should be equally substantial with an automatic opening feature operated by both remote openers for the vehicles and a key pad at the side of the entrance(s). This allows the client or the driver to enter and leave the property without having to get out of the car or be delayed unnecessarily outside the safety of the perimeter security.

It is important to select a strong, high quality type of gate that is known to have a proven track record for reliability. Security gates can either slide open or swing open, depending on the application, but they must all have heavy-duty hinges or rollers that will function smoothly and consistently. Clients' will have no patience with gates that tend to be temperamental or break-down and will simply leave them open, effectively nullifying the value of the entire perimeter system.

To further add deterrence to a fence or wall, it is possible to add outward curving wrought iron spikes or concertina razor wire. This may not be appropriate in exclusive residential neighborhoods but is highly recommended for rural properties, and the less visible back property lines in residential areas.

Where appropriate, flood lighting can be added to the perimeter to deny intruders the concealment of night or shadows and further deter approach. If constant lighting during the hours of darkness could be disturbing to the neighbors, then the lights should be activated by motion detectors or manually from inside the house.

With the perimeter secured, the next step is to look at the house itself. Few houses are built with security in mind, this only becoming a consideration after the owner has moved in. After an initial survey, especially on older houses and mansions, it is usually obvious that the antique locks and ornamental window latches are sub-standard. Many having not worked properly for several years. In some cases the doors and windows themselves will need to be changed.

When doing a site survey on a house, the initial walk through should be done with a locksmith who can give some immediate input as to the best type and cost of locks for particular applications. At a minimum, it may be necessary to re-key the entire house since the residents have often long lost track of just how many keys are in circulation.

In high threat cases, some doors will need to be reinforced or replaced and larger exterior windows may have to be replaced with Lexan or some similar bullet resistant poly-carbonate laminate. The object of all this being to physically deny a forced entry or at least delay it.

The last line of defense for physical security is the safe room. A room with a heavy door and secure lock where the occupants can secure themselves until the police or security response arrives to sweep and clear the property.

The purpose of the safe room, as with other physical security measures, is to deny access and further delay the intruder. Although large walk-in closets can be utilized, it is wiser to modify a bathroom to double as a safe room. This gives the occupants both fresh water and a source of relief if the police response is slow coming.

The basic modifications for a safe room would include a reinforced door with secure slide-bolt locks, internal steel shuttered windows, a telephone on a separate line, or a cellular phone, and a store of emergency equipment. Such items as blankets, flash lights, candles, matches, a fire extinguisher, and a firearm (if trained in its use) can all add to the occupants' comfort level. On a more sophisticate level, a closed-circuit television monitor can be tied in to the CCTV security system, allowing the principals to monitor external movements on the property.

ELECTRONIC SECURITY

The primary purpose of electronic security is to detect intrusion, and on more sophisticated systems, track and monitor the intruder. However, the secondary benefit from the appearance of CCTV cameras and perimeter sensors is deterrence.

Electronic security can vary from simple residential alarm systems to high tech motion sensing anti-intrusion systems. The cost can range from a couple of thousand dollars for a small house to over three hundred thousand dollars for a large estate, depending on the size of the property and the depth of the system.

As with physical security, electronic security can be installed on the perimeter or in the actual residence, each having advantages and disadvantages. The advantage of perimeter monitoring is that it gives the security team or principal an early warning of an intrusion and more time to react to it. The downside can be cost.

Cost becomes a significant factor on large properties, directly influenced by the length and depth of the desired protection. Perimeter detection systems, dependent on a number of sensors connected by cable and/or underground conduit, are usually designed and priced by the linear foot. The longer the property line, the more sensors required, the greater the cost.

The depth of a system refers to the number of overlapping detection and tracking systems utilized. For example, if a property is encircled by three levels of perimeter security—a fence sensor, a ground sensor and point-to-point IR beams—then the system can show not only the point of intrusion but can also track the direction of movement of an intruder. As good as this may seem, it can become very expensive and only adds more systems that need to be calibrated, maintained and monitored.

On most small urban dwellings, the detection system is placed right on the house, usually in the form of door and window contacts and interior motion detectors. However, on larger estates where there are a significant number of occupants and staff members, it is very difficult to secure the residence in this manner. Since there is almost constant movement in and out of the house, alarming it would only result in an unnecessary number of false alarms.

Author's Note: We have worked on large estates and properties where the principals often did not settle in for the evening until after 2 or 3 AM. Add to this the fact that maids and butlers were expected to stay on duty until the principals retired, and that some staff members even lived on property. In addition, cooks and maids often arrived or started their duties as early as 5 or 6 AM. This left only a two hour window in which there was no activity, so the motion detectors in and on the main house had to be disabled except when the occupants were out of town.

With electronic security, detection is only the first part of the system. It is the Closed-Circuit Television (CCTV) cameras that verify the type of intrusion and the number of intruders. Cameras can be either manually controlled, designed to pan to an intrusion automatically or may even be motion sensitive themselves. But all require that someone actually sit and watch the monitors to be of value.

The simplest form of CCTV is the single camera placed at a gate or door to verify the identity of a visitor before they are buzzed in. On the other end of the scale, a five or six acre estate may require as many as twenty or thirty cameras to have full coverage of the perimeter, entrances and parking areas. In addition, some clients may request additional cameras to cover an expensive art collection in the house, or a children's play area and swimming pool more for safety than security.

The design and implementation of a security system is an art form in itself, the best ones also having the potential for future expansion built into them. There is a large amount of basic ready to install hardware on the market, but the better system designers take the existing technology and customize it to better suit the location, its intended application and the lifestyle of the occupants.

It is strongly recommended that a professional systems design company be used to design a system and supervise its installation. The design company should be selected for its proven track record with similar systems and letters of recommendation from previous satisfied customers. They should also be able to supply photos and details of recently completed systems.

The most significant problem with many systems is false alarms or alerts. A poorly designed system or incorrectly applied equipment, can false because of a number of environmental factors, human errors or simply bad positioning. For example, ground sensors will be tripped by the roots of large trees blowing in the wind or by pounding surf on beach front properties. IR beams and micro-wave sensors can be tripped by small animals, curtains blowing in the wind, or even movement outside the perimeter. Motion and light sensitive cameras can be disabled by direct sunlight, car headlights, deep shadows, overhanging trees, rain and garden sprinkler systems. All electronics, not properly placed or water-proofed, can be damaged by water from drains, rain or sprinklers.

A system that continually falses, like the boy who cried wolf, will be shut down or simply ignored. For a system to be effective it must be utilized, maintained and calibrated regularly. The most common damage to perimeter security systems is caused by gardeners and maintenance men unaware of the location of wires, cables, sensors and junction boxes. Apart from educating the groundsmen, these need to be checked regularly for cuts, damage and alignment by the on-duty BG and the system's installers.

Pan-tilt zoom cameras with environmental housings

For corporate offices, where employees need a certain freedom of movement and image is important, overt physical security is generally not appropriate. What is more suitable is an electronic access control system either with specially coded cards or digital key pads. This gives those that need to have access freedom of movement but restricts the movements of unescorted visitors.

Key areas in the corporate office can also be covered with small CCTV cameras set-up to record 24 hours-a-day. These may not deny access but they do deter crime, letting people know their presence is being surveilled and recorded.

For high threat applications, an access control system can be monitored by cameras and manned by a security guard. This further deters intrusion by adding a human element, and is actually capable of denying unauthorized access.

CCTV monitoring system

GUARD SERVICES

Where the bodyguard moves with the principal handling his daily security needs, properties and buildings are usually protected by uniformed security guards. Even the US Secret Service has a uniformed branch to handle the property security for the first family.

For security to be effective, it must be complete and consistent. The most important reason for maintaining around the clock security is to prevent an intruder or kidnapper gaining access to a location while the principal is away. More than one celebrity has come home to find a fan hiding in their house.

To use highly trained bodyguards (and often highly paid), is a waste for property protection. Apart from the cost, the bodyguard will become bored watching monitors for more than a few days. The security guard is better suited to this job and is a more single minded, dedicated individual who will not be bored with this task.

If the threat level is high, the BGs should definitely be utilized for all aspects of security, but for the more routine assignments, the contract or in-house security service will be more cost effective.

As an added deterrent, the guard service can be supplemented by a K-9 guard patrol. Dogs are extremely effective when it comes to finding an intruder on a large, wooded property or even in a large house. In addition, where most criminals may be somewhat unimpressed by uniformed security guards or "rent-a-cops", they have infinitely more respect for a well trained German Shepherd or Rottweiler

As with the bodyguards, security guards must not be utilized for non-security related tasks. The purpose of the security guards is:

• To watch the CCTV monitoring systems
• To respond to intruders or alarm activations
• To patrol and inspect outer perimeters
• To control staff and visitor access
• To inspect, clean and maintain security equipment
• To supervise vehicle movement and parking
• To notify supervisors of defective monitoring equipment
• To maintain security and visitor logs
• To contact police when necessary

The position of uniformed security guard is generally a low paying job. These guards are not rocket scientists and are not hired for their creative thinking, initiative or imagination. They are more a single minded worker who is given a task and can hopefully be depended upon to do it competently.

• Security guards must be given specific instructions on all aspects of their duties.
• They must initially work under a supervisor or training officer until they have shown a solid grasp of their duties and are performing them to a satisfactory standard.
• Every security job site should have a simple but detailed manual of the duties and procedures for that location.
• Contact with the principals must be limited to responsible supervisors only.
• The principals must be briefed on the duties and limitations of the security guards. They must also understand the difference between their BGs and a regular guard.

All of the above are as much to protect the security guard's job as they are to contribute to the smooth running of an operation.

Good gates and fences are essential, but they must still be monitored by guards or CCTV.

Ground sensing systems require extensive trenching and landscaping.

PART III
OPERATIONS

"When it is expedient in operations, the general need
not be restricted by the commands of the sovereign."
—Ts'ao Ts'ao, in *The Art of War*

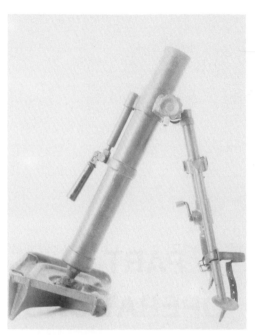

The mortar is crude but effective.

The Sagger anti-tank system has also turned up in terrorist hands.

19

OPERATIONAL SECURITY

Operational Security, or Op-Sec, is a significant element in all tactical operations. While friendly forces, through aggressive intelligence collection, try to learn as much as possible about the enemy, it is equally important that they practice good counter intelligence. They must deny the enemy any knowledge of their strength, deployment, defenses or future movement. This concept is also valid in executive protection.

The three main purposes for operational security within a protection operation are:

1. To deny criminals and terrorists information that may help them in formulating a plan or staging an attack on a principal.
2. To protect the private life of the principal and his family from the unwanted attention of the public and especially the parasitic tabloid news media.
3. To protect the principal's business interests and deny information to competitors, vendors, contractors, technology thieves and industrial saboteurs.

Operational security, just like counter intelligence work, is preventive and preemptive in nature. Once information has been leaked, it cannot be un-leaked. Either plans must be cancelled or the risks accepted. To ensure good operational security, two areas must be studied for leaks:

• The bodyguards and security staff
• The principal's own staff and family

THE BODYGUARDS

Operational security should become an active, conscious and routine part of bodyguarding. In addition, the principal has the right to expect that a sense of confidentiality be an integral part of the overall security effort.

For the bodyguards to disclose information directly related to the protection detail or security systems is not only unacceptable and unprofessional, it totally nullifies the value of both the procedures and the hardware. Any system that is known can be circumvented.

The following is just some of the information related to security that the BG should consider "need to know only" and avoid discussing outside of the security team.

- The nature and extent of the electronic security system
- Any key-pad codes required to open gates or disarm systems
- Which vehicles are armored and which are not
- Numbers for private phone lines into the residence or office
- Numbers for emergency phone lines hooked into security
- The time of movement of the principal to and from work
- Any details relating to future overseas travel

Apart from the security team and system, the bodyguards must also protect any personal or private information about the clients. This should cover not only the dirt, the scandal and the gossip, but any and all aspects of their personal lives.

The following are some of the subjects to be avoided:

- Details about the principals' personal lives
- Details about the house or its content
- The identity of friends and visitors
- The location of the children's school
- Information related to marital discord
- Information related to domestic disputes
- Preferred sports clubs, nightclubs and restaurants
- Domestic staff gossip and rumor

Obviously, with very famous or high profile clients, the bodyguards will find themselves constantly being pumped for information or gossip. This must be avoided with not only the press and strangers but also with friends and family members. A supposedly innocent and inadvertent comment getting back to a client can cost a BG his job. The BG must always remember that he is in a position of trust and that trust must be respected.

To reinforce Op-Sec, prior to employment, all security staff should be required to sign a confidentiality agreement that covers both the security team and the client. To further protect the client, the agreement should restrict unauthorized news interviews, press releases, articles and books relating to their work or duties on a particular contract.

THE STAFF & FAMILY

The staff and family can also be a source of leaks relating to security procedures and client movement, so it may fall upon the BG to educate all concerned in this area.

Idle conversation and gossip are the first things to be avoided but those are only the beginning. The trash that comes out of private residences or corporate offices can also give a wealth of information about an individual's personal life and habits. The average trash basket can contain letters, faxes, communications, credit card statements, cancelled checks, gas receipts, restaurant receipts, motel receipts, phone bills with numbers, copies of invoices, the carbon copies of documents, old dictaphone tapes, used airline tickets, frequent flier up-dates, old desk calendars, desk blotters with notes and numbers, subscription coupons, club membership reminders, etc, etc, etc.... Get the picture? A person's entire life and finances can be culled from the trash bin.

Fortunately, most people who work or live with the rich and famous are very conscious of the responsibilities. However, apart from general common sense, all staff and family members need to be schooled in the following:

• Do not give information to people who do not need it
• Be especially careful about talking on telephones
• Do not give out home addresses or phone numbers
• Do not release itineraries or travel information
• Do not discuss business strategies
• Do not discuss future business acquisitions
• Shred any documents related to future travel
• Shred any documents related to future business strategies

MOVEMENT & TRAVEL

Since foreign travel and public appearances bring with them increased exposure, it behooves the security director to cultivate a trustworthy and reliable corporate travel agent. Like the family and the office staff, the travel agents must be educated as to what is required of them from a security standpoint. Primarily this entails total confidentiality on all arrangements and the hand delivery of all itineraries and airline tickets.

Where possible, the principal and bodyguards should fly private and stay in private accommodation when traveling. But this is not always possible. On high risk assignments where the client must fly commercial and stay in hotels, it is not a bad tactic to make multiple airline bookings and multiple hotel reservations, only cancelling the unwanted ones at the last minute. Similarly, rental cars can be changed daily and different routes should be planned in advance.

The only areas that are hard to control are scheduled public appearances, important meetings and special invitation only functions. At these times the security team must adopt a heightened level of alert.

Author's Note: The following is example of not only stupidity and a lack of common sense but also a violation of basic operational security.

Some years ago we were working a safe house with a principal whose whereabouts were to remain unknown. All was going well until a BG we will call Snow, an ex-military policeman and normally reliable character, came on duty.

Snow, in the throws of new found love or lust, decided to give his work phone number to his new girlfriend. But instead of giving a cellular number, a beeper number or even the private security line number, Snow gives her the main house number. To compound the problem, he also told her the name of the principal and the location of the house.

So picture this. Phone rings, the principal picks it up and a female voice says, "Oh, is this you Mr X, can I speak to my Snow?". So much for Mr X's sense of security and privacy.

It is not surprising that big Snow lost his job. He also lost his girlfriend but luckily was able to get into a police academy and go on to become a cop.

Taut-wire systems

Passive infrared

Ground sensors

Anti-disturbance

20

RESIDENTIAL SECURITY

We know from past incidents that protecting the principal and his family at the residence is an important part of the security package. The residence being one predictable location in the principal's daily schedule.

Because of the level of wealth associated with those who have bodyguards, they do not generally live in regular sized houses but more often in mansions on large estates or ranches— and in some cases palaces or castles. Whatever the nature of the residence, the bodyguard will almost surely find himself pulling duty on the property.

In generic terms, property protection, either residential or corporate, is usually referred to as static security. This implies that a guard is anchored to a work station, with possibly some roving patrol work, from which he monitors a security system and points of ingress and egress for the property. Most professionally trained bodyguards will find static security duty mind-numbing and boring except when working high risk assignments. It is for this reason that static security is generally relegated to either a uniformed security guard service or the rookie bodyguards.

Apart from the routine 24-hour property security, the BG may periodically find himself pulling short stints monitoring a CCTV system, entrance or reception area. This often occurs when the principal is at his residence or office and does not require the immediate close protection of the BG. At this time, the BG will usually locate himself so as to best monitor and control access to the principal. However, there are limitations as to just how effective one BG can be in this situation.

WASHINGTON (Reuter) 10/29/94—The Secret Service identified the gunman who shot at the White House on Saturday as Francisco Martin Duran, a 26-year-old male from Colorado Springs, Colorado. At a White House briefing, Richard Griffin, assistant director of the U.S. Secret Service, in charge of protective operations, said Duran fired 20 to 30 rounds from an SKS Chinese semi-automatic rifle. Griffin said: "The president was in no danger what so ever."

Griffin said there was no reason to believe the attack was anything but the work of a lone gunman, but said the investigation was just beginning. White House Chief of Staff Leon Panetta told reporters that the gunman appeared to have fired randomly at the executive mansion. Bullets hit several parts of the building and at least one smashed a window in the press briefing room.

Panetta said the shooting obviously raised concerns about security for the president and would be discussed as part of an overall review of security initiated after a small plane penetrated defenses around the president's home six weeks ago and crashed into the White House lawn.

Investigation of these incidents will show that they were virtually unavoidable, and that the existing security procedures worked. The high fence around the grounds deters and denies easy access; the distance from the fence to the White House further makes approach difficult; the open grounds deny concealment to an intruder; and the thickness of the walls and bullet resistant materials used in the windows all but eliminate the probability of conventional ammunition penetrating the structure. Add to these the quick response of the uniformed branch guards, the constant proximity of DC police and the Secret Service snipers on the roof and the package is complete.

To totally eliminate assaults of this type, short of ringing the entire grounds with troops, tanks and high walls, would be costly, unsightly and impractical. This is in part due to the fact that the White House is not just the office and residence of the President, it is an important symbol of American freedom and an open democracy. "We the people" must feel that we have access to both our representatives and the symbols of our democratic system. Can you imagine some poor street merchant in Baghdad wanting to tour Saddam Hussein's palace? Considering the levels of distrust and political paranoia in any dictatorship, it is just not going to happen.

Although this type of random attack may scare the hell out of the occupants and rattle the security team, it can in no way be confused with a serious attack. With the advent of modern weapons, even military commanders recognize the vulnerability of fixed base defenses. The wood and stone forts of days gone by would quickly fall to modern weapons, high explosives, long range artillery, surface to ground missiles and aerial bombing. Even in a war zone, with all the might of the United States military, fixed location security cannot be guaranteed.

1983, October 23rd, 6:22 AM—A yellow Mercedes truck crosses the parking lot of the Beirut International Airport, crashes through a chain-link fence and comes to rest in the lobby of the terminal building, being used to house the 24th Marine Amphibious Unit. Seconds later, the 12,000 pounds of explosives in the truck detonates almost leveling the barracks, killing 241 Marines and injuring many others.

This act of terrorism, perpetrated by a dedicated religious fanatic could not be stopped. Yet a similar attempt at another location was foiled by one British military bodyguard who, upon recognizing a similar attack, managed to shoot the driver and stop the truck.

The key problem at the Marine barracks was one of mind-set on the part of the command staff. Firstly, they did not implement the necessary physical counter-measures to control vehicular approach; and secondly, did not put their troops on a high enough level of alert to respond to such an attack. Checkpoint guards were not allowed to carry weapons at Condition One and were unclear as to the rules of engagement (ROE).

At least the military learned from their mistakes and upgraded procedures in the numerous conflicts of recent years. An attempted repeat of the Beirut incident would have met far stronger resistance in Somalia, Saudi Arabia, Kuwait, Haiti and Bosnia.

However, these two incidents further illustrate the limitations of the lone bodyguard when trying to secure a property. At a minimum, property protection should be a team effort, and only then with the support of both electronic surveillance and physical counter measures.

ESTATE SECURITY

On short term celebrity contracts, the BG may be released after getting the principal safely back to the residence, or he may be required to stay on property. In some cases, the BG may be required to man some form of security monitoring system, be it a simple panic button or intrusion alarm or a more sophisticated active perimeter, CCTV monitoring system.

On some jobs, more typically with full-time personal security teams, the BG may be required to stay in the house with the principal, answering the door and serving dual function as a butler or personal assistant.

Other clients will expect their security package encompass not only the house and property but also the whole family. If there is a real threat, the family would be an opportune alternative target and the residence a choice predictable location. In reality, all this is beyond the scope of one bodyguard, but it does not stop many from trying. After all, a job is a job and there are not many good ones out there.

Whichever category the BG falls into, there are certain basic rules for operating in and around the residence. Some procedures are based on good security practice and common sense while others will be dictated by the client. To avoid any confusion, these must be discussed at length with the client, his business manager or personal assistant.

Many of the political problems that can be encountered are covered in Chapters 5 & 6, however, it is also helpful to have some written guideline or SOP manual, especially if there is more than one BG working a location.

ACCESS CONTROL

The primary duty of the bodyguard when working on an estate is to respond quickly to any threat to the principal or his family. But since attacks are not a daily occurrence, the BG's next duty will be to control the access of unwanted visitors. This is often complicated by the significant number of visitors who are welcome, along with staff, maintenance people and deliveries.

When working the estate, the BG will be expected to monitor the front gate, verify visitors and, in some cases, escort visitors to the client. This will require that the bodyguard be familiar with all the regular visitors and be supplied a current list of those with access. In fact, there should be two lists. One a list of close friends and associates who have free access at any time, and a second list, up-dated daily, of the expected visitors for that day or week.

To make this vetting process more efficient, there should also be a CCTV camera and voice box positioned at the front gate. This saves both time and shoe leather. The BG will also want to maintain a log of all visitors, especially maintenance personnel and service people. At any given time, the log should reflect who is still on property and which principals have left the property.

Where budget allows, and since the BG is already assigned to monitoring the gate, a full perimeter security system should be installed. This is the only way one man can realistically surveil a large property. The down side of this type of operation being that when the BG is working alone and responds to a suspected intrusion, no one is left in the guard shack to track the intruder on the security surveillance system.

If access is to be controlled effectively, there must be 24 hour coverage. Even when the principal is at work or traveling, the property must be secured. If the property is unattended at any time or openly accessed by service personnel, groundsmen and pool cleaners, there is a high probability that an intruder, stalker, obsessed fan or assassin could enter and lay in wait for the principal's return. More than one celebrity has been surprised by a fan hiding in their closet or bathroom.

It is simply too time consuming for the BG to have to sweep a large mansion or the grounds of an entire estate for possible intruders every time the principal returns. It is best to clear the property once and then keep it that way; then when required, doing periodic searches of the house, basement, staff quarters, storage areas, pool houses and wooded areas on the grounds .

THE GUARD SHACK

If a property and client warrant full-time security then there needs to be some form of room or office where the BGs can go to relax and from which to monitor the CCTVs and perimeter detection systems.

Over the years, we have heard this room called a security office, central monitoring, the communications center, but ultimately they all end up being referred to as the guard shack. But immaterial of the humble terminology, this room should not in any way be shack-like, untidy or unprofessional.

In most cases, the guard shack becomes not only a monitoring station but also a lunch room and a place for other BGs to hang out while waiting for their principal. This is not ideal since any off-duty or stand-by activity will distract the BG on duty from the monitors and zone board. However, few clients are willing to pay for both a guard shack and a recreation room.

In addition to the essential monitoring equipment, the guard shack should have:

• A multi-line phone system
• Radio chargers
• A large safe for guns and valuables
• A couch for visitors
• A small refrigerator & coffee pot
• Possibly a micro-wave oven
• Individual lockers

The guard shack should not have nude pin-up calendars, a supply of Playboy and Penthouse magazines, porno video tapes, a boom-box or stereo, empty pizza boxes or dirty laundry.

Extra guns or ammunition should be kept in the safe and not left lying around. There should be no alcohol on site or beer in the refrigerator. There should be a neatly kept phone log, visitor log and a notice board for messages and procedural changes. The phones should not be used for personal calls and the BGs should be dressed appropriately at all times. The guard shack is a place of business not home. The client should be able to walk in at any time, day or night, and see an alert, professionally dressed BG on duty—not a scene out of "Hawkeye's Swamp" in the TV series M.A.S.H.

Guest room being utilized as the guard shack

SECURITY PROCEDURES

A bodyguard should establish four basic routines when working estate security:

1. Initial familiarization with the house and property
2. Familiarization with the existing security system
3. A daily property and system check prior to each shift change
4. Standard response procedures for an intruder on the property

Upon arriving on a property for the first time, the BG must familiarize himself with the general layout of the house and grounds. Ideally, this should be a guided tour, done in daylight with someone intimately familiar with the property. The BG should pay special attention to gates, doors, and their function; locations of light switches and telephones; types of alarm systems and exterior lighting; safe rooms; staff and staff quarters; parking areas and garages; dead spots in the camera coverage; and any portions of the perimeter fence that may be damaged or over-grown.

If there is an anti-intrusion system, then the BG will need to be trained in its operation. This will include information on the types of detectors, the function of zone indication boards, CCTV tracking and monitoring, general maintenance, malfunction rates, reset procedures and expected off-property response by the police. The BG will also need access to the keys for both the house and cars and combinations for safes or coded key pads.

Upon arrival on shift, there should be a half hour overlap in BG hours so that the guard going off duty can brief the guard coming on duty. This overlap will also allow the new BG to walk the grounds and check the house.

A quick review of the log should reflect who is on property, any malfunctioning equipment, zones or cameras down, special requests from the principal, messages for the principal, the time for house phones to be shut down at night, any requested wake-up calls and the status of vehicles.

The most important security procedure that needs to be established on any estate is the response to an intrusion or threat. In most cases, this is two fold: 1/ What is expected of the principal and family; 2/ What is expected of the BG.

Again we see the limitation of one BG. When an intruder is suspected or identified on the property, does the BG go to cover the principal or begin a search for the intruder? Does he secure the principal first or go to the children's rooms?

Ideally, there should be a minimum of two guards, but barring that, the lone BG should go directly to the principal. Keep in mind that the principal, following paternal instinct, will go directly to the kids' rooms. If the client has spent some money on security planning, there will be a convenient safe room for the family to hold-up in while awaiting the cavalry.

Normally, the BG on duty will notify the principal of an intruder and direct him to go to the safe room. The BG then calls for back-up and goes directly to the principal's location, but unfortunately, must leave the monitors and thus not be able to track the intruder.

The BG, now with the principal and family, maintains contact with the responding supervisor or back-up through the use of hand-held radios or cellular telephones. He gives constant up-dates but stays off of the house phone lines since these can be monitored by an intruder picking up an extension.

The BG stays with the principal until the police or a back-up BG team arrives to search for the intruder and secure the premise. When all is secure, considering the scare for the family, the additional security should stay on site for the rest of the shift.

If there are two BGs on shift then one will go directly to the principal while the other monitors the system and up-dates the response team. If there is a security team of four or more, then one individual will monitor the cameras and system, one will go directly to the principal and the remainder, at least two, can respond to the intrusion or sweep the property.

CONFRONTING THE INTRUDER

Once an intrusion is suspected or identified, the BGs' first responsibility is to protecting the principal, but once that is assured, the team may chose to find and apprehend the intruder. In all honesty, there is nothing quite as satisfying as catching a villain in the act. Conversely, it is quite disconcerting to have an intruder escape without the opportunity to find out his identity or intent.

Making the decision to find and confront an intruder must be predicated by one important question. Am I trained and qualified to do this?

Security guards are usually only trained to "observe and report". Bodyguards are usually trained to "observe and protect". But very rarely do either group receive the necessary training to go on the offensive. Without the training that police officers get in this type of procedure, and a sound knowledge of street survival tactics, the protection specialist is better off staying with the principal and awaiting professional response.

If the decision is made to search for the intruder, personal safety becomes the paramount concern. The searchers, at least two, must move quietly and cautiously avoiding turning their backs on any uncleared areas. If the property has a sophisticated intrusion surveillance and tracking system then the guard on the monitors will be able to assist by talking the searchers onto the intruder's suspected location.

Before the search is begun, the back-up team should have been notified and, if warranted, rolling to the location. The search team should also have checked their weapons and flashlights and formulated a plan.

To detail the actual search procedures could take a whole book of its own, and these procedures will change from one situation to another and from property to property. Training and flexibility are the key elements. Suffice to say that if the BG has not been trained for this and has not practiced with the team under realistic conditions, then he is just as big a hazard in the dark as the intruder.

When searching:

- Always use a trained partner
- Wear body armor if available
- Utilize or be aware of cover where ever possible
- Do not turn your back on uncleared areas
- Practice good light discipline
- Practice safe weapons procedure
- Use ear pieces to silence radios
- Keep radio traffic to a minimum
- Move quietly and cautiously
- Communicate your observations to your partner
- Cover each other when clearing dark areas and doors

When initially confronting an intruder:

- Try to confront the intruder from behind cover
- Maintain maximum distance and get verbal compliance before approaching
- Be wary of a possible second intruder or partner
- Watch the hands for suspected weapons
- Have the suspect interlace his fingers behind his head
- Have the suspect go to the kneeling position and cross ankles
- If warranted have the suspect prone out with arms extended and palms turned upward
- One partner covers as the other goes in to cuff
- Always cuff before searching
- Communicate your status to the response team

For routine situations where the principal needs to call the BG, he should use the house phone, intercom or beeper. For emergencies, there should be a system of silent alarm panic buttons strategically placed throughout the house.

Procedures and supplies should also be in place for emergencies such as fire, flood, earthquake and other such natural disasters.

UNPROFESSIONALISM

Working on an estate or ranch is very different to the more conventional bodyguard duties in that it is very easy to fall into unprofessional habits. Most of these stem from the fact that over a period of time, the BGs begin to feel too relaxed and too comfortable.

This confusion does not occur when, for example, escorting a client to a black tie function. The only acceptable dress is a tuxedo and the BG is always alert for potential sources of danger. Similarly, when working executive protection of corporate security, business suits and sport coats are the order of the day. However, on an estate, especially at night, the dress code is more relaxed.

At first, the BGs will wear slacks and jackets with comfortable shoes, but after a while that may slip to black jeans and a windbreaker. Before long, guards are turning up in faded blue jeans, T-shirts and combat boots, or sweats and tennis shoes. On some contracts, like working for a rock-and-roll star, this may be acceptable and appropriate, but on an estate belonging to a senior executive, the appearance of the BGs should reflect the taste and status of the principal.

The problem is that when no comment is made about a particular style of dress or behavior, the BGs will take it a step further. Becoming so comfortable in a position that they lose sight of the fact that they are working and not relaxing at home.

If a lax attitude is permitted to go unchallenged, some individuals will push the limits by smoking and drinking on the job or even having women over while on night shift. Next comes raiding the client's refrigerator, borrowing video tapes, doing laundry on site, making long distance calls on the house phones, using the Rolls to run errands, taking advantage of household charge accounts at supermarkets and pharmacies, having friends stop by when working, and the list goes on.

To avoid this deterioration in professionalism, standards must be established in all aspects of dress, behavior and procedure. These should be documented, read and signed by all staff members.

Author's Note: One time I found it necessary to terminate a BG for drinking on the job. The individual then tried to sue for wrongful termination. Even though admitting to the judge that he had been drinking, his argument was that there was no written directive forbidding drinking on duty. I won the case but it seems that these things are important and that common sense does not always prevail in court. We now put everything in writing, in great detail.

THE SAFE HOUSE

Both federal and private sector protection teams periodically find a need for safe houses. For the US Marshal's Service and FBI it is most often for the purpose of protecting a key witness in a high profile court case. Usually drug or mob related. For the CIA it is to house a defector or spy during the long debriefing process.

For the private sector bodyguard there are several possibilities: a safe house to secure a client being threatened or stalked; a local private residence for a visiting VIP; a house for a mistress where the principal can visit with complete discretion; or a temporary residence for an individual experiencing a nasty divorce or high profile litigation.

A safe house should be a detached house since there are too many problems associated with hotels or condos. A hotel has too much public access to all floors; too many staff members; and too little control over the phone system and food preparation. In addition, hotels are like very small towns, ripe with gossip and speculation. Short of taking over a whole floor with a large team of BGs, hotels are simply too public.

The same is true of most condos and apartment buildings that have too many nosy neighbors and poor access control.

A detached house on the other hand, carries a certain expectation of privacy, especially if the client and BGs avoid acting in a suspicious manner. When moving into an established neighborhood, it is important that everything appear normal and that there be not too much unnecessary late night movement.

A house can be rented under a different name, using the pretext of a writer needing seclusion, newly weds wanting privacy, a convalescing patient, or a wealthy senior executive just visiting the area on business.

Security around a safe house is similar to an estate but dependent more on secrecy and discretion than physical or electronic security measures. Never-the-less, the house should be selected for maximum distance from other houses, natural privacy afforded by walls or trees, easily controlled access points, and secure covered parking for vehicles. It is best if the property has only one primary gate or entry point and that there be a direct access from the garage into the house. It helps if the protectee or BG team is able to drive right into the garage and close the doors before entering the house.

In additional, cars should be changed regularly; BGs must attempt to blend into the neighborhood; phone conversations on house phones should be limited; grounds should be maintained; all normal garbage, mail and delivery routines followed; and the principal briefed on how to act like the perfect neighbor who simply seeks privacy.

Fences, guards and open areas all add to White House security.

21

CORPORATE SECURITY

Corporate security and executive protection makes up the bulk of private sector bodyguard work, matched only by supplying protective services for celebrities and the entertainment industry. It is therefore important that a BG understand the dynamics of corporate life and the necessary security procedures.

The corporate office, like the estate, has its own internal political structure. Just as the praetorian guard is responsible for the emperor, the BG usually answers directly to the principal, who is probably the CEO or owner of the corporation. But it is also important for the BG to know exactly who constitutes the "inner circle" and which administrative assistants handle the boss's personal business and have the authority to make things happen. The principal's personal assistant is the one person who can give the BG some early warning or heads-up on the principal's plans and movements.

The very nature of the corporate structure, from the most junior executive to the chairman of the board, creates a competitive, often cut-throat environment where the players aggressively claw their way up the corporate ladder. To have direct access to the owner or CEO is a major advantage in this race. Knowing this, the BG can view corporate employees in two groups: those who have direct access to the principal and those that would like to have access. Because of the BG's daily contact with the principal and ability to move freely in both his business and personal life, the BG may be viewed as one avenue of approach, or at least a source of inside information on the future plans of the principal.

Another mine-field for the BG is the fact that on any given business day, there will be executives who are in favor and those that are out of favor. This is a fluid situation directly affected by an employee's performance on a given contract, negotiation or deal. To avoid the appearance of disloyalty, it is therefore important for the BG to limit his contact with the staff and not get drawn into the office politics. The BG must try to restrict his communications to those essential to the security, travel planning and daily movement of the principal.

This can be difficult for the bodyguard who has worked for one principal for some time and is invited and drawn into the various social functions that revolve around the corporate family. It is difficult to refuse all of these events, birthdays, weddings, bar mitzvahs and Christmas parties, so at best, the BG must remain conscious of the sensitive position that he holds and avoid any discussion of the principal's personal life or business strategies.

SECURITY CONSIDERATIONS

Part of the threat assessment process in corporate security is to establish which other companies or organizations share the same building as the client. Even though the client's organization may occupy one or two complete floors of a high-rise building, that still leaves several other floors that could have occupants of a higher threat level than the principal.

Author's Note: On one contract, our client owned a multi-story building but his organization only occupied two floors. Most of the other tenants were a cross section of bankers, lawyers and business types, all except one other entire floor which was the consulate for a Middle Eastern country. This significantly raised the overall threat level since our client could have been targeted as the building owner and therefore "a friend of" that country. Or he could have simply become a victim of collateral damage created by an attack on the consulate.

Barring any obvious known threats, corporate office security begins at the principal's assigned parking space and works inward from there. His personal parking should be unmarked, well lit and close to the entrance or elevators. If security has a chase vehicle, a parking space should be made available in close proximity to the principal's space. Valet parking attendants should be briefed on any special handling or parking arrangements for the principal's car. They should also be encouraged to be observant and to report any unusual activity.

The parking area, entrance and elevators are the areas of highest potential risk for the BG. They provide an attacker with a predictable location, the easiest access, surveillance and an avenue of escape. Any attempted penetration into the inner offices would be restricted by access control systems and making escape more difficult.

For kidnappers, the best time to hit the principal is enroute to the office, slowing for an intersection or entering the parking structure, but before he comes under the security coverage of his office and staff. The underground parking structure, out of public view and off the streets, also offers an excellent opportunity for the snatch.

The main lobby of the corporate office should have uniformed security or information officers who have CCTV monitoring of all accesses and lobbies. The actual reception area for the CEO's offices should have video surveillance, carded or coded access control, with a receptionist who can buzz visitors in when necessary.

The reception area should be the holding area where unescorted visitors wait until the executive they are to meet comes to greet them. From there, a visitor should have to pass the front receptionist, the principal's assistant and the BG before having direct access to the inner sanctum.

The bodyguard should select, or be provided, a convenient office or small room, close to the principal's, and if possible, with a video feed from the lobby, elevator and reception CCTV cameras. If there is a system of panic buttons in the key senior executives' offices, then the monitoring should also be pulled into the BG's control room.

After controlling the access of personnel, the protection specialist should also consider mail, package and delivery control. Couriers and messengers should leave all deliveries with the front receptionist, but the packages they deliver must be checked. This could be a duty for the BG, or if there is already a well set-up mail reception room, packages should be screened through there. All suspicious or unexpected deliveries should be carefully investigated. (See Chapter 17 for procedures).

Another collateral duty for the BG could be to brief all office staff on basic security awareness, a healthy suspicion of strangers, telephone procedure and the importance of confidentiality concerning the principal's plans and movements.

Lastly, if they do not already exist, the BG should work-up a set of written guidelines covering his duties and response procedures for the corporate office, then having the principal read and authorize them.

DAILY ROUTINE

The daily routine for the corporate bodyguard will revolve around the principal's schedule and work habits. If the principal routinely heads to the office at 8:00 AM then the BG needs to be checking the cars at 7:00 and ready to roll at 7:45. However, this schedule can change, so the principal's AM meeting times should be confirmed with his personal assistant the night before. It is also a good habit to confirm directly with the principal as he is delivered back to the residence in the evening.

Author's Note: When working corporate clients, I would send one team to collect the principal in the morning and one team directly to the corporate office to check that location. The team at the office would clear the principal's personal office and bathroom, verify access codes for that day, check radios and monitors, and then wait in the parking area for the arrival of the principal. The chase team would follow the principal into the parking area and then hand-off to the office security team when they were given the "all OK" sign.

Upon first arriving at the office, the BG will escort the principal to his office, then begin his morning checks. These could include:

• Phone the residence security team and verify safe arrival
• Verify that office access codes have not been changed
• Check with the principal's assistant for schedule changes

- Call down to building security for any incident reports from the night before
- Talk to the building maintenance supervisor about any expected maintenance activity in the principal's area
- Check that all monitors and cameras are on line
- Check that all radios and cellular phones are charged and functioning
- Check the location and condition of any emergency equipment

After all the checks are done, the BG will usually settle in to monitor the CCTVs and observe visitors.

At lunch time, a number of things can happen. If the principal has a luncheon meeting at another location then the BG will usually go with him. If he eats in the executive dining room or penthouse private club, then the BG will usually eat in his office or may be able to slip out for half an hour. The best solution, to avoid having to leave the monitoring station, is to either bring a packed lunch or have it delivered.

Whatever the procedure, the BG must be equipped with a pager, radio or cellular phone so that he can be called back quickly. Most principal's are understanding of the necessary creature comforts of their security staff and make allowances. However, if the threat level warrants, then a relief BG should come in to cover the lunch period. Another solution is to schedule the BG shift change at noon, allowing the replacement to stay with the principal until 8:00 p.m. or even midnight.

When the principal leaves in the afternoon or evening, the BG will accompany the principal to his car or limousine and then either hand-off to the chase team, follow in a chase vehicle or ride with the principal. The BG should be in a heightened state of alert during the movement through the parking structure, driving to the residence, approaching the residence and until safely within the walls.

COUNTER MEASURES & PROCEDURES
The following are a list of possible counter measures that could be employed to improve office security.

- Control all office access
- All visitors should be escorted
- Restrict after-hours access to the offices
- Secure and check executive washrooms
- Maintenance closets should have locks
- ID badges should be worn by all employees in large corporations
- Fire protection equipment should be inspected regularly
- The principal should have a safe room attached to his office
- Emergency supplies should be maintained for natural disasters, fires, injuries or siege situations
- All publicity releases should be vetted by security
- Incoming mail should be routed through a screening process
- Parking structures should be secured
- Principal's travel itineraries should not be released

To conclude, corporate security can be a difficult task, since the principal still needs to work and many people need to have access to him on a daily basis. The corporate office will usually have a known address that can be easily accessed by the public, maintenance personnel and delivery services. In addition, the client may not be the only tenant in an office complex.

All of these factors create a situation where sound security procedure is often compromised or sacrificed for the sake of public image and business efficiency.

Substantial access control systems used at many embassies

Limos and chase cars lined up, guarded and ready to go

Author (left) and team working in Greece. Bus is for guests and staff.

22

GOING MOBILE

Although the rich and famous may feel safe within the high walls of their estates and offices, to enjoy their fame and fortune they must be able to venture out into the real world. Unfortunately for many, because of their status, it is difficult to move freely in public without being recognized or drawing unwanted attention. Even the most powerful businessmen and politicians can be intimidated by the simple daily pleasures that the average citizen considers routine.

For those who do not wish to be confined by their own celebrity, there are only two practical solutions. Either try to conceal one's appearance under a ball cap and sunglasses and take the risk of recognition, or hire a security team or bodyguard. The down side of the security team is that this often draws even more unwanted attention, where as a single BG may be less effective but a lot more discreet.

For bodyguards, going mobile with a client is not only their most important function, it is also one of the most difficult. Unlike out of town or overseas trips that are carefully planned, moving around the home town or city is more of a spontaneous, daily, less organized affair.

If a BG is a full-time employee, he is prone to be called upon at any hour of the day or night to go mobile with a client. It may be dinner at a local restaurant, a movie, shopping, the need to meet with a friend, a trip to the beach or park, or a myriad of the other distractions that make life interesting. Whatever the occasion, the BG must maintain a constant state of readiness.

There are however, several things that the motivated BG can do to make his job a little more manageable and a little less confusing. The first priorities are preparation and planning. If the BG knows his principal well, he will be able to anticipate certain moves based on prior experience and the principal's normal daily routine. The BG will also find it helpful to cultivate a working relationship with the principal's secretary or personal assistant. Either of these individuals can give the BG some early warning based on the principal's plans or appointments.

There are also more general procedures that the BG can implement:

- The principal's car should be kept clean, gassed and ready
- Security chase vehicles should be kept gassed and ready
- Chase vehicles should be parked so that they are ready to pull straight out
- The BG should have petty cash on hand for tips, valet parking, movie tickets or minor incidentals
- The BG should keep a suitable change of clothes in his car for various occasions
- Radios, cellular phones and pagers should be kept turned on at all times
- Secretaries, butlers and limo drivers should be instructed to notify the BG at the first indication that the principal may be going out

The simplest way to anticipate a principal's movement is to just ask the principal what his or her plans are for the day. Some BGs are intimidated by talking directly to the principal, but if there is no personal assistant to ask, this is still the best way to avoid embarrassing confusion or delay. Luckily, most principals are creatures of habit and after even a few weeks of employment the intelligent BG should have a good grasp of his duties. However, the professional should never become complacent and must always anticipate the unexpected.

As soon as the BG is notified of a pending movement, he should ascertain the following:

- What is the ultimate destination
- How many in the principal's party
- How many BGs are required
- What is the appropriate dress for the occasion
- What time are they expected to arrive at the location
- Method of transportation; personal vehicle, limo, etc
- Should the BG ride in the car or limo, or take a chase vehicle
- What is the expected function of the BG at the event
- What is the expected departure time from the residence
- Are there any secondary stops or destinations

The ultimate destination, in most circumstances, will dictate the dress, and the number of principal's or family members may affect the number of BGs. The destination may also dictate the method of transportation and the function of the BGs both enroute and upon arrival. The most common destinations are social engagements, restaurants, nightclubs, movies and shopping. For most occasions, parking will be a problem, so it is preferable to have a dedicated driver(s) drop both the principals and the BG(s) at the location and then stay with the car(s). This avoids the problems incurred with either finding parking or valet parking.

When looking for parking, there is no guarantee that one will be able to find adjacent spaces for both the principal's vehicle and the security chase car. With valet parking, there is not only the inconvenience of waiting while they find car and keys, but the fact that the car may be left unlocked and unattended. If valet parking must be used, the car should not contain any valuables or security equipment, and particularly no weapons. In addition, there should be no keys except the ignition key on the key ring and the registration or anything with addresses or personal information should be removed from the car. This avoids the problems commonly associated with leaving both house keys and a home address in a car with a minimum wage valet parking attendant who may have possible criminal tendencies.

SOCIAL ENGAGEMENTS

Social engagements can range from a private dinner at a friend's house to a celebrity black tie affair. Between these two fall a wide range of weddings, cocktail parties, political events, museum and gallery openings, conferences, bridal showers, bachelor parties and charity luncheons.

As stated above, the key to success is being prepared and organizing some form of early warning. If there is time or opportunity for some advance work then the BG should take a drive to the location to, one, learn the route and identify the drop-off point and, two, scope out any potential problems with the public or press. If there is no time to actually drive to and from the location, the BG should at least get out a map and familiarize himself with the best possible route.

Another helpful tactic is to ascertain who has security responsibility for the particular event and to make direct contact with the director or shift supervisor. By notifying the host security of the principal's impending arrival, they can make parking available and alert the BG of the current crowd status and best drop-off points.

The function of the bodyguard upon arrival will often be dictated by the principal and the type of event. In general, at smaller and more exclusive events, the BG should give the principal room to socialize, hang back and try not be noticed. In some cases, the principal may feel so safe at the event that he will request the BG to stay with the cars. At larger events with more strangers, the BG should stick closer to the principal and make his presence a little more felt. Again, when in doubt, the BG should ask the principal what he is comfortable with.

At most events, if there is an on-site security presence, they should anticipate the arrival of other protection specialists and make food, refreshments and a rest area available.

RESTAURANTS

Everyone has their favorite little restaurants but it is safe to assume that a principal will also frequent the best restaurants in town. At any given time there will be a number of well known restaurants where the who's who like to "see and be seen". They all go to considerable lengths to become known to the owner, chef or maitre d' so that they get that little extra personal treatment and choice tables.

The professional bodyguard, even though probably not able to afford these establishments, should familiarize himself with all the top restaurants in his town, with particular attention to the exact address, phone numbers, route, parking and main entrance.

When working clients who frequent these restaurants, it is advisable to keep a small notebook with the phone number and the name of the maitre d'. This allows the BG to call ahead, confirm reservations and alert the maitre d' of a principal's arrival.

Reservations should always be made in advance, especially if the principal has a preferred table, there is a large group or if an additional table is required for the BGs. Making reservations is normally the domain of the private secretary but it is not uncommon for this task to fall to BGs if they are also working estate security.

Where possible, the BG should make friends with the maitre d' or at least introduce himself. This will create a mutually beneficial arrangement where the principal will always get the select table and the BG can call the restaurant when the principal is inevitably running late. The BG can also call the maitre d' when they are five minutes away from arrival so that they can ensure the table is cleared and ready. The more important the principal, the better the cooperation the BG can expect.

When first entering a restaurant, or during the advance, the BG should note the locations of entrances, emergency exits, bathrooms and telephones. If possible the principal should have a well placed table away from the serving areas and positioned so that there is not constant foot traffic passing by. The more activity around the table, the more difficult it is for the BG.

If the BGs are to eat in the same restaurant at the same time as the principal, they should select a table at a discreet distance, facing the door but not so that they are directly facing the principal. The principal should not have the feeling he is being watched. It is actually preferable that the BGs not eat at the same time since this can be a distraction but it is periodically unavoidable.

If the BGs must eat, they should make it known to the waiter or waitress that they need to eat immediately and be finished with the bill paid before the principal's party. They should skip the appetizers, order a simple main course only, order no wine or alcohol, request the check as soon as practicable, or have it added to the principal's bill. If the BGs are paying their own bill but with the principal's money, they should leave a reasonably generous tip so that they will be guaranteed good service on the next visit.

Rather than taking a table it is preferable to eat at the bar, especially if that also affords a view of the principal's table. The BGs should be particularly alert when the principal goes to the bathroom and should go at the same time.

The BGs can have the head waiter notify them when the principal requests his check or has ordered dessert or coffee. This will give them time to have the cars brought around and to prepare for the departure.

NIGHTCLUBS

Escorting the principal to a nightclub can be one of the more hazardous parts of a bodyguard's duty, especially if the club has a rough reputation or the principal is escorting a particularly beautiful wife, girlfriend or date. Or for that matter, if the principal is herself a beautiful woman.

The dangers are not the same as those associated with terrorists, kidnappers or assassins, but more drunks, jerks, scum-bags and slimeballs. The same individuals who have no class, wear too many gold chains, cannot stop from staring at women, and generally make a nuisance of themselves.

The BG should stick very close to the principal when passing through crowds and in crowded places such as popular nightclubs. In reality, there should always be at least two BGs, one for the principal and one for his lady. Again, a little advance work can go a long way. By calling ahead, the BG can make sure that the principal's party is cleared at the door and that they have reserved a good table or booth.

If an advance team is available, even one extra BG, they should go ahead to the nightclub to actually select and secure the table and meet with the manager and doormen. A booth is preferable to a table and should be well away from the band and speakers but selected with a view of the dance floor in mind, and easy access to bathrooms and exits. If necessary, the advance team should be authorized to order a bottle of the clubs best champagne to be placed on the table to guarantee the reservation. A two hundred dollar bottle goes a long way toward getting the head waiter's attention and letting the club know that someone is coming who expects VIP treatment.

Once the necessary palms have been greased and the table reserved, the BGs should go to the door to await the arrival of the principal. As soon as the party pulls up, they can be whisked straight through the all too familiar crowd at the door and directly to their table. It is also good form for the BG to make the effort to introduce the club's owner or manager to the principal so that he will continue to be well received as a VIP guest.

At some of the more exclusive clubs and "members only" type establishments the principal may feel quite safe, but at the crowded hard rock clubs, meat markets and flesh-pots, the BGs will definitely earn their pay. With two BGs, one should take responsibility for the principal and the other the lady friend. If the lady is particularly stunning, equally well known or dressed provocatively, then the BGs must escort her to the lady's room and when crossing to the dance floor.

Note: On special assignments where the principal wanted to low key the security, I would take a female bodyguard along so as to appear as just another couple on a date. In this manner we were able to stick close to the principal on the dance floor and the female BG could accompany his date into the bathroom. This only works if both BGs can remain focused on the job and are not distracted by the less formal social atmosphere.

In general, the BGs should let the bouncers or club manager handle any unpleasant encounters with creeps and weirdos. The management will be very conscious of the importance of the principal and make every effort to assure his or her comfort.

One particularly annoying individual is the no-class lecher who cannot stop himself ogling the principal's date. This can prove very disconcerting in the confines of a club, especially if the principal is an older gentleman accompanied by a young model or actress. If the club management cannot take care of this problem, then it is sometimes appropriate for the BGs to indulge in a little subtle intimidation. Most self professed playboys and "latin lovers" are not fighters and will become equally uncomfortable with too much attention from the BGs. However, the best solution is to simply tip the club's bouncer to just toss the jerk's skinny butt out of the club, for whatever reason.

When working as part of a BG team of two or more, a game plan to handle confrontations should be worked out before entering the club. If the BGs are routinely armed, it is sometimes advisable to have one or two go unarmed so that they are better prepared to handle physical altercations. It is much easier to fight in a crowded, confined space if one does not have to worry about being disarmed or a gun falling from its holster in a tussle. This leaves the armed BGs free to cover or evacuate the principal.

Before leaving, the waitresses should be well tipped, along with the manager and bouncers if it is appropriate, especially if the principal likes the club and intends to return in the near future.

MOVIES

Trips to the movies fall into one of three categories; regular public showings, industry showings and special premiers. Premiers are not too much of a problem in that like special events they are planned ahead of time, extra security and police coverage are laid on and most people choose to have a limousine drop-off and pick-up. In most part the biggest problem comes from the press and the adoring fans of the stars.

Industry showings are also little problem in that they are either on a studio lot or in a reserved theater. Either way, they are organized, planned, on private property and have on-site security in place.

The tricky one is the unplanned, spontaneous idea to go to a movie in the afternoon or evening. Again, prior preparation and planning is the secret to success.

- The BG must establish what movie, what cinema and what time the principal wishes to go.
- The BG should also try to find out how many in the principal's party and how many BGs are required.
- At the first indication, the BG should call the cinema to confirm show times and theater locations
- The BG can also find out if shows have been selling out or if seating is well below capacity

- The staff should then send someone ahead to buy sufficient tickets for both the principal's party and security
- This individual can then hold a place in line or wait at curbside for the principal to arrive
- When the principal arrives, the advance man can either take them directly into the cinema or hand-off to the chase team
- The advance can then park the cars and stay with them, monitoring a radio for the signal from the CP team that the principal is on the move

The close protection team should have small flashlights for emergencies in the theater, and attempt to sit directly behind the principal and his party. If this is not possible, the BGs should sit one empty seat away on either side of the group. If the threat level is very low, then the security team may chose to give the principal more space and sit a few rows back, but on the isle and with a clear view of the principal.

Where a BG is working alone and no advance warning is given, the best he can do is to make sure he is appropriately dressed, usually sport casual, has a small flashlight and petty cash for incidentals. He should still attempt to sit one row back and to the side so that he has a clear view of the party.

The BG should not get engrossed in or distracted by the movie. He should not get suckered in to running for pop-corn and sodas, but he should escort the principal and family members to the bathroom.

SHOPPING

Now for the big one—the curse of all bodyguards—going shopping with a female principal or the wife or girlfriend of the principal. It is important to clarify here that there is a difference between purchase specific shopping trips and major non-specific expeditions. Handling security for a principal that needs to shop for something in particular is a routine part of BG work, but escorting his mate on a veritable feeding frenzy of excess is more than any man should be required to endure.

Author's Note: It may seem from this section that I harbor a somewhat negative attitude towards women's shopping habits. Without offending women in general, I offer no apology except to say that I am a product of my experience. I have personally never met a client's wife or girlfriend who did not have a well earned black belt in shopping, some with an almost single-minded addiction, typifying waste and decadence at its worst. I have seen women shop, not because they needed something for themselves or their children, but out of pure boredom; for revenge on whoever must pay the credit card bills; and just to establish prestige in the more exclusive stores. This is not a pretty sight to witness and can scar a thinking man's mind for life.

Most men and women of power and importance have little time for the frivolity of shopping, preferring instead to have trusted personal assistants do it for them. Even when it comes to clothes, most clients have personal tailors who came to their home or office, or have an assistant buy a wide selection of clothing, sending back what they did not like. However, on rare occasions, even the President of the United States will venture into a shopping mall or up-scale department store to purchase Christmas gifts or something for someone special. In these cases it is time for security as usual.

For the women of these powerful men, it is a whole different story. They shop "because they can" and in some cases it becomes a major part of their pampered existence. Many principal's will even tolerate this one excess in return for the woman's devotion and companionship.

In many cases, the BG assigned to the woman is hired not because she realistically needs security but more to protect the principal's interests. In other words, the principal may harbor some basic male insecurities about his trophy "Barbie" going out by herself. Again, not to be confused with the happily married wife and mother of his children.

From the "Barbie's" point of view, the BG is only there to spy on her, to keep her company, to drive the car, carry the packages and in some cases supply the principal's plastic (credit card).

Since some shopping duty is unavoidable in a BG's career, he should at least understand the dynamics and plan ahead. The first rule is to set down in one's Conditions of Employment that BGs are not porters and should not to be utilized for non-security tasks. The BG should also make it clear from the outset that carrying anything in his hands only impedes his ability to function effectively as a BG.

Next, establish an efficient way to go shopping. This can be done by recommending that in addition to the BG, a non-security staff member or assistant accompany the lady on all outings. It would then be this person's responsibility to pay for the goods, carry them or arrange delivery to the house. An alternative is to simply pay for the goods or put them on account and then have the shop deliver them directly to the house later in the day.

Since many shopping trips can run ten to twenty thousand dollars an outing, cash payment is not practical. In most cases, credit cards are the order of the day, but unfortunately, some women do not have the patience to wait while the credit card is run through and approved. To overcome this, it is advisable to have several credit cards so that one can be left at a store as the shopper moves onto the next. At the end of the spree, someone can be sent back to collect the cards and goods.

Getting to the shopping mall is usually by limo but in many cases the lady will prefer to drive herself and have the BG follow in a chase vehicle. This is so that she can use this valuable drive time to talk on the cellular phone without being over-heard by the principal's spy, the BG. If she does wish to meet someone privately, this also allows her to run a few stop signs or red lights and ditch the BG in traffic. *(Trust me, it happens, and you can bet it will be "the guards fault" when retold later to the principal).*

Another problem with the chase car method is that when the lady needs to hit a particular store, she will stop in a red zone in front and jump out, forcing the BG to do the same. This racks up a lot of parking tickets, and in some cases can even result in returning to find the cars towed. This makes the limo a better option or utilize at least two BGs so one can jump and run while the other deals with the cars.

Another danger of shopping with the principal's wife or girlfriend is that in some cases, she will actually befriend the BG and treat him as a confident. This in itself is not all bad, but then she has the tendency to want to buy clothes and gifts for him as well. Some BGs even take advantage of this relationship and drop less than subtle hints about things that they "like or need but can't afford".

Accepting gifts or clothes is both dangerous and unacceptable. For some BGs, having clothes purchased for them could simply be viewed as the uncontrollable "collateral damage" of the wife's assault on an upscale department store, since when she buys she buys for anyone. Like a child, she sees the BG as just one more doll to dress. This however may offend the principal who is not only paying the shopping bills and the BG's salary, he may also feel threatened by the lady's attention to the BG.

In the situation where the principal or his wife indicate that the BG does not possess the suitable up-scale wardrobe to accompany them in public, then an appropriate clothing allowance should be formalized in the BG's conditions of employment.

CONCLUSION

In all the above situations requiring the BG to go mobile with the principal, prior preparation and planning will greatly simplify the job. Requesting early warning of a movement from either the principal or a staff member is the single most important consideration. If there is no time to actually drive routes and visit locations, then a few phone calls can still be helpful. In all cases, cars should be gassed and ready to go and the BG should have appropriate changes of clothing on hand. The BG should never be hesitant about recognizing his own limitations recommending to the principal that a second or third BG be brought in to facilitate the movement.

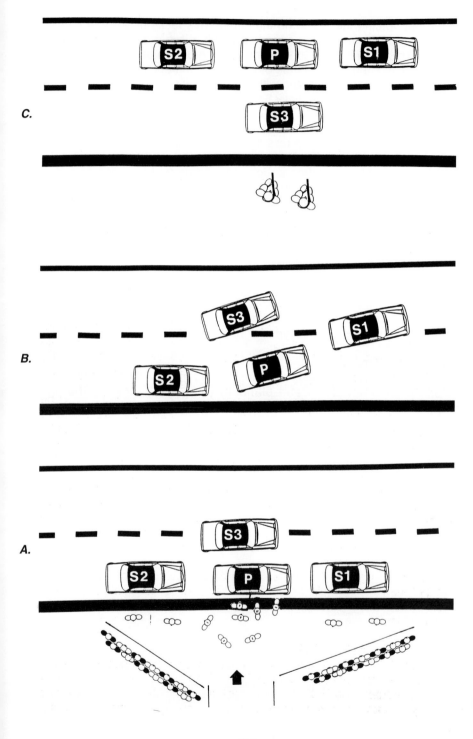

23

SPECIAL EVENTS

Apart from the routine movements and social commitments that a principal has around town, there are also special high profile events that must be considered by the BG. Working one of these events is usually beyond the capability of one BG but he or she should at least know how to interact with the other official and private sector security personnel.

The types of functions that would constitute special events could be political or charitable fund raisers; dinners with Heads of State or similar world leaders; diplomatic visits; important public speaking engagements; star studded celebrity galas or awards ceremonies; high profile weddings and funerals; lavish birthday bashes for the rich and famous; and openings or dedication ceremonies.

Because of the personages involved and the nature of these events, it is important that every aspect, from catering to entertainment, run smoothly and that security be tight. Each of these events can create unique security problems that are only compounded by the large number of behind the scene staff, often massive press attention and the potential for uninvited gate crashers.

For the bodyguard, these events can be divided into two groups; those which he and the principal must attend, and those which his principal is hosting. Obviously, the later being the more demanding from a security point of view.

ATTENDING AN EVENT

Fortunately, the invitations for special events are usually sent out weeks and often months ahead of time, giving principals time to arrange their schedules and RSVP. Unfortunately, if the BG is not a full-time employee or is not in the information loop, he may not find out about it until the day before. At the first notification of an impending event the BG should establish:

1. The time and location of the event
2. The appropriate dress code
3. The time his principal would like to arrive
4. The number of guests in the principal's party
5. The method of transportation to the event
6. The official drop-off point for limousines
7. The required size of the principal's security team

Next comes the more specific security considerations:

• Will the BG or team enter the event with the principal?
• Have "All Access" passes been arranged for the security team?
• Is there an event security coordinator?
• Who will be the on-site security supervisor?
• Are there special security registration formalities?

At some events, like the Academy Awards, because of the high priority placed on member and guest seating, no provision is made inside the auditorium for bodyguards, and in fact, attendees are requested not to bring their own security. These events are so well choreographed, and access so well controlled, that without an invitation no one is getting in.

If an event does permit BGs, then the BG must have the same "all access" pass as his principal. If the principal has a VIP lounge or backstage pass, then the BG must be supplied with one also. At most organized events, an official security pass will get the BG into more places than even the principal has access.

The drop-off at some events is timed and choreographed for both efficiency and the benefit of the news media. Guests will have not only invitations but also required arrival times and drop-off areas. It is not appropriate to have two big stars arriving simultaneously and having to share the television cameras, just as it would be unwise to bring two feuding Heads of State to a summit conference at the same time and through the same entrance.

Author's Note: It is important to note that security is not always the principal's first consideration at these events. The day before escorting a principal and his guests to a private sector gala event, quite some years ago, I had run the advance work, met with the event coordinators, found the least congested route to the auditorium and selected the most suitable entrance—from a security stand-point.

On the festive day, we flew in to a private local airport and motorcade into town to a hotel without problem. Later that evening approaching the event in the limo, I identified myself to a police sergeant at one of the barricades, and was able to by-pass all the congestion at the main entrance slipping my principal's party into the auditorium—no fuss, no muss.

The principal was impressed but his date had very different ideas. She had been preparing for this event for some time, had bought a very expensive original designer gown, had flown in her own hair and make-up girl, and by God she was going to make a grand entrance in front of all the cameras and spectators. So it was back to the limos and around the block to sit in traffic for another thirty minutes to get dropped off at the red carpeted, flash-bulb popping front entrance.

Prior to arriving at any event, the BG or team leader should make contact with the event's security coordinator. In some cases this may be another bodyguard or security company but in many it will be a local police representative or the Secret Service Special Agent in Charge. It is preferable to arrange to meet the security coordinator at the site the day before an event, but if time and distance do not allow, then the BG should at least talk with him on the phone.

The BG should let the coordinator know who his client is, the size of the entourage and how many on his protection team. The coordinator should be able to then arrange the necessary passes and supply any maps, timetables or seating charts that the BGs may find helpful. At the site, the BG should confirm where his client will sit, who is at the nearby tables and where the nearest emergency exits are located.

If the event is an official government function where the President, Vice President or First Lady are in attendance, then the Secret Service advance team will require not only a list of all attending security personnel, but may also require background information and copies of their weapons permits. At some events, private security are not permitted to enter with weapons, while at others the Secret Service will issue small color-coded lapel pins to BGs so as to identify those who are armed. Since security at official events is quite tight, and everyone goes through metal detectors, most principals are safe enough inside without the need for armed escorts.

When arriving at large events, the BG can either escort the principal's party directly to their table or hang back and allow the event ushers to handle that. Normally, once the principal is seated at an event, the BG will move to the nearest edge of the room where he can observe the principal's table. The principal should know where to look to see his BG if he should need him. Only on rare occasions at big events will the BG actually sit with the principal's party or at a nearby table.

The BG should watch anyone approaching the principal's table and be observant for any signals from the principal. If the principal moves about the room, the BG should move with him at a discrete distance. If the principal goes to the bathroom, the BG should go in and wash his hands at the same time.

When it comes time to leave, it is always advantageous for the principal to leave a little early and beat the crowd at the limo pick-up point or valet parking. The limo drivers must be kept on immediate stand-by for the duration of the event and if the BG has radio communication with them, he can call them up to the entrance early. Lastly, the limo drivers should never be told that they can leave for an hour or two during an event since the principal or one of his party may become bored or sick and decide to leave at any time.

HOSTING AN EVENT

When the principal is hosting an event, the protection specialist's job is considerably more complex, especially if entrusted with overall security coordination. Now the BG becomes the point of contact for other security directors, BGs and Secret Service advance teams. To get the ball rolling, the most important initial considerations are:

• Date and location of the event
• Nature of the event
• How many guests expected
• Who is the guest of honor
• Who is the event coordinator

The very nature of an event and the caliber of invited guests will have considerable impact on the security planning. Obviously an informal political luncheon for a hundred guests will draw less attention than a $1000-a-plate charity fund-raiser dinner for a thousand guests. Similarly, if the event is an annual gala affair and a well publicized gathering of the rich and famous, then security will become a large undertaking.

Planning and preparing for a large event can begin weeks or even months before the actual day. The sooner that security becomes part of the information loop, the more time the security coordinator will have to do a professional job. Planning can be broken into four areas: long term, which may be weeks ahead of time; short term which would be the week leading up to the event; and then the day before and finally the day of.

As the day approaches, the security coordinator will become totally consumed with "sweating the details". The assumption can never be made that someone else has taken care of some important detail. Even jobs that are delegated must be followed up and verified completed by the coordinator.

Long Range Planning:
• Ascertain the location for the event
• Verify the number of expected guests
• Research possible threats related to the cause or individual that the event may represent
• Establish the condition of the fences, walls and gates on site
• Walk the site to estimate the number of security personnel required
• Consider what level of communications will be required
• Look over the limousine drop-off point
• Consider where the valet parking will park the cars
• Consider a suitable location for arriving news media

- Meet with principal to discuss security requirements
- Discuss the budget limitations for security
- Order improvements to the physical security
- Order necessary changes to the CCTV surveillance system
- Order "All Access" ID badges for security and key staffers
- Order "limited access" badges for caterers and workers
- Select and notify the necessary security personnel and specialists
- Meet with any police or governmental security representatives for expected dignitaries; ie President, Governor, Ambassador, Mayor, Chief of Police, etc.

In the long range planning phase, it is advantageous for the protection specialist to do some research into the actual event and location before discussing security with the principal or his delegate. This will allow the coordinator to discuss the security manning and requirements with more specificity.

The event planner should also be part of the information loop. Most principals who have the necessary finances and resources to host a large political or charitable fund raiser will also have a staffer assigned to handle these events. This staffer can be very helpful to the security coordinator since he will be in direct contact with the invited dignitaries and celebrities. He or she can also supply the necessary guest lists, and lists of the workers employed by caterers, valet parking, rental companies and event management.

Short Range Planning:
- Verify all of the above
- Meet with Secret Service advance teams if necessary
- Continue to improve the physical and electronic security
- Ensure scheduled security personnel are available
- Test security communications systems
- Make catering arrangements for visiting security
- Meet with the event coordinator for any changes or up-dates
- Brief the principal on security progress to date

The Day Before:
- Again, verify all of the above
- Establish positions or zones for security personnel
- Brief security on their duties and responsibilities
- Brief security teams on dress and equipment requirements
- Establish shift rotations, back-ups and rest breaks for the security teams
- Begin monitoring traffic on and off the property

The Day Of:
- Check that the command and communication center is up and running
- Check that all cameras and intrusion systems are operational
- Walk the property and inspect the outer perimeter fences and walls
- Assemble, inspect and brief security personnel
- Issue lists of authorized workers and expected guests
- Test all portable radios and ear pieces
- Assign security personnel to their positions or zones
- Continue monitoring all traffic on and off the property

For the security coordinator of an event, the day starts early. Several hours before the guests begin arriving the security team must begin tightening the security on the property and if necessary, meet with Secret Service to perform bomb sweeps with the K-9s.

As the hour of the event draws closer, the security should be settling into a routine of securing entrances and verifying identities of workers. Security will also be required to coordinate with other security advance teams, political advance teams, fire marshals inspectors, local police representatives and possibly Secret Service.

Author's Note: At some events, for example during presidential primaries, we have had to deal with as many as sixty official security and law enforcement types. On one occasion I had 23 of my own personnel, an 8 man Secret Service advance team, 2 navy EOD specialists, 4 local police uniformed officers, 2 fire marshals, 2 members of LAPD intelligence, and several State security agents. Then when the candidate's motorcade arrived we had an additional dozen Highway Patrol motor officers, several more Secret Service agents, a half dozen LAPD and Beverly Hills uniforms and a few private bodyguards. All were well taken care of in a separate on-site area set-up to cater to their needs.

If the event planners have done their job well, there should be a lull in activity as all preparations are completed well before guests begin arriving. If the event coordinators are less than well organized then there will be frenzied activity right up to the time that guests begin rolling in.

Apart from general event safety, security and access control, the security coordinator must also consider the actual close protection for the principal during the event. In addition, if the event is at the principal's residence, then security must be assigned to prevent theft from or damage to the interior of the residence.

Once the event has begun, security falls into three areas: outer perimeter, zone and close protection. Outer perimeter is responsible for fences, walls, gates, valet parking and access control to the property. They will also respond to suspected intrusions detected by the monitoring station.

Zone teams are assigned to discreetly patrol specific areas such as the main house, the kitchens, press areas, back-stage, or restricted access areas.

The close protection personnel will be assigned to cover the principal, his family and/or key visiting dignitaries or celebrities. In some cases BGs may also have to be assigned to make hotel or airport pick-ups of arriving guests of honor.

All security personnel should be alert for uninvited gate-crashers or intruders, but should be especially alert during the arrival and departure of the guest of honor. Security should also be observant for petty theft or souvenir hunters when the guests are leaving and when the caterers and workers are cleaning up.

When the guests and workers have left, security must do a thorough sweep of the entire property, including basements, closets, garages, cars, storage areas and gardens for any intruder who may be in hiding.

CONCLUSION

All of this may seem beyond the capability or responsibility of the humble bodyguard, but it is indicative of the type of assignment that a dedicated and motivated individual can expect if he or she stays in the business.

The secret to success in event management and security coordination is meticulous attention to detail and constant communication with the organizers. The security specialist must not only plan for the expected, but spend some time and effort anticipating the unexpected. Even though one should never become too complacent, the more experience one accumulates, the easier big events become.

Motorcade

BGs moving with a slow motorcade

Suburban chase vehicle with heavy weapons and medical supplies

24

ADVANCE WORK

Advance work is the term used to encompass all of the preparations and planning made prior to the arrival of a principal or delegation at a specific site, city or country. The purpose of advance work is to improve both the security and efficiency for the operation, and when done well is the mark of a true professional.

For a high profile protection detail like the Secret Service, advance work is not only an essential when traveling ahead of the President but is also utilized on a local level. For any security team, whether visiting a foreign country, a business meeting out of state or simply a charity event in the next town, advance work can eliminate many of the annoying inconveniences associated with travel. When done correctly, it also creates a more efficient and professional image for the security team.

When handling security for a well known public figure, or large group or delegation, the work done by the advance team becomes a critical part of the operation. It is even more important if the group is scheduled to make several stops, in a number of cities or countries, all on the same itinerary. The effectiveness of the close protection security measures are directly related to the thoroughness of the advance work, so it is important that the advance be handled by the most experienced and reliable agents.

For the private sector bodyguard working alone, advance work is a luxury that can only be indulged in when time is permitting. In most cases, the lone BG accompanying the principal, is unable to move ahead to make site surveys or arrangements. At best he may be able to get on the phone and reconfirm travel plans, hotels and limo pick-ups. If the budget allows for additional BGs, it is preferable to send at least one ahead to personally confirm reservations, drive expected routes, make site surveys, coordinate local cooperation and arrange ground transportation.

Advance work can encompass many tasks depending on the purpose of the security assignment, some being only indirectly related to security. On any given movement, the principal is going to travel somewhere, require ground transportation, attend some function and require local accommodation. So even if the security team is not actively involved in the travel and event planning, they should at least be in the information loop and study how these may affect security.

In breaking down the tasks of the advance team or individual body-guard, we find that advance work falls into one of three categories: Travel related, Visit related and Security related.

TRAVEL RELATED

Travel related planning and bookings are the most common form of advance work with which the BG will have to deal. This can include air travel, both private and commercial; ground transportation, including limos, luggage vans and rental cars; and accommodation in either hotels or private residences. In some cases it may also encompass ships or luxury motor yachts.

To ensure that no detail is overlooked or forgotten it is recommended that the BG develop specific checklists for the different aspects of the operation. In the initial stages of any planning, the BG should:

- Collect phone numbers for the principal's assistant and travel agent or bureau
- Obtain copies of all itineraries and timetables
- Reconfirm all travel plans through the travel agents
- Ask the principal about any special security or travel considerations
- Establish what travel documentation or inoculations are needed by the principal, security and guests
- Do basic research on the countries or cities to be visited

Airlines:
- Establish whether the principal intends to fly private or commercial
- If private get the names and contact numbers for the scheduled pilots
- If commercial reconfirm all reservations
- Ensure the seating is to the principal's liking—smoking / non-smoking, aisle / window.
- Confirm that BG seating is within view of the principal
- Check luggage space or weight restrictions
- Check short and long range weather reports
- Confirm airline departure and arrival times
- If the advance team leader, utilize flight time to review hotel and ground transportation checklists

Hotels:
- Reconfirm all reservations for the principal and guests
- Reconfirm all reservations for the security team
- Ensure that the security rooms are close to the principal's suite. Have hotel fax floor plans if necessary.
- Ensure that the principal's suite is stocked with the appropriate foods and beverages
- Ensure that the hotel kitchen or chef is aware of the principal's dietary restrictions or favorite dishes
- Arrange for advance check-in of the principal's party to reduce time in the lobby
- Collect room keys and sweep rooms for devices or surveillance equipment
- Tip the concierge and/or manager generously in advance to ensure good service

Ground Transportation:
- Reconfirm limos and rental cars
- Confirm that the vehicles are the type and color that the principal prefers
- Reconfirm a separate luggage van if necessary
- Obtain vehicle baby-seats if necessary
- Obtain local street maps and tour guides
- Get the names and contact numbers for all drivers
- Note the license plate numbers of the vehicles, especially if they look similar
- Brief the drivers on the routes to be used and appropriate speeds
- Arrange for a BG who knows the route to ride "shotgun" with the lead vehicle
- Arrange a BG to ride "shotgun" with the principal vehicle
- Familiarize oneself with the local road system and road rules
- Drive all expected routes that will be used in and around the city

Since the protection specialist will be interacting with many people in the travel and hotel industry, it is advisable to have personal business cards made up that will serve as an introduction. As the BG meets these people, he should also collect their business cards for future reference. This allows him to have key points of contact at hand and to be able to simply pick-up a phone and make confirmations or changes to the bookings. If the trip requires a low profile security effort, the advance man can have cards made up identifying him as an administrative assistant to the principal or a travel consultant.

Many security specialists live by their card-file folders and find them very useful for future contracts. Now however, there is a more powerful tool for the traveling BG—the lap-top PC computer or power notebook. With a portable lap-top the BG can now run a variety of business programs and keep more complete records of his work, including:

- Security and travel checklists
- Client files and personal data sheets
- Day, week and monthly appointment planners
- Past, current and future itineraries
- A variety of phone number and business card files
- Useful points of contact with airlines and hotels
- Liaison personnel with local government or law enforcement
- Preferred hotel rooms or airline seating for various clients
- Special requests from the principal and his party
- Clubs and restaurants frequented by clients
- Personal files on security staff
- Medical information on clients and their guests
- Emergency contact numbers for all traveling personnel
- Details on known threats or stalkers
- Essential travel document numbers and issue dates
- Daily expense records

A small powerful computer also allows the BG to run a complete world atlas program with geographical, climatic and time-zone information; and a street map program for the entire U.S. and most major cities around the world. In addition, the BG can run a secure fax-modem hook-up to his office, corporate headquarters or the travel bureau, effectively by-passing any eavesdroppers on the local exchange or hotel phone system.

VISIT RELATED

After all the travel and accommodation plans have been made and confirmed, the advance team can turn their attention to the purpose for trip or movement. This could be business, pleasure or often a combination of the two.

If it is business, then meetings need to be confirmed and routes driven to and from the necessary addresses. In some cases, the companies or organizations to be visited will supply their own cars, limos and drivers, greatly simplifying the BG's work.

If the purpose of the visit is pleasure, then the BG will need to confer with both the travel bureau and the principal as to what points of interest they wish to visit; what restaurants they would like to eat at; what shows they wish to attend; and what sporting activities they would like to participate in. In some cases, the principals may have no idea, leaving it up to the advance team to find the best restaurants, nightclubs and recreational opportunities.

In most cases, the BG will be required to either make or confirm reservations at tennis clubs, gyms, golf courses, health spas, beauty salons, and country clubs. In some cases, the principals may also request snow ski equipment, ski instructors, scuba equipment, lessons, fishing boats, water skiing, horse riding, four wheel drive vehicles, or whatever their personal interests or sports. In all cases, the advance man should actually visit these locations to confirm the reservations, look over the facilities and learn the best routes.

SECURITY RELATED
While handling all of the above travel and administrative considerations, the advance team can also integrate the more important security considerations into the planning. This is part of the advantage of making many of the reservations. For example, it is better to select a hotel suite with security in mind than to try and figure out how to secure a suite that is a cracker box. Hotel penthouses with card-coded elevators are obviously preferable to ground-level suites with numerous balconies and windows.

Apart from the flight in, the BGs will have two primary functions; to ensure secure ground transportation and to secure the hotel or residence. In most cases, these functions are no different to the routine security at the principal's main residence and movements around the home town. (Covered in Chapters 20 & 22).

The quality and efficiency of the security advance work really is the mark of professionalism, covering:

- Preparation for the expected
- Preparation for the unexpected
- Anticipation of the client's needs or wants
- Anticipation of the client's family & associates' needs
- Understanding of local custom and procedures

Security advance checklist:
- Evaluate local threat level based on past criminal or terrorist activity
- Consider local weapons restrictions
- Consider local radio frequency restrictions
- Check with the travel bureau for official travel advisories
- Study local newspapers for current crime statistics and political stability
- Research any key dates to be avoided such as elections, protests, manifestations, past wars, etc
- Check for international health advisories for that region
- Liaise with US embassy if necessary
- Liaise with local law enforcement if necessary
- Visit suitable hospitals and meet with English speaking doctors
- Evaluate hotel for general efficiency and cleanliness
- Evaluate in-house security procedures at the hotel
- Meet with hotel security manager
- Select restaurants for security, access and parking
- Check airport arrival areas and procedures
- Inspect all vehicles for safety, comfort and handling
- Ensure that local limo drivers are safe and competent
- Select routes that avoid slums, housing projects, open markets and heavy traffic congestion

Part of the advance work is to learn local customs and protocols.

*The author with a state limo that was supplied to his delegation
while visiting China (1983)*

Even though reservations may have already been made, if there are any changes in the city or region, such as political or civil unrest or a rapid increase in crime, the advance team should notify the principal and advise postponement of the trip. Similarly, if upon inspection the selected hotels or cars appear to be dirty, unsafe or unsuitable, this should also be communicated to the principal.

If all this is beyond the capability of the lone BG, he can at least let his fingers do the walking. When the BG returns to his hotel room or is on standby, he should be on the phone making arrangements or confirming the next day's reservations.

Note: I have two interesting stories related to the importance for advance work. The first, a contract in Milan, Italy in the early eighties. I had flown in a few days early to make all the necessary hotel and ground transportation arrangements, and had even taken a crash course in Italian, so was feeling quite confident. The day before I had driven the route, from the same airport at which I had arrived, to the hotel at the same time, in the same expected traffic conditions without problem. That morning I had confirmed from the hotel that all flights were on time so arrived at the airport two hours early with limos, luggage vans and my own rental car.

What surprised me at the airport was that my client's flight number was not on the arrival board. After a few enquiries I was informed that there were in fact two airports in Milan and his flight was scheduled to arrive at the other one, clear on the other side of the city. After a mad dash across town, I arrived just in time to see my client's plane touch down, but would not have if I had cut the time closer at the first airport. The moral of the story is always give yourself plenty of extra time for the unexpected.

The other story comes out of St Lucia in the Caribbean. My client was scheduled to arrive about midnight on a private jet that had refueled in Miami. Myself and the advance CP team arrived at the St Lucia airport well before midnight to find that the airport had closed. And I mean dark, deserted, nobody.

Luckily we found the tower controller just pulling out of the parking lot so struck a deal($) with him to man the tower until our client arrived. But that was not the end of it. He informed us that we also needed an immigration official and a customs official to process the arriving party. After a few phone calls to now sleepy officials, we were able to convince($) two to return to the airport just for our plane. They did not own cars so we also had to send a car and driver to collect them.

To compound the problem, the client's jet was delayed out of Miami, and the longer the delay, the more convincing($) the officials needed. By the time the Gulf Stream dropped onto the tarmac, I felt like we had bought the whole damn airport. Fortunately, American dollars go a lot further in the islands than they do in the US or Europe.

CONCLUSION

The more the BG does advance work, the easier it gets, especially if revisiting locations on a regular basis. Based on past trips, everyone involved will know exactly what the principal and security expect. However, it is still recommended that the BG discuss each trip with the principal with a view to changes in both travel and security arrangements. These suggestions or changes should be noted or entered into that lap-top PC for future reference.

Author working advance in Bangkok with Thai police representative

25

WORKING OUT OF STATE

Working out of state assignments requires much of the same planning and advance work of international travel but is considered some what less complicated. There are several reasons for this including no language barrier, no monetary exchange problems, a greater similarity in laws and regulations, and easier access to travel planning information.

However, even taking into consideration all of the above, there are still different laws and regulations governing security work in any given state or city.

ADVANCE WORK

As stated in Chapter 24, competent advance work plays a key role in successful out of state travel. The BG's first task is to ascertain the type of visit, the intended business or vacation, and the level of expected local cooperation. The level of cooperation will often be affected by the importance of the principal and the influence of the local contacts.

Author's Note: Several years I had one of the easiest advances in my career. My team was to handle the security for an important individual attending a major charity event in Denver, Colorado. Having not worked in that city before, I flew ahead to handle the advance.

Upon arrival in Denver and beginning my advance routine, I discovered that the sponsor of the event was so well known and respected in that city that I received total cooperation from both the event organizers and the Denver Police Department. In addition, the sponsor's personal security detail went out of their way to make my team welcome and facilitate any needs that arose.

As with any advance, the first order of business is to obtained itineraries, travel information, local maps, hotel information and details on any local firearms restrictions.

If scheduled to work in a state or city where one has not worked before or has no direct point of contact, it is best to try and take advantage of the principal's corporate or official contacts. If the purpose of the visit is business, then there will be some company or individual with whom the principal is scheduled to meet. If the purpose is political, then the principal will be meeting with the President or some other elected representative. Either way, both these groups will have organizations and administrative assistants who can be of considerable help to the advance team.

If the principal has traveled to a city or state before, but without a particular BG, the principal's personal assistant should be able to supply the BG with a list of preferred limo services, car rental companies, past problems or local points of contact.

The BG should get into the habit of making notes for future reference and collecting business cards from any points of contact or particularly helpful individuals. It also pays to drop a short note of appreciation to these people upon returning home.

As with any travel assignments, the more the BG travels, and the more often one returns to particular cities, the smoother things run.

TRAVELING WITH FIREARMS

Many bodyguards perceive traveling with firearms to be one of their biggest problems, but that is often because they are so locked on to the concept of having to have a gun to be of value. It is not unlike the Freudian observation of men, their guns and their penises—no gun equates to no manhood. This could not be further from the truth since most professionals know that it is the brain that is the BG's most valuable asset.(Well, not for every one!?)

Not to make too light of the subject, traveling with firearms can be a problem for the private sector BG, particularly to cities like New York and Washington, D.C. Even though the need for a gun is slim, most professionals still feel more confident and better prepared with that chunk of iron on their belt.

The actual travel with the firearm is not usually a problem, it is at the final destination where the regulations may be a problem. When flying domestically within the United States, most commercial airlines allow passengers to transport firearms as long as they conform to certain federal regulations. This is not just for police and security personnel but for sportsmen traveling to shooting competitions or hunt reservations.

The actual regulations can be confirmed with each particular carrier, but in general they are as follows:

- Firearms and ammunition may not be carried on the person or in cabin baggage without official identification and completion of the necessary forms.
- Firearms may be transported in checked luggage as long as they are unloaded, in a locked rigid case and separated from the ammunition.
- Firearms must be declared at check-in and inspected by airline personnel.

- Some airlines limit the amount of ammunition and require that it be in an identifiable factory box.
- The passenger must sign a special baggage tag, declaring the weapon to be unloaded, that is then placed in the bag.

These are only a guideline so the traveling BG should contact the particular carrier for their interpretations or changes. Failure to comply to federal and airline regulations can cause delays at the airport, loss of the firearms or even result in arrest.

Author's Note: While passing through airport security, one of my team members was discovered to have a single round of ammunition in the bottom of his carry on bag. It was the same bag that he routinely used for the range and the bullet had become trapped under the lining. To make a long story short, he was delayed, questioned, searched and lectured on aviation regulations before finally being released.

On another trip, twenty minutes after checking our bags, my partner was called to the check-in desk. It seems he had checked his hull baggage without unloading his weapon and this had shown up on x-ray. Luckily he was a federal agent so after IDing himself and unloading the weapon we were permitted to continue. A private sector BG could have expected a lot more heat on this transgression.

If flying by private jet, the BG will generally board and deplane at a small airport or Fixed Base Operator (FBO), by-passing all the inconveniences of public airport check-in and security.

The real problems for the bodyguard begin upon arrival at the final destination. Not all states or cities have the same regulations when it comes to carrying concealed weapons, many being unreasonably restrictive for both BGs and law abiding citizens.

Although many bodyguards possess concealed weapons permits, these are a State permit, issued by local law enforcement, and do not apply to other States. Even though some States may recognize the permits of a neighboring State, this is purely a courtesy and not a right to carry. Since there is no such thing as a federal weapons carry permit for private sector bodyguards, the BG must find some other way of obtaining authorization to carry out of State.

Some states do not even permit off-duty police officers to carry when staying or traveling outside of their jurisdiction. Others are very accommodating and permit anyone with peace officer status to carry in their States. This is some advantage to police officers moonlighting as BGs but even they cannot carry in such places as Washington, D.C.

On some occasions, a BG may get an official authorization to carry in the line of duty based on his home State credentials. If the BG has contacts with local law enforcement, this can greatly facilitate the process.

Another option is to have the principal's influential associates or local contacts arrange some special clearance with local law enforcement.

There are also some chief's of police who will give an unofficial sanction for concealed carry, but the BG should keep in mind that "unofficial" isn't worth squat if the proverbial "shit hits the fan".

If it appears that there is no legal way to carry concealed, the security team leader may opt to hire local police officers or licensed bodyguards to augment his team.

Lastly, it may seem obvious to some, but US bodyguards must realize that Canada and Mexico are not part of the United States. Many guns have been confiscated from American BGs entering or operating in these countries, some even having to do jail time for their sins. Puerto Rico, although a US protectorate, is also a different country with very strict gun laws brought about by the influx in the drug trade.

THE CORPORATE JET

Many successful businessmen and celebrities own their own private jets and many more routinely charter aircraft for both domestic and foreign travel. Some own smaller jets like the Lear or Falcon for domestic travel but will charter larger Gulfstreams or 727s for longer overseas flights. Helicopters being used strictly for short hop local flights of usually less than a hundred miles.

The protection specialist should have a working knowledge of executive air services and know how and where to charter aircraft suitable to a particular assignment. Size, cost and range are the three most common considerations, but since aircraft can vary in range and passenger capacity based on the configuration of the cabin and fuel tanks, the following should be used only as a general guide.

Aircraft	Passengers	Range(approx)	Hourly Rate
Gulfstream III	11-15	3,800 sm	$3,950
Gulfstream II	10	2,800 sm	$3,500
Falcon 50	9	3,100 sm	$2,900
Challenger 601	10	3,800 sm	$3,400
Falcon 20	8-9	1,200 sm	$2,100
Learjets	7-9	2,000 (max)	$1,400
Citations III	8	2,200 sm	$2,100
Hawker 700	8	2,200 sm	$2,100
Westwind II	7	2,400 sm	$1,650
Sikorsky S76	6-8	300 sm	$2,195

Aircraft are usually billed based on the time the engines are actually turning and burning, but the above costs do not include additional overnight rates, catering, landing, parking or international fees.

From a security perspective, corporate aircraft are very vulnerable to attack by snipers or shoulder fired rockets while sitting on the tarmac and during take-offs, landings and taxiing. There have also been incidents reported of sabotage, instrument tampering and fuel contamination but these are not common in the United States.

The owner of any corporate jet or security advisor should insist on some basic precautions both when the aircraft is hangared and when traveling. These may include:

- Access should be restricted to authorized personnel only
- Aircraft should be locked and secured when not in use
- On high risk assignments, 24 hour security must be assigned to the aircraft
- The pilot should be present during fueling to test for contamination
- The pilot should be present for any maintenance that needs to be done while traveling
- Preflight inspection should include a search for any suspicious packages not part of the normal flight equipment
- Security seals should be used on fuel filler caps and doors when the aircraft is left unattended
- Fuel should be inspected for contamination prior to take-off
- Company logos should be removed from aircraft and identifying registration or "N" numbers reduced to the smallest size allowed
- The FBO and ground handlers should be instructed to contact the pilots or BG immediately if there are any accidents or unusual activity near the aircraft
- Before any departure, the air frame should be inspected for damage that may have occurred while parked. It is not unusual for a taxiing pilot or ground handler to accidentally clip the tail or wing-tips of a parked aircraft, especially at night, where there is a lot of student pilot activity or at very congested FBOs.

Private and charter air travel definitely gives more flexibility in travel planning allowing a principal to depart at will or travel to other cities with the minimum of delay. However, the BG should still try to give the pilots as much lead time as possible of any departures or changes in destination. This will allow them to prep the aircraft, obtain necessary flight information and file flight plans.

As a security precaution when chartering a jet, the BG should request both the names and physical descriptions of the pilots from the charter company. Also, since principals are known to change their plans at a moments notice while traveling, the BG should ensure that he has 24 hour contact numbers for the pilots, at their hotels or on the nationwide pagers that many now carry.

Another convenience and security consideration of executive air is that cars and luggage vans can be driven right up to the aircraft with no fuss or delay. However, smaller charter jets often have space, weight and luggage limitations that larger commercial jets do not. For some clients who insist on traveling with mountains of baggage, it may be necessary to send staffers on ahead on commercial flights with the excess baggage.

Because of limited passenger space, not all private aircraft have flight attendants, so the BG should familiarize himself with all in-flight emergency procedures, equipment and exits. This will include emergency oxygen, life vests, floatation cushions, extinguishers, crash landing procedures and emergency escape door operations.

Corporate jets have limited baggage space but the BG should still inventory all bags being loaded.

When flying private, clients and security can usually drive right up to the jet.

Author's Note: Apart from general maintenance problems and ground delays, I have personally been on three charter jets that have had in-flight problems. The first was a navigational equipment problem, the second a broken windshield and the third and most serious, the cabin began to fill with smoke. All required immediate landing; the windshield took twelve hours to repair before continuing; but the smoke problem was more scary so the principals refused to re-board that aircraft. This caused a several hour delay, at a small airport with no facilities, waiting for a replacement to be flown in to pick-up the group.

WINTER SKI RESORTS

Most celebrities when in search of the sun will vacation at some exotic location in the Caribbean or South Pacific, but when in search of winter activities, most will select an exclusive ski area in the US such as Aspen, Colorado. For this reason, the well rounded BG should make sure that he is not only capable of running operations in these areas, but that he is also a strong skier. What value is there in having a BG who is incapable of the same sports activities as the principal and his family?

Ski resorts are not considered high risk areas when it comes to violent crime or terrorism, but theft and property crimes can be quite high. One only has to see all the expensive boutiques and the furs and mink coats hanging in every restaurant and hotel to know that the pickings are good for the criminally inclined. One factor that keeps crime to a minimum is that most ski resorts are in remote mountain communities, that in winter have only one road in and one out, making escape difficult.

The novice BG should not be alarmed by the number of people running around in ski masks in resort areas. Skiers had these long before international terrorists and armed robbers made them synonymous with violence and intimidation.

There is not much difference in the advance work, except for some necessary study into local weather and ski conditions and the appropriate related equipment and clothing. As Scandinavians like to say, "There is no such thing as bad weather, only bad clothing". This is especially true for the BG who may be out in the elements considerably more than his clients.

Vehicle selection and driving skills are little different for those hailing from warmer climates, requiring 4WD, snow tires, chains or a combination of all of the above. The BG may also find that there are no cellular phone nets in some areas and that hand-held radios do not have the same range in the mountainous terrain.

As to ski equipment, the BG need not be a ski pro but he should have enough experience to select equipment for his clients based on their size and ability, and to be able to help a novice client with skis and boots.

Since ski slopes, ticket offices and pro shops can become crowded in the morning, the BG should get ski passes, rent or buy equipment, have skis tuned and book instructors the day before skiing. It is advisable to always have local ski instructors accompany the principal skiing since

Author and team member with two instructors checking the runs before the principals hit the slopes of Aspen

Author at celebrity ski races in Aspen. The Trumps are skiing up in background

they know the mountain, can assist the principal, and most importantly, jump the long lift lines. There is also a certain accepted status amongst celebrities in having one's own ski instructors booked for the season.

When it comes time to actually go skiing, it is best to let the ski instructors handle the principal's ski related needs, leaving the BG free to concentrate on security. Professional ski instructors are very adept at dealing with clients of all skill levels and, knowing all the local gossip and every other celebrity on the mountain, even add to the more social aspects of skiing. Instructors cultivate and cater to their more important clients knowing that their return business and tips are directly proportionate to the client's enjoyment of the whole experience.

One security related advantage of ski equipment is that it makes everyone look similar on the slopes, apart from a few bright splashes of color, and that the hats, ski masks and goggles conceal almost anyone's identity.

One of the bodyguard's most important roles when skiing with a client is to supply protection from idiots and hot-doggers bombing down the mountain barely in control. This activity is frowned on by ski patrol and those who insist on doing it pose a real risk to slower skiers traversing the slopes.

The BG or BG team should develop a technique of staying up hill from the principal, traversing parallel and at the same speed. This does two things; it blocks down-hill bombers and allows the BG to ski down to assist the principal if he or she hits a "snow snake", falls or looses a ski. If the BG gets below the principal, it becomes a hard slog back up to help with a problem.

If skiing with the principal's children, the BGs must be even more alert for the dangers of faster skiers. Apart from still having a ski instructor, the BG should also make an effort to educate the kids on ski etiquette and to steer clear of the middle of the runs. At the same time, the BG must make the experience fun for the children, resting or going into the warming huts whenever they complain of cold or fatigue. On some occasions, it is best to just leave the skis in the truck and go get some hot chocolate or throw a few snowballs with them.

Most clients are not hard-core skiers so will not be first on the lifts in the morning or last off of the mountain in the evening. Most will ski only in the best weather, preferring to stay to the less demanding runs. Others are known as the "crack of noon club", getting on the mountain at about 11:50 AM when it is warm, skiing to the most popular restaurant on the mountain, and then skiing down afterwards. And that is their prerogative since they are paying all the bills.

In the evening, towns like Aspen really come alive with a host of fine restaurants and designer shops that will rival any in the world. After dinner there is no shortage of lively bars and nightclubs to keep the night-owls going until the dawn hours.

As discussed in other chapters, the BG should make a point of surveying all these establishments and introducing himself to the owners or managers. This goes a long way toward guaranteeing the best tables and service for one's clients.

A final note on resort etiquette. Apart from all the glitz and glamour, these are still very small tight-knit communities where everyone knows everyone and gossip is rampant. The BG must be polite with everyone, tipping ski instructors and waitresses well if future good service is to be expected. When shopping with a client, warn him or her that even though shopkeepers will happily take their money, big city shitty attitudes will not endear them to the natives.

Lastly, since parking is a premium in resort towns, especially near the ski lifts, the principal's will more than likely collect a few parking tickets. The BG should make sure that all tickets are paid at city hall before leaving town.

IDS Team escorting special aerospace loads from California to New Mexico

26

GOING INTERNATIONAL

Every rookie bodyguard, and even a few of the more experienced, dream of the opportunity to join the big time and go international with their trade. They fantasize about jet-setting around the world, staying in the finest hotels, protecting some multi-millionaire or even billionaire. All the time foiling the plots of international terrorists and ruthless kidnappers.

Well, time to wake up and smell the roses. Those who work or have worked international protection know that it is not all glitz and glamour. It is more a world of late night flights, airline meals, jet lag, lost luggage, antiquated phone systems, language problems, and the frustration of endless small details and bureaucratic BS. All the foreign countries, exotic peoples, majestic hotels and lavish dinners are blurred by the long hours, constant travel, weird time zones and lack of sleep.

There is no argument that international protection work can be interesting and challenging, or that there is increased danger. The threat levels definitely increase, especially when working countries that have a history of terrorism, civil unrest or anti-American sentiment, but the threat is not the only thing that increases. The logistical problems of transportation, accommodation, language, money, food, medical assistance and local cooperation also become more complex. Fortunately, in many countries there exists the international language of "money talks," and most clients who can afford professional protection can also afford local facilitators who will fall over themselves to be of help.

The logistical, language and cultural problems become especially evident in places like Asia and Africa. At the same time, every major hotel seems to have enough brown-nosing assistant managers, whose sole purpose in life is to suck up to rich visitors, so getting anything done is only a few dollars away.

Before addressing the specifics of international bodyguarding, the BG must first decide if he is even qualified for this type of assignment. The excitement and anticipation of working in a foreign country must be tempered with a serious reality check. The BG can start by asking himself such questions as:

- Do I have the travel experience or language skills to run an international operation?
- How much do I know about the country to be visited?
- Are my passport, shots and travel documents up to date?
- Will my military experience in Germany help me in Central America?
- What will I do for weapons?
- Should I contact the local police or are they too corrupt?
- What is the local attitude toward Americans?
- Do I have local contacts who can assist me?
- Can I expect any embassy support or cooperation?
- Am I skilled at driving on the left (wrong) side of the road?
- How do I even ask directions if I get lost?
- If not qualified to run the operation, am I at least qualified to escort a client overseas?

These are all pertinent questions that must be addressed before taking on such an assignment.

There are innumerable executive protection companies who claim global capability and expertise in international terrorism, but few have any actual experience at all. When looking at their brochures and promotion literature, the reader gets the impression that they all use the same printing company or just copy each other's brochures since they all tend to use the same catch-phrases—"VIP Protection", "International Executive Security", "Counter Terrorism", "International Bodyguards", "International Threat Assessment"....ad nauseam.

Again, this is a case of "buyer beware". Just because the owner of a local protection agency vacationed in Europe one year, or took a client to Mexico City on one occasion, this does not prepare them for the complexities of international security.

Author's Note: Having traveled internationally since I was sixteen, worked or trained in over thirty countries, lived in three of those and being bi-lingual, my move to international operations was an easy transition and logical use for my talents. However, I often wonder how all those bodyguards who claim to be international experts ever got their experience.

Having been heavily involved in European and Middle Eastern counter terrorism and special operations training since the early eighties, I also wonder how some local BG suddenly becomes an "international executive protection and counter terrorism expert", without ever having left the continental United States.

I do know from first hand experience, that there are a select number of very competent ex-Secret Service agents, US intelligence types, and special forces operators in the business, since these are the same ones that I have run into in Asia, Europe and the Middle East. There are also a smattering of Israelis, British SAS, German GSG-9 and French GIGN types kicking around the globe. But for every one of these legitimate "consultants", there are dozens, if not hundreds of over-weight ex-cops, young academy wash-outs, nightclub bouncers, PIs and opportunists with ads in the yellow pages and glossy business cards claiming the same experience.

Simply traveling with a client or sticking close to a principal in a foreign city does not require any great level of expertise on the part of the body-guard. But this also falls far short of the value that a professional protection specialist can be to a client. The principal's safety when traveling, comes from the meticulous prior planning and preparation, not the 220 pound bullet magnet who will be taken out with the first few rounds from a terrorist's weapon.

Apart from years of travel experience and hopefully being multi-lingual, there are several more basic things that a BG will need before ever contemplating international security. First and foremost, anyone intending to travel needs a passport, and yet there are many BGs looking for work who have never taken the time or effort to apply for one. Along with the passport, the BG will need the necessary visas or entry permits for all the countries on the itinerary and the appropriate vaccines, shots or inoculations for most of the under developed ones. Next on the list are major credit cards and an international driver's license. The credit cards, preferably American Express, Visa and Mastercard, being essential to make bookings, obtain rental cars and confirm hotel reservations, and in some instances for emergency cash.

After those prerequisites, the BG will need a good general knowledge of world geography, followed by a more detailed study of any country the BG anticipates visiting. This will include geography, political status, existing sub-national conflicts, the monetary system, predominant religions, local laws, customs and language.

ADVANCE WORK

Much about advance work has been covered in previous chapters, but handling an individual or delegation in Athens or Barcelona is not quite the same as a trip to Houston or Miami. Where travel and hotel reservation services are computerized, efficient and quite reliable in the US, in some other countries they still seem to be operating in the dark ages of miscommunication, telegrams and 4x6 file cards.

The advance man's first order of business will be to arrange for the same limo service that the principal will be using a few days later, to pick him up at the airport. This is a test of the limo service's punctuality and professionalism, and will give the BG the opportunity to evaluate both the quality of the vehicle and the driving habits of the driver.

Next comes the hotel. Most often a client will stay at the best hotel in town, but if this is to be the first visit to a particular city for a principal, the hotel should be evaluated for efficiency, cleanliness and suitability. Some clients do not mind the old-world hotels but they have notoriously small rooms, old plumbing and decrepit phone systems. Most executives, politicians and business types prefer to stay in modern international hotels with larger suites, American style plumbing, modern phone systems and cable TV. In addition, because of the design and construction materials, modern hotels are far more secure than the older ones that one can literally break into with a pocket-knife.

Another reason to check out the hotels is that in some cases, the hotel may have no record of the reservation and be already full booked. In which case the BG must get on his horse and make other arrangements.

Anytime the advance man comes across these problems and needs to start making changes, it is important that he call back to corporate HQ, the travel bureau or directly to the client to up-date them on the situation. Once the BG starts making new reservations or changes he must be constantly aware of the particular client's needs and wants. Unless a BG knows his client very well, prior approval on all changes is essential to protect both his reputation and job.

After the hotels are squared away, the BG will move on to learning the streets and running the routes to and from scheduled meetings or events. This is best done in a self-drive car and will require reliable, up-to-date road maps, usually available from the rental car companies.

FLYING

If the principal and guests are flying commercial, the advance team will need to know the air carrier, flight number, scheduled arrival time and correct airport terminal. The airport is important since the principal may not fly in to the same airport as the advance team. Some cities like New York, London and Paris have more than one international airport.

The advance man must also stay in constant contact with the airlines and travel bureau to confirm that the flight is on time and that the principal actually boarded the flight.

To facilitate arrival in a foreign country, it always seems preferable to fly in on a private jet. This not only allows the principal to usually enter through a smaller and quieter airport, it also tends to send a message to local officials that someone of importance is arriving. In most cases they will just wave the group through customs after stamping passports.

In semi-third world countries, most minor government functionaries are intimidated by wealth and power, but at the same time, the advance team must be wary of those officious little bureaucrats who wield their small amount of authority like pocket-sized Napoleons. Without greasing($) the wheels of authority and the right respectful attitude, nothing moves across their desks.

Author's Note: In more than one country, there are several of these always irritating and often infuriating little pencil-necked paper shufflers who are alive today only because it was against the law to kill them at the time. Joking? Maybe!

One disadvantage of utilizing charter jets, apart from the forty thousand plus dollars it may cost to fly to Europe, is that any delays on the ground caused by the principal or his party may carry heavy penalties. Since these jets are often scheduled to pick-up a new group soon after they drop one off, any delay caused by one client causes an expensive reaction down the chain. In some cases requiring the charter company to dispatch a second aircraft incurring additional fuel and crew costs.

ARRIVAL PROCEDURES

If the hotel is already aware of the wealth and importance of the principal or delegation, the advance team should have the hotel send a representative who speaks the language to the airport, to facilitate arrival and handle any paper work($) or formalities.

Arriving in any foreign country, at the first point of entry, the principal, his entourage and CP team will be required to clear immigration and customs formalities. In most cases, the group will be waved through after a perfunctory passport check and visa stamp. To further facilitate this transition, arrival forms should have been issued and completed in flight and one person should have been delegated to handle all the passports.

If the principal or BG is traveling with a large amount of cash or negotiable instruments these should have been recorded with US Customs before departure. They should also be declared at arrival in a new country since some countries have strict laws governing the movement of cash and the exchange of local currency.

Worse than monetary violations are illicit drug violations. Recreational drug use may be flaunted in the United States and even tolerated in some countries, but there are many where drug possession carries long prison terms and even the death penalty.

A professional BG does not want to be anywhere near clients who may be drug users or abusers when going through customs in any country, especially returning to the US. If a client is busted with drugs, all bets are off and the bodyguard needs to cover his own ass. This is one reason that the international BG needs to be particularly selective about who he protects and with whom he travels. If a questionable client requests that the BG fly ahead with his bags, the BG should either search every bag or just say no thanks.

Another area where the arriving passengers may have problems is excessive amounts of medicines or prescription drugs. These should all be in well marked bottles and it is recommended that one also carry a letter from one's doctor detailing the medical condition that requires those medications. This is also true for the CP teams trauma kits, medical supplies or oxygen systems.

After drugs and money comes guns. Another advantage of flying private is that the apparent importance of the principal may help facilitate any problems that the BG or CP team may have with firearms. In some countries, officials have been known to just shrug and pass the BGs through knowing that they were carrying firearms but not really wanting to open that can of worms. There is a certain assumption that if an individual can afford a private jet, travels with a large entourage and a bejewelled wife, then he needs security.

If this occurs, the BGs must keep in mind that overlooking the weapons or even quiet approval does not constitute an official permit to go armed in that country. You can be sure that if there is a problem while in country, the airport official will deny any knowledge of guns and dump full responsibility back in the BG's lap.

The BG's underlying thought behind carrying "unofficially" in a foreign country, should be whether or not the BG is willing to do time in that country's jails. If one has seen the movie "Midnight Express" or talked to someone who has been locked-up in a Mexican jail, the answer will be most definitely not.

Guns often create more problems than they are worth in many countries, but there are also countries and cities where it would be unwise to take a client without armed protection.

Author's Note: Over the years I have carried firearms in several countries under both government and police authority, but in others we have operated in the gray area of sanctioned but unofficial activity.

On one trip we were to escort a client to England to attend a special event with members of the British royal family. This obviously facilitated arrangements for the client but precluded any of the security team going armed. As with most Commonwealth countries, the Brits are a little funny about firearms, and even the Secret Service has limitations placed on them in England, Australia and New Zealand.

On another trip to a country in Eastern Europe, shortly after the hijacking of TWA 847 out of Athens, government officials were so keen to revitalize their tourist industry that they supplied my whole team with official concealed weapons permits so that we could handle security for an important U.S. businessman. We were even permitted to carry in airports and on commercial flights.

While working in Asia, in a country where guns are also very restricted, it was necessary for me to hire a local police sergeant as an escort so that I could go armed in the city. They knew it was a potentially dangerous place but simply wanted an official presence should the bullets start flying. In retrospect, even though carrying a gun added to my personal sense of well being, having an official who spoke the local language was actually far more valuable than the guns.

Each country's laws and regulations relating to firearms must be researched before the BG considers carrying on the job. Some will issue permits under strict conditions for particular situations, some will not issue permits at all, while others can be quite reasonable. In some countries, civilians are not permitted to carry 9mm, .45 ACP or any military caliber weapons, but under the right circumstances, permits for .38 Special revolvers are possible.

To conclude, some country's international airport procedures are far more strict than those at the overland border check-points that they share with their neighboring countries. Considering the relatively short distances between countries in Europe, in some instances it is easier to fly into one country then drive across into the other. This is especially true for the advance team who may be traveling with radios, hardware, trauma kits and counter surveillance equipment that they do not wish to explain.

Hotel supplied armored limo used by the author in Bangkok

Author (right) running a seach and rescue operation in Taiwan

IN COUNTRY

Movement within a foreign city is much the same as any similar sized city in the US, complicated only by language barriers, unreadable street signs, and the erratic driving habits of many foreign drivers. In most instances, the use of the hotel limousine service will minimize these complications and prove to be a convenient form of ground transportation. Where distances are greater and facilities allow, charter helicopters are another efficient method of travel.

In cities where one wishes to low key the principal's presence and movement, it may be preferable to pass on the convenience of limos and use self-drive rental cars. In larger cities like Paris and Rome the Mercedes 500 will not draw any undue attention, but in other cities BMWs may prove lower profile and more economical. The key factors in vehicle selection are that whatever vehicle is used it must first have all the necessary features for evasive driving and yet still blend into the local environment.

Up until recent years, mobile communications were a problem when traveling abroad but with the boom in electronics the security team now has several options. For short range communication, the team can utilize their own hand-held VHF or UHF radios or purchase inexpensive ICOM type radios in country. If traveling with the same radios used in the United States, the BGs should be aware that their use may be restricted in some countries where a radio operators license is required. In others, the frequencies used in the US may be restricted and limited to police or military use only.

Author's Note: To overcome some of the problems that we have had traveling with our Motorola radios, and since we already do a lot of maritime security work, we now carry a set of marine-band radios. These are not only legal but in common use all over the world, especially around marinas and in coastal cities.

For longer range communications, many international hotels and car rental agencies will make cellular telephones available to their guests or clients (at an additional cost). Cellular phones can also be linked to portable computers, that have a fax/modem feature, for document transmittal.

For the real professionals who want hassle free global communications, there is now a range of brief-case sized satellite communications (SATCOM) units available to the public. Anyone having worked on ships will be familiar with the large SATCOM systems that they use, but until recently, the small portable stuff was solely the domain of the military. For around fifteen thousand dollars (like all new technology that should be coming down) the BG or principal can flip open a brief-case, tune in a satellite and talk directly to anyone in the world.

A final and less expensive option that an advance team may find useful is global satellite pagers with alpha-numeric features. With the use of a telephone or PC modem, these allow the principal or CP team to immediately notify the advance team leader of any changes or problems with the itinerary.

When traveling in many countries, there is another danger, far more insidious than terrorists, that the security team must anticipate. That is contaminated water and food poisoning. This is especially a problem in under-developed countries or tropical regions like Mexico, Central and South America, the Pacific Islands and much of Asia and Africa.

Analysis of the waters in some these countries has shown the presence of some 30 different viruses including typhoid, polio, salmonella, hepatitis and cholera, not to mention a host of other bacteria and gastro-intestinal parasites.

Knowing this, the BG team must be careful where and what they eat, making every attempt to stay with well cooked food and bottled water or drinks. Even the smallest amount of microscopic contamination can, at the least, result in a bad case of diarrhea, sweating, dizziness, weakness and dehydration. On the other end of the scale, some food poisoning can result in serious illness and death.

Before departure from the US, the team should ensure that they have all the necessary shots, but once in country, must still pay special attention to personal hygiene, washing their hands, eating only in the hotel or good restaurants, avoiding uncooked foods and local markets, and stocking-up on purified bottled water. Even brushing ones teeth or taking a shower places the individual at risk of digesting local water and the accompanying bacteria.

Since this is a very real problem that can take a whole team out of the game faster than an ambush, it is advisable that the team also carry a supply of suitable drugs and preventive medications.

Tipping is another task that BGs will have to deal with when traveling. The amount of the tips should be discussed with the principal or his or her assistant before departure. In general, most principals are generous people who appreciate good service so tip quite generously, and since the BG is acting on their behalf, should follow their lead. Where it is usually appropriate for someone to tip ten to fifteen percent in a restaurant where service is not included (Non Compris), wealthy people often tip at least twenty percent. But only if the service is good.

Again, tipping and expenses must be discussed with the principal to ensure that everyone is on the same program. In addition, the BG should keep a detailed expense sheet of all tips and expenses so that there is no question of misuse, honesty or reliability.

Author's Note: Expense sheets are something that I am very particular about with my teams. When given thousands of dollars of the principal's money for both the team's and the principal's expenses, it is all too easy for some BGs to forget that this is not their own money. My personal expense sheets are detailed accountings, up-dated on a daily basis, and when moving a lot, often several times a day. After two weeks on the road, these sheets become dog-eared, full of notes and up-dates in a variety of pen and pencil colors, but always accurate.

I become very suspicious of the individual who does not keep daily notes or up-dates his sheets regularly, and then at the end of a contract, turns in a neatly printed sheet all in the same pencil. I am also suspicious of expenditure amounts under single headings with no dates and in nice round numbers. For example: tips—$1,000, hotels—$4,000, rental cars—$2,000, food—$1,500, etc.

On my sheets, although not as neat and sometimes coffee stained, the principal or accountant can see exactly how much I spent on each tip or expenditure and on what date. Big round totals just leave too much room for the less trustworthy individual to pad his expenses and take advantage of the system. One should also be suspicious of this individual if he has no daily log or back-up when queried.

While on the subject of honesty and appropriate behavior, there must be some consideration given to the bodyguards' off-duty hours. If there is only a single bodyguard traveling with a client, then there will be no off-duty time. When not actually with the principal, the BG should be in his hotel room on-call and ready to move.

If part of a larger team, then there may be some rotation and off-duty time. The BGs should conduct themselves in a professional manner, avoiding wild activities, drunken behavior, fights, strip joints, or any other activity that could prove embarrassing to the principal. In fact on most jobs, since one could get called back to duty at a moments notice, there should be no drinking at all. The BGs should also keep in mind when getting rowdy, that they are in a foreign country where the judicial system may not be as lenient as in the US.

HOME LIFE

The bodyguard who plans to frequently work international assignments, can expect a few problems on the home front. More than one marriage or relationship has gone down the toilet because "What's his name" is always off "chasing terrorists". Apart from always being away, the problem is further compounded by the fact that loved ones will have a problem equating jet-set travel, exotic locations and first-class hotels with work. To them, not grasping the long hours and hard work involved, this is just too much like vacation. The only damage control that the BG can do is to phone home often, send postcards and bring back lots of souvenirs.

Limos and luggage vans arriving at a rented chateau just outside of Paris

Two of the IDS Team in France

Off-duty BGs relaxing with some archery at the chateau

From a security standpoint, there are both advantages and disadvantages to luxury motor yachts.

The H&K 91 is the civilian version of the G3-SG1 and its .308 caliber make it well suited to the longer ranges that may be encounteed on the high seas.

27

MARITIME SECURITY

Author's Note: Because of the number of maritime security operations that we ran in the Mediterranean, Caribbean and Aegean, this became something of a specialty for my team. It was hard work but enjoyable duty since many of us were "water people" with a love of boating, most water sports and prior military experience in diving and ship-board operations.

Sailing has long been considered "the sport of kings", but there are also many non-royals who own boats or enjoy spending time on the water. One only has to visit the Principality of Monaco to realize that the large majestic motor yachts, more like small ships, packed into the harbor are a popular diversion for the rich and famous.

Although maritime security is something of a protection specialty, any bodyguard could find himself working for a principal who either owns or likes to charter luxury motor yachts. Where many Saudis and Europeans own yachts in the Mediterranean, and wealthy Greeks have yachts in the Aegean wealthy Americans tend to prefer summer charters in that area. Some of those same yachts that are available for charter will relocate to the Caribbean in the winter.

American businessmen who own large boats tend to dock them in Miami, cruising the Bahamas and eastern sea-board in summer and the warmer waters of the Caribbean in winter. Although there are a few boats on the West coast, docked in San Diego or Marina Del Rey, the colder Pacific waters are not as suited to cruising.

Even though charter yachts are expensive, running twelve to twenty thousand dollars a day, they are the essence of luxury and convenience. Instead of having to move from hotel to hotel, packing and unpacking, a principal can board a yacht in one port, settle back and just relax. At the principal's whim, the yacht can up-anchor and move anywhere his heart desires. In one or two weeks one can cruise the entire South of France and Italy, enjoy the casinos of Monte Carlo, sun-bathe in St Tropez, hit the film festival in Cannes or shop in Rome, all from a luxurious floating hotel. In the Caribbean one can cruise islands and visit exotic locations that are all but inaccessible by any other means.

If one chooses to scuba dive, water ski, wind surf or jet ski, one has merely to ask the crew and the equipment will be prepared. In the evenings, the choice is a formal black-tie dinner, a more casual but stylish feast or burgers on the back deck. Get the idea!!

Now back to reality. There are several good reasons for the principal to have security on board when cruising. Large motor-yachts are such an obvious representation of super wealth, especially when cruising under-developed areas off of Central or South America, the Caribbean or South China Sea. In addition, piracy is not dead and luxury yachts are still an easy target for both criminals and drug runners. In fact, one of the first questions asked by the principal who has not cruised before will be if there is any piracy activity in the selected area.

MODERN DAY PIRACY

Piracy is still alive and thriving in some parts of the world but luckily the Mediterranean is not a high risk area. Pirates no longer carry cutlasses or swing down from the rigging, but they still prowl the coastal water ways preying on the weak or vulnerable.

Piracy is most prevalent in the South China Seas, West Africa, Southern Caribbean, South America, and to a lesser extent Indonesia and the Philippines. The largest operations being off of China.

In the Philippines, endemic corruption and patchy law enforcement makes piracy a growth industry. A few pirates are in jail in Manila, but too few for the amount of piracy going on. The financial rewards are just too great and the potential for capture too slim for the small boat pirates not to take advantage of the situation. The locals feel that the Singaporians are the real pirates who routinely go armed.

Some shipping companies feel that the pirates are employed by "pirates in pinstripes", businessmen and insiders, who have knowledge of both commodities and manifests, and control many of the attacks. They practice a form of sea jacking where they steal an entire ship, typically a cargo vessel with a cargo they can move on the open market.

The pirates use fast boats to get alongside the targeted vessel then round up all the crew and put them in one cabin. They will tie up the crew, lock the cabin door and not hesitate to kill any resistors.

While still at sea they will change the ships name, and with prepared documents, register the new name under a flag state. They will then forge bills of sale to finish process.

The pirates will pick areas where ships must slow for tight straits or narrow channels and usually operate near international boundaries so as to easily escape pursuit.

One of the major problems in the orient is state supported piracy, particularly by China who targets ships out of Hong Kong, usually smaller cargo ships of weaker flag countries such as Vietnam, Korea and even Russia. They are primarily after cars and electronics and are willing to venture out of Chinese waters in unmarked, grey-painted naval patrol boats. Again, they will modify the ship's charts to show that the ship strayed into Chinese waters, and will then make the ship's captain sign the altered charts thus seizing the ship and cargo.

Fortunately, no US flag ships have been attacked to date in the South China Sea, but this is not so with smaller pleasure craft off of Florida and the Bahamas.

Dopers and drug runners out of Miami, South Florida, and Columbia have been known to utilize luxury yachts knowing full well that they are seldom searched coming into US waters. In addition, many large yachts carry fast cigarette boats that are popular for high speed night dope runs in and around the Florida Keys and everglades.

Ships that work waters where piracy is a problem have developed a few simple counter measures to reduce the probability of their being selected as a target. They are:

1. Keep an alert deck watch for any approaching vessels or activity
2. Turn search powerful lights on all approaching vessels
3. Hang fire hoses on railings to be used to repel boarders
4. Pull boarding ladders and keep all exterior doors locked at night
5. Utilize anti-collision radar to detect approaching vessels when steaming and at anchor

For more information and up-dates on piracy, protection specialists can contact the International Maritime Bureau who are very active in investigations of this problem. On the other hand, the IMO—International Maritime Organization—has shown very little willingness to seriously address piracy.

PLANNING

Enough about pirates since they are really not a significant threat to clients who wish to cruise the more popular ports of the Mediterranean, Aegean or Caribbean.

Before embarking on a cruise, both the principal and the protection specialist must do some careful planning. Firstly, all parties concerned must understand some of the limitations of luxury yachts and cruising. Even 100' and 150' motor yachts have a shortage of space and the cabins and closets are not what one would expect in an international hotel. Ship-board living can be quite confining, and if the principal has invited too many guests, or even a few obnoxious ones, this unique experience will quickly become the cruise from hell.

A 200' yacht may have accommodations for 12 but there is also 17 crew members plus staff and security to consider. A smaller 100' vessel may have 4 state rooms, a crew of 12 but no cabins for BGs.

In general, because of small cabins and closets, it is recommended that the principal and his wife or girlfriend take two cabins or state rooms for themselves, and then only invite the minimum number of guests that they know they can get along with under confined conditions. A boat is not like a hotel where one can just get another suite, go for a walk or get away for a while.

Children are another important consideration. Boats, like swimming pools, are a potential hazard for young ones, except now they are surrounded by deep water. If the children are to be taken along, then they must be not only educated to the dangers of boat life but also have nannies or minders who are strong swimmers.

Two unpredictable factors that are difficult to plan on are weather and sea state. When wind, rain or storms come up, so does the sea, and in the tropics, these can come and go quite unexpectedly. When the sea gets rough, all the captain can do is run for the nearest port and weather it through. Hopefully, in the right season, it will pass, but no amount of moaning by the guests can change mother nature.

The planning process really begins when one decides on the area one wishes to cruise and then contacts a charter agent. There is a wide range in charter costs, depending on size, passenger capacity, number of crew, level of luxury, and additional deck equipment such as power boats, jet-skis and wind-surfers. Bigger is usually better, but one must also consider the age of the boat and the time since the last refit, when looking for real quality.

The only problem with really big yachts occurs when they cannot enter certain marinas or small harbors. In this case there are two options, neither very appealing to the guests. If the seas are calm, the boat can anchor outside of the harbor and the guests will shuttle in by tender boats; or one can dock in the nearest commercial port. Either way, the guests may not enjoy riding in the small boats, especially if in evening attire, and they will definitely not like the scenery of a dirty commercial wharf.

From a security stand-point, anchoring out is preferable to tying up in a big port where crime is often rampant, but then security is not always the guests' first concern. Their first choice will generally be to pull into an exclusive marina alongside other luxury yachts, but baring that they will generally chose the comfort of port over anchoring out, unless it is really calm.

When it comes to actually planning an itinerary, the principal must first do a little research and then take some advice from the charter operator and ship's captain. When in doubt, one should listen to someone who has actually cruised the selected area, and most often that is the captain.

In the South of France, the most popular areas are St Tropez, Cannes, Nice, Monte Carlo, and Corsica, with most yachts basing themselves out of Monaco. In the Italian waters, many visit Naples, the islands of Capri and Sardinia, and the picturesque bay of Portofino. From Viareggio one can visit the leaning tower of Pisa, and from the ports of Fiumicino or Civitavecchia one can drive into Rome for the day. People intending to vacation in French waters will often fly into Nice but board their yachts just over the border in the Italian port of San Remo, so as to avoid French cruising taxes.

If it is Spanish waters one seeks, then one can meet the boat in Majorca on the island of Palma, cruise to the island of Ibiza, and then continue up the coast to Barcelona. From there it is a short hop back to the South of France.

For Greece, one can board in Athens and just cruise the well known islands of the Aegean, or meet the boat further west on the island of Corfu (actually off of Albania) in the Ionian Sea. From Corfu, one can cruise down through the Ionian Islands and pass through the Corinth Canal to get back to Athens. Once in the Aegean, one can cruise to the islands of Crete, Hydra, Mykonos, Delos, Rhodes and Santorini, even venturing up into Turkish waters if one wishes. Again, there are tax advantages to boarding some ships in Italian waters before entering Greek waters.

In the Caribbean one can cruise the chain from south to north or north to south, usually staying on the lee-ward side of the islands. Popular stops are Barbados, St Lucia, Guadeloupe, Martinique, St Kitts, St Barts, Antigua, St Martin/San Marteen, and the Virgin Islands.

In the Pacific, some of the best cruising is off of north-eastern Australia, and in particular the Great Barrier Reef. One will normally fly into Brisbane and then connect to a domestic flight up to Cairns to meet the boat. Apart from the diving and underwater wonders of the Barrier Reef, one can stop in at the wildlife park on Heron Island, the luxury resort of Hayman Island, the tranquility of Lizard Island, and the rain forests near Port Douglas.

For the BG or team leader, his concerns are less sight-seeing oriented and more related to selecting qualified personnel and the necessary equipment. There are obvious advantages to selecting BGs who have strong water skills and preferably some small boat handling experience. The sources of the best operators are military units like the US Navy Seal teams, British Royal Marine SBS, federal agents with maritime VIP/DVP training, or police officers who have served with emergency services or port police units.

From the private sector, bodyguards with advanced scuba certifications, lifeguard experience, skipper tickets, or aquatic sports experience should be considered first. Non-swimmers or those prone to seasickness are definitely off the list.

As for equipment, marine radios and nautical charts are essential, and scuba gear, small compasses, night vision goggles, warm jackets, wet-weather gear, deck shoes, shotguns and long rifles are desirable.

ADVANCE WORK

When doing the advance, the team leader should arrange for the charter operator of ship's agent to meet him at the nearest airport since this is usually the same way that the principal's group will be met. Most charters include ground transportation to and from the nearest airport.

In addition to road maps for all the ports-of-call, the advance will also need nautical charts to be able to study the lay-outs and docking facilities at each location. Upon arrival at the boat, and after the required greetings and pleasantries, the advance should have the captain or first officer give a full tour of the vessel. The team should then:

- Evaluate the exterior for cleanliness, paint damage or marine growth, and if necessary, recommend that the crew do some maintenance before the principal arrives
- Inspect the overall condition of the interior with special attention to the master stateroom
- Give the captain any up-date to the principal's itinerary
- Brief the captain and chief steward on any special requests by the guests
- Brief the chef and stewards on any dietary considerations and food preferences
- Give the chief steward the stateroom and cabin allocations for guests and staff
- Inspect the on-board security system, deck cameras and CCTVs
- Request to inspect any weapons carried on board, and if necessary ensure that the captain has them under lock and key
- Learn how to operate the bridge radios, portable radios and SATCOM system
- Learn how to operate the small boats and tenders
- Confirm that there are adequate Coast Guard approved life-vests

Even though plans are always flexible and open to change, the sooner the captain has the final itinerary, the sooner he can reserve dock space at scheduled ports or marinas—the more popular ones being quite congested in high season.

The BG should familiarize him- or herself with the function of the ship's equipment, particularly the radio room (left) and communications equipment

BGs should learn to operate the tender boats.

Passing through the Corinth Canal in Greece

OPERATIONS

The daily routine when staying on a ship is much like a hotel, except that the scenery can keep changing. Guests will rise, generally eat breakfast in the salon, go ashore if in port for some shopping or sight-seeing; return to the boat for lunch, generally served on deck; relax, sun-bathe, try some water skiing, or go scuba diving; have drinks on deck at sunset, and then either eat on-board or go ashore for dinner.

After dinner they may visit the casinos, catch a show or go to a night club—or all three. Somewhere around two to four in the morning they will return to the boat, maybe hit the ship's salon for a night-cap or late dessert and then retire for the night.

If the boat is to move at night, it is best to bring up the anchors before the guests are asleep and then not drop them again until morning. When steaming, the BGs can catch some sleep, but if staying in port they may need to pull a deck watch rotation. The other advantage of moving at night is that the guests will wake-up in a new port or location without having wasted an entire day steaming at sea.

General security considerations:
- Keep a BG on deck at all times, especially when in port
- If working alone, have crew members assigned to deck-watch at night
- Lock all exterior doors at night and have the principal lock his state-room door just as a precaution
- Retract gang-ways, boarding ramps and ladders when not in use
- Stow any ropes or bumpers hanging over the sides so as to make boarding more difficult
- Bring small boats and tenders on deck at night
- Watch children closely when on deck or playing around water
- BGs should try to catch-up on sleep when the boat is steaming from port to port
- Have the captain call ahead to have ground transportation waiting
- Have BGs waiting on the dock or ready to go ashore with the principal whenever the boat is at anchor or in port
- Monitor all traffic at the boarding ramp and discourage crew members from bringing guests on board

When working the French Riviera and the west coast of Italy, it is rec-ommended to have a shore based security team driving ahead to make restaurant and nightclub reservations and to arrange additional ground transportation.

Most boats cruise at 12 to 20 knots when moving from port to port, whereas a car doing 60+ MPH (100+ KPH) can make the same distance in a fraction of the time. Since the boat is following the coast, the shore team can still communicate with them by use of marine radios.

When in port, the shore team will handle the coverage if the principal comes ashore, leaving the others to handle boat security. This also puts at least one car, that has already been thoroughly checked-out, at the principal's immediate disposal.

When the boat is tied up at dock, the shore team can handle security surveillance from the vehicles parked near-by. This allows them to observe any attention the boat or its guests may be getting without having to look too obvious, standing at the railing or near the boarding stairs.

Author's Note: On long contracts in the Med, I prefer to use an eight to twelve man team, with half of the team moving ahead of the boat with me, ensuring that all arrangements have been made. I will also personally handle the principal's security team when he comes ashore, leaving the other BGs free to cover the boat and guests.

To cover any 24-hour a day operation, takes at least three two man teams just to secure the boat, with an additional two to four BGs to handle the principal, his wife and his children's close protection ashore.

On some operations we will have as many as three or four cars driving ahead of the boat from Rome to Monte Carlo and on around to St Tropez. This alleviates the difficulties often involved with reserving luxury rental cars like the Mercedes 500. In some cases we have even had to drive 500s down from Paris, knowing that ultimately the clients will finish their business or vacation there anyhow.

Rear docking is recommended to facilitate security but the boarding ramp should still be retracted at night.

DIVING

Where the threat level warrants, it is advisable to have scuba equipment on board and qualified divers on the protection team. Anytime one is sitting in port or at anchor, there is always the possibility that a bomb could be placed beneath the boat. The only way to protect against this or to detect a device in place is to have divers swim the bottom of the hull several times a day. Especially at night and just before the boat is scheduled to leave port.

Even if a group does not wish to kill the principal or boat owner, a small charge could be timed to disable the boat at sea for the purposes of boarding, piracy and kidnapping.

With this type of threat in mind, it is advisable that a team leader select some team members who have formal training in hull search procedure, explosive identification and basic EOD. Even though the divers would not try to dislodge or disarm the device for risk of triggering it, they should at least be able to make some educated observations as to its size and origin.

Apart from explosive devices that may be designed to sink or cripple the ship, smugglers have been know to attach drug pods or other contraband to the bottom of ships that they believe will not be searched entering a foreign port. By being seen to dive the ship on a regular basis, these activities would be discouraged or detected before they became an embarrassment to the charterer or owner.

Lastly, many clients may enjoy the sport of scuba diving, so the BG or team should at least be able to inspect the ship's diving equipment, assemble it, perform safety checks and accompany the client on a dive. If a client or his guests are avid divers, then the BG team should receive advanced training in both divemastering and the handling of diving related medical emergencies. (See STTU's SRT Diver book for additional information on this subject)

Author preparing to check the hull while working a detail in the Caribbean

Author working with U.S. Customs checking ships for drug pods

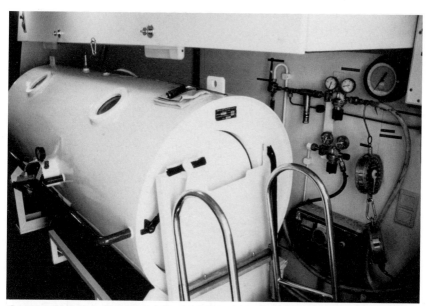

Some private yachts are equipped with recompression chambers to handle diving-related injuries.

When in port, the boarding ramp must be watched 24 hours a day.

Author awaiting the arrival of his clients in the Italian port of San Remo

28

CONCLUSION

Bodyguarding can be an interesting and rewarding profession if approached with the right attitude and motivation. As in any job, there are those who put out a good effort and others who are just spinning their wheels waiting for some better opportunity. Unfortunately all too many bodyguards are either failures at a long list of other careers, or disillusioned police officers and military types who can find no other field in which to utilize their training.

It is perfectly acceptable to use BG work as a stepping-stone to another career opportunity, but while working as a BG you should act like a professional and try to do the best job possible. It is important to keep in mind, that whatever you may choose to do in the future, you will always be judged on past performances. So even if waiting to get into a police academy, working your way through college, or aspiring to be an actor, you should still be the best BG that you can be, and this means training, studying and paying special attention to the small details in planning.

For the individual who wants to make a career in the security profession, there are numerous lucrative opportunities. Any intelligent bodyguard, with time and experience, can move up to the position of team leader, shift supervisor or advance man. Some choose to start their own businesses hiring other BGs to do the grunt work. There are also many opportunities in the security consulting and systems design business, or more steady managerial positions as corporate security directors.

However, the doors to these opportunities are only opened to motivated individuals who are willing to study, train and grow with the business. Most employers of bodyguards can understand a young man or woman who has drive and ambition, but no one will tolerate an individual who is just spinning his or her wheels until something better comes along.

CYA

CYA is the military abbreviation for "Cover Your Ass" and refers to the need to be cognizant of all the little things that can come back to bite you in the rear. So pay heed to these final words since bodyguarding can be both a legal and political minefield.

First, be a professional, act like a professional and only seek legitimate employment. Do not work for people with shady dealings or whom you cannot respect.

Next, establish written conditions of employment and job descriptions before going for an interview or starting work. These should send a clear message concerning the acceptable security related duties for a bodyguard.

Learn all that you can about the job, work locations and the principals. Identify the other staff members who can be of help to you but be wary of those who simply wish to use your friendship to get closer to the principal.

When you see activity that you believe to be inappropriate or inconsistent with good security, log it and report it to a supervisor or directly to the principal. However, avoid getting caught in turf wars between feuding husbands and wives or corporate office personnel.

Make use of written checklists in all aspects of your work and try to develop a checklist mentality when sweating the details. Keep duty logs when working at corporate offices or estates so that all activity is recorded for future reference.

Treat employers, principals, their families and friends with polite but reserved professionalism. Do not try to become their friends or become overly familiar in your daily contact with them. When you fall from favor with one, you fall from favor with all.

Do not bring your personal problems to work or try to involve the principal in your personal or business affairs. This is especially true with financial and legal problems.

Do not try to take advantage of the principal's position to gain access to other important people or seek employment in other areas. This can only be viewed as disloyal and even dishonest.

When traveling, keep meticulous details of all expenditures and cash usage so that your ability to handle money or honesty can never be called into question.

In this litigious society, think twice before touching anyone and seek legal advise immediately if you do have to use physical or deadly force.

Keep in mind that working on private property, in corporate offices or on estates, affords certain rights and protections that do not carry over into public areas. Understand the legal rights and limitations of a private sector bodyguard before starting an assignment.

Do not be a "cowboy" by constantly looking for opportunities to flash your piece. It is better to never show a weapon, to the point where principals will actually have to ask if you are even carrying a gun since they have never seen it.

TEN COMMANDMENTS
1. Thou shalt act like a professional at all times
2. Thou shalt obey thy supervisor in all things
3. Thou shalt sweat the details
4. Thou shalt practice diligently to maintain all skills
5. Thou shalt treat all information as sacred and confidential
6. Thou shalt not partake of alcohol or illicit substances
7. Thou shalt not flash thy piece or leave it unattended
8. Thou shalt not abuse thy position of trust
9. Thou shalt not abuse thy client's property
10. Thou shalt not borrow thy client's car or wife

DOOM ON YOU IF YOU DO!

Remember: if it gets to this point, you have already made major mistakes!

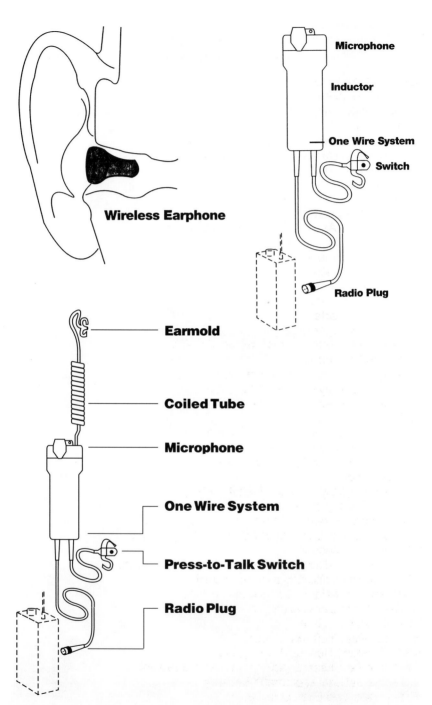

Wireless Earphone

Microphone

Inductor

One Wire System

Switch

Radio Plug

Earmold

Coiled Tube

Microphone

One Wire System

Press-to-Talk Switch

Radio Plug

TEA wireless Collarset II (top) and more conventional Collarset III (lower)

Appendix A
GLOSSARY OF TERMS

ACP—Automatic Colt Pistol
AO—area of operation
AP—armor piercing ammunition
AR—assault rifle
ASP—small retractible baton used by raid teams
B&E—Breaking and Entering / burglary
BFA—blank firing attachment
BG—bodyguard
BS—bullshit
CAR—Colt Automatic Rifle
CAT—Counter Assault Team (Secret Service)
CONUS—Continental United States
CN—chemical agent / mace
CP—Close Protection
CP—command post
CQB—close quarter battle
CQS—close quarter shooting
CS—chemical agent / gas
CST—Counter Sniper Team, Secret Service
CT—counter terrorist
DEA—Drug Enforcement Administration
DELTA—US Army counter terrorist team
Det Cord—high explosive priming fuse
DSS—Diplomatic Security Service
DVP—Distinguished Visitor Protection
EMT—Emergency Medical Technician
EOD—Explosive Ordnance Disposal
EP—entry point
ESD—Emergency Services Detail (LASD)
FBG—flash bang grenade
FBI—Federal Bureau of Investigation
FLETC—Federal Law Enforcement Training Center
FPS—feet per second
GIGN—Groupe d'Intervention de la Gendarmerie Nationale
GPS—global positioning system / satellite
Grain—unit of weight / 437.5 grains = 1 oz.
GSG-9—West German counter terrorist team
HK—Heckler and Koch
Hook-up—handcuff and arrest
HRT—Hostage Rescue Team (FBI)
IA—Immediate Assault plan (or Immediate Action)
IDS—International Diplomatic Security
IED—Improvised Explosive Device
IR—infra red

KEVLAR—strong bullet resistant material used in vests and stocks
Keep—actual hostage location in the stronghold
Kg—kilograms, 1 kg = 2.205 pounds
LAPD—Los Angeles Police Department
LASD—Los Angeles Sheriff's Department
Lbs—pounds, 1 pound = 453.592 grams
M—meters, 1 meter = 3.28 feet / 1.09 yards
MO—Modus Operandi / Method of Operation
MOA—minute of angle (1.047" at 100yds)
MM—millimeter = 0.04 inches
MP—military police
MSG—Marine Security Guard (US Embassies)
MV—muzzle velocity
Nietzsche—(1844-1900) German philosopher
NOMEX—a fire retardant material
NVGs—night vision goggles
OC—Oleoresin Capsicum, a mace-like pepper spray
PC—personal computer
PD—police department
PI—private investigator
Point—lead man in a team
PPD—Presidential Protection Detail
PPS—Personal Protection Specialist
PT—physical training
ROE—rules of engagement
SAS—Special Air Service (British Army CT team)
SATCOM—satellite communication system
SBS—Special Boat Service (Royal Marine Commandos)
SEALs—Sea Air and Land US naval commandos
SEB—Special Enforcement Bureau, LASD
SF—special forces
SMG—submachine gun
SOCOM—Special Operations Command
SOG—special operations group
SOP—standard operational procedure
SOTG—Special Operations Training Group (STTU and USMC)
SPEC-OPS—special operations
SRT—special response team
S/S—stainless steel
STTU—Specialized Tactical Training Unit
S&W—Smith and Wesson
SWAT—special weapons and tactics
TAPS—Tactics—Accuracy—Power—Speed
TSCM—Technical Surveillance Counter Measures
TL—Team Leader
UC—undercover agent
USMC—United States Marine Corps

USN—United States Navy
USSS—United States Secret Service
UXB—unexploded bomb
VIP—very important person
VP—Vice-President
Zero—sight setting where POA = POI

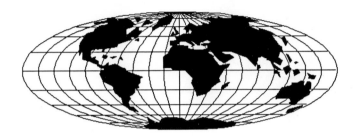

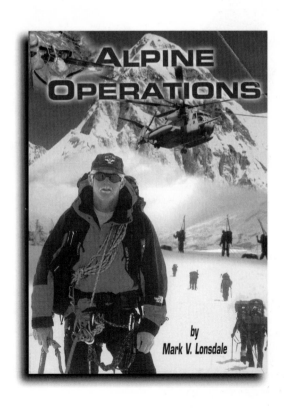

ADDITIONAL TITLES
AVAILABLE FROM S.T.T.U.

Appendix B
ADDITIONAL READING

ADVANCED WEAPONS TRAINING for HRT—Mark V. Lonsdale, STTU

CQB—CLOSE QUARTER BATTLE— Mark V. Lonsdale, STTU

RAIDS—Mark V. Lonsdale, STTU

SNIPER COUNTER SNIPER—Mark V. Lonsdale, STTU

SNIPER II—Mark V. Lonsdale, STTU

SRT DIVER—Mark V. Lonsdale, STTU

PROVIDING PROTECTIVE SERVICES—Richard Kobetz

EXECUTIVE SAFETY & INTERNATIONAL TERRORISM—Tony Scotti

IN THE GRAVEST EXTREME—Massad Ayoob

PROTECTING THE PRESIDENT—McCarthy & Smith

TERRORISM—Brian Jenkins—Butterworth Publishers

THE TERROR NETWORK—Claire Sterling

LIVING IN TROUBLED LANDS—Patrick Collins

TERRORISM—HOW THE WEST CAN WIN—Benjamin Netanyahu

THE CULT OF COUNTER TERRORISM—Neil Livingston

THE CRIMSON WEB OF TERROR—Chapman

TECHNOLOGICAL TERRORISM—Clark

COUNTER ATTACK—Dobson & Payne

POLITICAL TERRORISM, Volumes 1 & 2—Facts on File

THE DIARY OF CHE GUEVARA—Bantam Books

THE ART OF WAR—Sun Tzu

MAO TSE-TUNG ON GUERRILLA WARFARE—Brig.General Griffith

H&K USP .45 ACP similar to the US Socom offensive handgun

Beretta 92F with Sure-Fre light mount

Appendix C

EQUIPMENT SUPPLIERS

TACTICAL EQUIPMENT:
BIANCHI INTERNATIONAL – 800/477-8545; Fax 909/676-6777;
www.bianchiinternational.com
BLACKHAWK INDUSTRIES – 800/694-5263; 757/436-3101;
Fax 757/436-3088; www.blackhawkindustries.com
BOLLE GOGGLES – 800/628-2740, Ex1628; Fax 303/543-0834
CMC RESCUE – 800/235-5741; 805/562-9120; Fax 805/562-9870;
www.cmcrescue.com
EAGLE INDUSTRIES – 314/343-7547; Fax 314/349-0321; 400 Biltmore Dr,
Suite 530, Fenton, MO 63026; www.eagleindustries.com
SAFARILAND – 909/923-7300; Fax 909/923-7400;
3120 E. Mission Blvd, Ontario, CA 91761; www.safariland.com
SAFETY SYSTEMS CORPORATION – 630/653-1103;
www.safetysystemscorp.com
SHOMER-TEC – 360/733-6214; Fax 360/676-5248
STREICHER'S – 800/367-3763; Fax 800/566-6776; 763/546-1155
TAC-ORD – www.tac-ord.com; 208/288-1450; Fax 208/288-1451
TACTICAL & SURVIVAL SPECIALTIES – 540/434-8974;
Fax 540/434-7796

WEAPONS, SCOPES & ACCESSORIES:
ROBAR COMPANIES – 623/581-2648; Fax 623/582-0059;
www.robarguns.com; 21438 N. 7th Avenue, Suite B, Phoenix, AZ 85027
WILSON COMBAT – 800/955-4856; www.wilsoncombat.com;
2234 CR 719, Berryville, AR 72616
D&L SPORTS – P.O. Box 651, Gillette, WY 82716; 307/686-4008
LEUPOLD & STEVENS – 503/646-9171; www.leupold.com;
PO Box 688, Beaverton, OR 97075
METRO TACTICAL – 800/735-7030; www.metrotac.com
SHOOTER'S CHOICE / VENTCO – 440/834-8888; Fax 440/834-3388;
www.shooters-choice.com; 15050 Berkshire Industrial Parkway,
Middlefield, OH 44062
HECKLER & KOCH – 703/450-1900; Fax 703/406-2361
HSM AMMUNITION – 406/777-2106; Fax 406/777-3908;
www.montana.com/hsm
VULPES VENTURES (custom ammo) – 630/759-1229
FEDERAL CARTRIDGE CO – 612/323-2300; Fax 612/323-3890
SIERRA BULLET CO – 800/223-8799; www.sierrabullets.com

CUSTOM HANDGUNS:
WILSON COMBAT – 800/955-4856; www.wilsoncombat.com;
2234 CR 719; Berryville, AR 72616

D&L SPORTS – P.O. Box 651, Gillette, WY 82716;
   307/686-4008
ROBAR, 21438 N. 7th Avenue, Suite B, Phoenix, AZ 85027;
   602/581-2648; Fax 602/582-0059; www.robarguns.com
NOVAK'S - P.O. Box 4045, Parkersburg, WV 26104;
   304/485-9295; Fax 304/428-6722
JAMES CLARK - 336 Shootout Lane, Princeton, LA 71067;
   318/949-9884; Fax 318/949-9829
LES BAER CUSTOM - 29601 34th Ave, Hillsdale, IL 61257;
   309/658-2716; Fax 309/658-2610

EXECUTIVE PROTECTION SCHOOLS:
EXECUTIVE PROTECTION INSTITUTE – Arcadia Manor, Route 2,
   Box 3645, Berryville, VA 22611; 703/955-1128; Fax 703/955-1130

SHOOTING SCHOOLS:
THUNDER RANCH - HCR 1, Box 53, Mountain Home, TX 78058;
   210/640-3138
ISI – P.O. Box 950254, Mission Hills, CA 91395; 818/786-1165
TACTICAL FIREARMS TRAINING TEAM (TFTT) – 714/8468065;
   www.directactiongroup.com
SIG ARMS ACADEMY – 603/679-2003; academy@sigarms.comreco
GUNSITE TRAINING CENTER – P.O. Box 700, Paulden, AZ 86334;
   520/636-4565; Fax 520/636-1236

TACTICAL TRAINING:
STTU – Specialized Tactical Training Unit
   Fax 310/829-0868; www.sttu.com; Email STTUHQ@aol.com
BLACKWATER – 877/425-5987; www.blackwaterlodge.com
CMC RESCUE SCHOOL - 800/227-9281; Fax 800/235-8951;
   www.cmcrescue.com
NTOA – www.ntoa.org
TEES – Tactical Explosive Entry School – 800/950-8337; 662/781-9423;
   www.tees-training.com

BODY ARMOR:
ARMOUR OF AMERICA – www.armourofamerica.com
U.S. ARMOR – 11843 East Smith Ave, Santa Fe Springs, CA 90670;
   562/949-1733; Fax 562/949-1501; www.usarmorcorp.com
PROTECH – 20 Keeler St, Pittsfield, MA 01201; 800/234-3104;
   413/499-3104
PROLITE ARMOR SYSTEMS – 800/645-4443; www.publicsafetymall.com
RBR ARMOR – 800/672-7667
SECOND CHANCE – 800/253-7090; 231/544-5721;
   www.secondchance.com
SAFARILAND – 909/923-7300; Fax 909/923-7400; www.bodyarmor.com

DRIVING SCHOOLS:
SCOTTI SCHOOL - 10 High Street, Suite 15, Medford, MA 02155;
800/343-0046; 617/395-9156; Fax 617/391-8252
BONDURANT SCHOOL - P.O. Box 51980, Phoenix, AZ 85076-1980;
800/842-7223; 4809610143
BSR - P.O. Box 190, Summit Point, WV 25446;
304/725-6512

VEHICLE ARMOR:
VEHICLE SYSTEMS DEVELOPMENT (VSDC) – 1271 W.9th St, Upland,
CA 91786; 909/981-3236
O'GARA-HESS & EISENHARDT – 9113 Le Saint Drive, Fairfield,
Ohio 45014; 513/874-2112; Fax 513/874-2558; www.ogara.com
KERAMONT CORP. – 4231 S. Fremont Ave, Tucson, AZ 85714;
602/889-9503; 800/388-2848; Fax 602/294-0107
EXECUTIVE ARMORING (EAC) – 4836 Whirlwind, San Antonio,
TX 78217; 512/654-3905; Fax 512/654-8105
ARMOR HOLDINGS / PROTECH – 20 Keeler St, Pittsfield, MA 01201;
800/234-3104; 413/499-3104; Fax 413/443-1572

BREACHING TOOLS & STUN MUNITIONS:
B-SAFE Industries – 508/252-3769; Fax 508/252-3470;
www.swattools.com
FEDERAL LABORATORIES – 904/741-5400
MK BALLISTIC SYSTEMS – 800/345-1504; www.mkballistics.com
UNIVERSAL PROPULSION – 800/525-3501

DEFENSIVE TACTICS:
REDMAN – 10045 102nd Terrance, Sebastian, FL 32958;
800/327-6812; Fax 407/388-9859
SPAR PRO / PRO-LINE – PO Box 38, Gatesville, TX 76528;
800/606-7727; 254/865-7221; Fax 254/865-8011

KNIVES & MULTI-TOOLS:
BENCHMADE KNIFE COMPANY – 503/655-6004; Fax 503/655-6223;
www.benchmade.com
BUCK KNIVES – 800/735-2825; Fax 800/733-2825; www.buckknives.com
COLD STEEL – 800/255-4716; www.coldsteel.com
GERBER LEGENDARY BLADES – www.gerberblades.com
LEATHERMAN TOOL GROUP – 503/253-7826; Fax 503/253-7830;
www.leatherman.com
SPYDERCO – 800/525-7770; 303/279-8383; www.spyderco.com

LIGHTS & HEADLAMPS:
PRINCETON TEC – 609/298-9331; Fax 609/298-9601
PETZL – www.petzl.com
PELICAN PRODUCTS (Lights & Cases) – 310/326-4700; Fax 310/326-
3311; 23215 Early Ave, Torrance, CA 90505; www.pelican.com
SURE-FIRE – 714/545-9444; www.surefire.com

PACKS:
GREGORY – 800/477-3420; Fax 909/676-6777; 909/676-5621;
100 Calle Cortez, Temecula, CA 92590; www.gregorypacks.com
BLACKHAWK – 800/694-5263; 757/436-3101; Fax 757/436-3088;
1133 Executive Blvd, Chesapeake, VA 23320;
www.blackhawkindustries.com
EAGLE INDUSTRIES – 314/343-7547; Fax 314/349-0321; 400 Biltmore
Dr, Suite 530, Fenton, MO 63026; www.eagleindustries.com

RESCUE & MEDICAL:
ADVENTURE MEDICAL KITS – 800/324-3517; Fax 510/261-7419
CHINOOK MEDICAL GEAR – 970/926-9277; Fax 970/926-9660;
www.chinookmed.com
CMC RESCUE INC – 800/235-5741; 805/562-9120; Fax 805/562-9870;
PO Drawer 6870, Santa Barbara, CA 93160-6870; www.cmcrescue.com
CONTERRA Inc – 360/734-2311; Fax 360/738-2241;
www.conterra-inc.com
DYNA-MED – 800/854-2706; www.dyna-med.com
OUTDOOR RESEARCH – 800/421-2421; Fax 206/467-0374;
www.orgear.com
SOS – Survival On Snow - 780/973-5412; Fax 780/973-3318;
www.sos-find.com

ROPES:
CMC RESCUE, Inc. – 800/235-5741; 805/562-9860; Fax 805/562-8260;
www.cmcrescue.com
NEW ENGLAND ROPES / MAXIM – 508/678-8200; Fax 508/679-2363;
www.neropes.com
PMI – 800/282-7673, 706/764-1437; Fax 706/764-1531;
www.pmirope.com
STERLING ROPE – 207/885-0330; Fax 800/755-ROPE;
www.sterlingrope.com

COMMUNICATIONS & RADIOS:
TEA Inc. LASH – 310/457-7401; 914/763-8893; Fax 914/763-9158;
www.swatheadsets.com
MOTOROLA – www.motorola.com

INSTRUMENTATION - ALTIMETERS, GPS, COMPASSES, ETC:
GARMIN – 913/397-8200; Fax 913/397-8282; www.garmin.com
BRUNTON – 307/856-6559; Fax 307/857-8282; www.brunton.com
620 East Monroe, Riverton, WY 82501
NIELSEN-KELLERMAN (Kestrel) – 800/784-4221; 610-447-1555; Fax
610/447-1577; www.kestrel-instruments.com or www.nkelectronics.com
SUUNTO – 800/543-9124; 760/931-6788; Fax 760/931-9875;
2151 Las Palmas Dr, Suite G, Carlsbad, CA 92009

CATALOG SALES:
CMC RESCUE, INC – 800/235-5741; 805/562-9860; www.cmcrescue.com
SAFETY SYSTEMS CORPORATION – www.safetysystemscorp.com
SHOMER-TEC – 360/733-6214; Fax 360/676-5248
TACTICAL & SURVIVAL SPECIALTIES – 540/434-8974; tacsurv@gte.net

STTU BOOKS available from:
STTU – Fax 310/829-0868; www.sttu.com/books;
   Email: STTUBooks@aol.com
Amazon Books – www.amazon.com
Barnes & Noble Books – www.barnesandnoble.com
Calibre Press – 800/323-0037; www.calibrepress.com
Paladin Press – 800/466-6868; www.paladin-press.com
Shomer-Tec – 360/733-6214; Fax 360/676-5248
Tactical & Survival Specialties – 540/434-8974; tacsurv@gte.net

USEFUL WEBSITES – HEALTH & TRAVEL:
CENTERS FOR DISEASE CONTROL AND PREVENTION – CDC
   Fax info service: 888/CDC-FAXX - www.cdc.gov
TRAVEL HEALTH INFORMATION SERVICE: www.travelhealth.com
INTERNATIONAL SOCIETY OF TRAVEL MEDICINE: www.istm.org
AMERICAN SOCIETY OF TROPICAL MEDICINE & HYGIENE:
   www.astmh.org
STATE DEPARTMENT TRAVEL ADVISORIES – http://travel.state.gov

www.sttu.com

NOTES

NOTES

NOTES

NOTES

NOTES

NOTES

NOTES

NOTES

NOTES